THE LIVES OF CHILDREN:

The Story of the
First Street School

CLASSICS IN CHILD DEVELOPMENT

THE LIVES OF

Introduction by
John Holt

CLASSICS IN CHILD DEVELOPMENT

♣ ADDISON-WESLEY PUBLISHING COMPANY, INC.

Reading, Massachusetts   Menlo Park, California
New York   Don Mills, Ontario   Wokingham, England
Amsterdam   Bonn   Sydney   Singapore
Tokyo   Madrid   San Juan

CHILDREN

*The Story of
the First Street School*

GEORGE DENNISON

 A Merloyd Lawrence Book

The publisher wishes to thank Taylor Stoehr for thoughtful
assistance in preparing this new edition.

Introduction by John Holt first appeared in *The New York
Review of Books.*

Library of Congress Cataloging-in-Publication Data
Dennison, George, 1925–
    The lives of children : the story of the First Street School /
George Dennison ; introduction by John Holt.
        p.   cm.—(Classics in child development)
    "A Merloyd Lawrence book."
    ISBN 0-201-55045-8
    1. First Street School. 2. Socially handicapped children—
Education—New York (N.Y.) 3. Learning disabled children—
Education—New York (N.Y.) I. Title. II. Series: Classics in
child development (Reading, Mass.)
LD7501.N514D46   1990
372.9747′1—dc20   90-36035
                                                                            CIP

Cover design by Joanna Bodenweber
Set in 10-point Caledonia

ABCDEFGHIJ-MW-93210
First printing, May 1990

* Introduction *

For some months, when speaking to teachers or to anyone else concerned with education, I have said that while there were many recently published books on education (my own among them) that I thought they should read, if they felt they had time for only one it should be *The Lives of Children*. It is by far the most perceptive, moving, and important book on education that I have ever read, or indeed ever expect to. For while I hope that in years to come we may learn much about human growth and development that we do not now know, I doubt that any one book will advance our understanding as much as this one.

It describes the lives of twenty-three children in the small private school in New York in which Dennison taught, and which has since been disbanded. They were black, white, and Puerto Rican in equal proportions. All were poor, half were on welfare, and about half "had come to us from the public schools with severe learning and behavior problems." They were, in short, children of the kind that our giant educational system conspicuously, totally, and hopelessly fails to reach or to help. This school, spending no more money per pupil than the city's public schools, did not fail. The children got well, grew, learned.

This book must be seen also as a destroyer of alibis and excuses. We cannot say any longer that we do not know why we are failing, or that we do not know what has to be done instead, or that we cannot afford to do it. If we go on failing much longer, stunting and wrecking as we have the lives and spirits of millions of children, it can only be because for peculiar and dreadful reasons of our own that is what we really want to do.

What the book is about may be summed up in Dennison's statement, that might well be on every wall of every school of education in America, that "the business of a school is not, or should not be, mere instruction, but the life of the child." He continues:

> The really crucial things at First Street (School) were these: that we eliminated—to the best of our ability—the obstacles which impede the natural growth of mind; that we based everything on reality of encounter between teacher and child; and that we did what we could (not enough, by far) to restore something of the continuum of experience within which every child must achieve his growth. It is not remarkable that under these circumstances the children came to life. They had been terribly bored, after all, by the experience of failure. For books are interesting, numbers are, and painting, and facts about the world.

The key ideas are *reality of encounter* and the *continuum of experience*. There is no reality of encounter between adults and children in most schoolrooms (or homes, for that matter), because most teachers do not feel free, do not dare, either to let the children say or to say themselves what they really feel and think. Their concern is that nothing shall be said or done in the classroom that might get them into trouble—and the trouble they can get into is real enough, as is clearly shown every year by the experience of brave and honest teachers. But what is worse is that they are neither brave nor honest enough to admit that their primary concern, the overriding reason for everything they make or let happen in class, is staying out of trouble.

It is bad enough that thousands of teachers all over the country who in their hearts would like to assign, for example, *The*

Catcher in the Rye are afraid to do so. But children might learn a great deal about education and society—much more than is in their civics books—if their teacher said to them, "I know a book that I think you would enjoy and from which you would get a great deal, but I don't dare assign it to you, I don't even dare tell you its name, for fear that some of your parents, or some people in the community, will kick up such a fuss that I will lose my job—and I can't afford to lose my job." Here might be the foundation for a real curriculum and a great deal of honest talk and true learning. Our schools pretend, not altogether hypocritically or dishonestly, to be much concerned with morality, but as Dennison says, "an active moral life cannot be evolved except where people are free to express their feelings and *act upon the insights of conscience*" (italics mine) and this freedom hardly exists anywhere in our schools.

Of an incident in which a teacher took time, to a degree unthinkable in most schools, to help two children settle a bitter quarrel (but *they* settled it, not she), Dennison writes:

> . . . [the children's] self interest will lead them into positive relations with the natural authority of adults, and this is much to be desired, for natural authority is a far cry from authority that is merely arbitrary. Its attributes are obvious: adults are larger, are experienced, possess more words, *have entered into prior agreements among themselves*. [italics mine]

This last is of critical importance. I do not know of a more compact or complete definition or at least description of what we mean by the elusive word "culture." The children, living in this culture, sense it all around them, sense that in spite of its bewildering variety it must make some sense, and want more than anything else to find out how it works. What nonsense it is to speak of children living in "unstructured" situations—no one does, every human situation has a structure—or to assume that children are indifferent to the real nature of the world and society around them, and will learn nothing about it unless it is crammed down their throats.

Dennison continues:

> . . . When all this takes on a positive instead of a merely negative character, the children see the adults as protectors and as sources of certitude, approval, novelty, skills. In the fact that adults have entered into prior agreements, children intuit a seriousness and a web of relations in the life that surrounds them. . . . These two things, taken together—the natural authority of adults and the needs of children—are the great reservoir of the organic structuring that comes into being when arbitrary rules of order are dispensed with.

Organic structuring; the natural authority of adults: these are two more of the key ideas that are central to this book. In a hundred places Dennison describes how children playing, working, or even fighting—some of the best descriptions in the book, and the most significant, are of fights—will out of their needs and desires find a way to create a natural order, an order that works, and out of which further activity, growth, and order may develop. Dennison points out, "the way they find is neither haphazard nor irrational, but is a matter of observation, discernment, generosity, intelligence, patience." Remember again that the children of whom he is speaking were labeled by their public schools as unteachable and incorrigible.

Elsewhere he speaks of "the barrier of compulsion," by which he means simply that in proportion as we demand or hold over children the power to compel we give up and lose the power to influence and help. One particularly moving passage—and there are many others—makes this point well:

> So many adults these days live in a world of words—the half-real tale of the newspapers, the half-real images of television—that they do not realize, it does not sink in, that compulsory

attendance is not merely a law which somehow enforces itself, but is ultimately an act of force: a grown man, earning his living as a cop of some kind, puts his left hand and his right on the arm of some kid (usually a disturbed one) and takes him away to a prison for the young—Youth House. I am describing the fate of hundreds of confirmed truants. The existence of Youth House, and of the truant officer, was of hot concern of two of our boys. They understood very well the meaning of compulsory attendance, and understanding it, they had not attended. We abolished that act of force, and these chronic truants could hardly be driven from the school.

Like Dennison, I have for some time now urged that we abolish or at least greatly relax the laws requiring compulsory attendance. No other change I advocate, however radical, provokes such a terrified and hysterical response. Proposals to wipe out half the human race with hydrogen bombs do not generate one-tenth as much anger. People say shrilly, "If we didn't make children go to school, they would never go, they would run wild, etc.!" No one seems to consider that children do not run wild on the 180 or so days a year they do not go to school, or that, as Paul Goodman once pointed out, in at least one instance statistics showed there was more juvenile crime when school was in than when it was out. In any case, these fears about what children would do if not locked up in school are groundless for many reasons, but this above all others—they need us! At least, they need whatever in us is real and helpful and interesting, and in any of us there is far more of this than we are ever allowed to make available to them in school.

The heart of the book—if one can speak of such a thing in a book virtually every page of which contains more truth than can be found in most writings on educational psychology—is the third chapter, only eleven pages long. It deals largely with the learning problems of twelve-year-old Jose. Dennison begins:

Here we come to one of the really damaging myths of education, namely, that learning is the result of teaching, that the progress of the child bears a direct relation to methods of instruction and the internal relationships of curriculum . . . To cite these as the effective causes of learning is wrong. The causes are in the child. When we consider the powers of mind of a healthy eight-year-old—the avidity of the senses, the finesse and energy of observation, the effortless concentration, the voracious memory—we realise immediately that these powers possess true magnitude in the general scale of things. . . . Why is it, then, that so many children fail? Let me put it bluntly; it is because our system of public education is a horrendous, life-destroying mess.

There is no such thing as learning (as Dewey tells us) except in the continuum of experience. But this continuum cannot survive in the classroom unless there is reality of encounter between the adults and the children. The teachers must be themselves, not play roles. They must teach the child, and not teach "subjects." . . . The continuum of experience and reality of encounter are destroyed in the public schools (and most private ones) by the very methods which form the institution itself. . . .

Continuum of persons and experience; reality of encounter. What these or the lack of them mean in real life is made achingly clear in Dennison's description of Jose and of his work with him.

Jose had failed in everything. After five years in the public schools, he could not read, could not do sums, and had no knowledge even of the most rudimentary history or geography. He was described to us as *having* "poor motivation," *lacking* "reading skills," and (again) *having* "a reading problem.". . .

To say "reading problem" is to draw a little circle around Jose and specify its contents: syllables, spelling, grammar, etc. . . .

By what process did Jose and his school book come together? Is this process part of his reading problem?

Who asks him to read the book? *Someone* asks him? In what sort of voice and for what purpose, and with what concern or lack of concern for the outcome?

And who wrote the book? For whom did they write it? Was it written for Jose? Can Jose actually partake of the life the book seems to offer?

And what of Jose's failure to read? We cannot stop at the fact that he draws a blank. How does he do it? What does he do? . . . Is he daydreaming? If so, of what? Aren't these particular daydreams part of Jose's reading problem? Did the teacher ask him what he was thinking of? Is his failure to ask part of Jose's reading problem?

Printed words are an extension of speech. Reading is conversing. But what if this larger world is frightening and insulting? Should we, or should we not, include fear and insult in Jose's reading problem? . . .

Jose's reading problem is Jose. Or to put it another way, there is no such thing as a reading problem. Jose hates books, schools, and teachers, and among a hundred other insufficiencies—*all of a piece*—he cannot read. Is this a reading problem?

A reading problem, in short, is not a fact of life, but a fact of school administration. It does not describe Jose, but describes the action performed by the school, i.e., the action of ignoring everything about Jose except his response to printed letters.

With these few words Dennison shows up for the empty and pretentious and pseudo-scientific nonsense it is the whole structure of mystification (specific reading disability, aphasia, dyslexia, strephosymbolia, etc., *ad nauseam*) and quackery that has been erected in recent years by our self-styled specialists in Reading and Remedial Reading. Some may feel the word "quackery" too strong. It is carefully chosen. Our doctors of medicine do not hesitate to call chiropractors quacks, but chiropractors, and even faith healers, have probably done more good and less harm in their fields than our reading experts in theirs.

Dennison then describes Jose's behavior during a typical early reading lesson. The description is enough to break your heart, and to make you wonder later how our tens of thousands of psychologists and related experts can have been so blind and stupid as to have ignored for so long the importance of such behavior, which must have been duplicated, and must still be duplicated, by hundreds of thousands of poor and despised children all over the country. He continues:

. . . We need only to look at Jose to see what his problems are: shame, fear, resentment, rejection of others and of himself, anxiety, self-contempt, loneliness. None of these was caused by the difficulty of reading printed words—a fact all the more evident if I mention here that Jose, when he came to this country at the age of seven, had been able to read Spanish and had regularly read to his mother (who cannot read) the post cards they received from the literate father . . . in Puerto Rico. For five years he had sat in the classrooms of the public schools literally growing stupider by the year. . . .

Obviously not all of Jose's problems originated in school. But given the intimacy and freedom of the environment at First Street, his school-induced behavior was easy to observe. He could not believe, for instance, that anything contained in books, or mentioned in classrooms, belonged by rights to himself, or even belonged to the world at large, as trees and lampposts belong quite simply to the world we all live in. He believed, on the contrary, that things dealt with in school belonged somehow to school. . . . There had been no indication that he could share in them, but rather that he would be measured against them and found wanting. Nor did he believe that he was entitled to personal consideration, but felt rather that if he wanted to speak, either to a classmate or to a teacher, or wanted to stand up and move his arms and legs, or even wanted to urinate, he must do it more or less in defiance of authority. . . .

One would not say that he had been schooled at all, but rather that for five years he had been indoctrinated in the contempt of persons, for contempt of persons had been the supreme fact demonstrated in the classrooms, and referred alike to teachers, parents, and children. For all practical purposes, Jose's inability to learn consisted precisely of his school-induced behavior.

Two things must be said here. The first is that *contempt of persons* is precisely and above all else what is taught, and learned, in almost every classroom in almost every school in the country, public or private, black or white, rich or poor, "good" or "bad." It is what our educational system brings about, and in many places is intended, as directly and specifically as basic training in the Army or Marines, to bring about—contempt for others, contempt for self, the need and ability to get a sense of identity and worth only by submitting oneself to the demands of a superior and oppressive force and acting as its agent in oppressing others.

The second has to do with the word "belong." Our educational system, at least at its middle- and upper middle-class layers, likes to say and indeed believes that an important part of its task is transmitting to the young the heritage of the past, the great traditions of history and culture. The effort is an unqualified failure. The proof we see all around us. A few of the students in our schools, who get good marks and go to prestige colleges, exploit the high culture, which many of them do not really understand or love, by pursuing comfortable and well-paid careers as university Professors of English, History, Philosophy, etc. Almost all the rest reject that culture wholly and utterly.

The reason is simple, and the one Dennison has pointed out— their schools and teachers have never told them, never encouraged or even allowed them to think, that high culture, all those poems, novels, Shakespeare plays, etc., belonged or might belong to them, that they might claim it for their own, use it solely for their own purposes, for whatever joys and benefits they might get from it. Let us not mislead ourselves about this. The average Ivy League graduate is as estranged from the cultural tradition, certainly those parts of it that were shoved down his throat in school, as poor Jose was from his Dick and Jane. The entertainment highlight of the class dinner at my 25th college reunion, and the nearest thing to a cultural event during the whole weekend, was a low-comedy parody of grand opera. It seemed to be just what most of my classmates expected and wanted.

Dennison continues:

> The gradual change in Jose's temperament drew its sustenance from the whole of our life at school, not from minuscule special programs designed especially for Jose's academic problems. And not the least important feature of his life (it was quite possibly the most important) was the effect of the other children on him. I mean that when adults stand out of the way so children can develop among themselves the full riches of their natural relationships, their effect on each other is positively curative. . . . This is the kind of statement that many professionals look upon askance and identify as Romantic, as much as to say that the sphere of the world rides upon the tortoise of their own careers.

The development or demonstration of this is one of the most important parts of the book. Precisely because it depends upon so many specific incidents, it cannot well be summarized or even represented in a brief quote. Equally important, and equally hard to summarize, is the relationship of the adults to these interactions, the ways in which they use, and the children make use of, their natural authority. This matter—the proper relationship in a non-coercive school between the old and the young— is immensely important, and is not well understood, or even understood at all, by many people in such schools, or by teachers in more conventional schools who would like to make their classrooms more free but do not know exactly what they would do, what their task and function would be, if they gave up their present roles of straw boss, cop, and judge. As Dennison wisely points out:

If compulsion is damaging and unwise, its antithesis—a vacuum of free choice—is unreal. And in fact we cannot deal with the problem in these terms, for the real question is not, what shall we do about classes? It is, What shall we do about our relationships with the young? How shall we deepen them, enliven them, make them freer, more amiable, and at the same time more serious? How shall we broaden the area of mutual experience?

How did Jose get to his first reading lesson? What facts and conditions led to his going there?

. . . he suffered because of his inability to learn. He was afraid to make another attempt, and at the same time, he wanted to.

We established a relationship . . . spent several weeks getting to know each other, roughly three hours a day of conversations, games in the gym, outings, etc. We lived in the same neighborhood and saw each other in the streets. He knew me as George, not as "teacher."

He understood immediately that our school was different, that the teachers were present for reasons of their own and that the kind of concern they evinced was unusual, for there were no progress reports, or teacher ratings, or supervisors. . . .

He understood that I had interests of my own, a life of my own that could not be defined by the word "teacher." And he knew that he, though not a large part of my life, was nevertheless a part of it.

Now given this background, what must Jose have thought about my wanting to teach him to read? For I did want to, and I made no bones about it. . . . The fact is, he took it for granted. It was the right and proper relationship, not of teacher and student, but of adult and child. . . .

And so I did not wait for Jose to decide for himself. When I thought the time was ripe, I insisted that we begin our lessons.

My insistence carried a great deal of weight with him, since, . . . he respected me. . . . My own demands were an important part of Jose's experience. They were not simply the demands of a teacher, nor of an adult, but belonged to my own way of caring about Jose. And he sensed this. There was something he prized in the fact that I made demands on him. This became all the more evident once he realized that I wasn't simply processing him, that is, grading, measuring, etc. And when he learned that he *could* refuse—could refuse altogether, could terminate the lesson, could change its direction, could insist on something else . . . we became collaborators in the business of life. . . . It boils down to this . . . we adults are entitled to demand much of our children. . . . The children are entitled to demand that they be treated as individuals, since that is what they are. . . . There is nothing in this process that is self-correcting. We must rely on the children to correct us . . . (to) throw us off, with much yelling and jumping, like a man in a pair of shoes that pinch his feet.

 . . . I have mentioned conflict just here because I have always been annoyed by the way some Summerhillians speak of love, of "giving love" . . . we cannot give love to children. If we do feel love, it will be for some particular child, or some few; and we will not give *it*, but give ourselves, because we are much more in the love than it is in us. What we *can* give to all children is attention, forbearance, patience, care, and above all justice. This last is certainly a form of love; it is—precisely—love in a form tht *can* be given, given without distinction to all, since just this is the anatomy of justice: it is the self-conscious, thoroughly generalized human love of humankind.

And if we do not have justice in our schools, how will we have it in our society, and if we don't what will become of us? Perhaps, though I have left much unsaid, and am haunted by the possibility that I may have left unsaid just what might have drawn to this book some who otherwise may not read it, this is the place to end this review.

 For, as we see in Dennison's pointed and moving discussion of sexual freedom among today's young people, or his comparison between the oppressed Russian peasant boys in Tolstoy's school and the far more deeply oppressed and demoralized city boys in his own, or in any one of a number of other places, this is a book about our unhappy society—sick, sadistic, self-destructive, mystified, and manipulated at every level by self-serving experts and con men, and heading however waveringly toward war abroad and some kind of dreadful native variety of Fascism at home. There is still much we can and must do to stop this slide to disaster—we have that much freedom. But we must recognize that we are almost certainly too stunted and broken in spirit, too full of fear, greed, envy, self-doubt, self-contempt, disappointment, and rage to be able to create for the first time a society that is truly human, just, honest, and peaceful, with some reasonable prospect of survival. To do that, we must have the help of a new generation of people far more intellligent, more kind, more loving and respecting of life than most of us can ever hope to be, and our only chance of getting such help is by making our schools, as Dennison has shown us how, into the kinds of places in which such people can grow. Perhaps, if enough of us, many millions of us, read this book, take it to heart, try in every way we can to put its not too difficult lessons into practice, we may yet save ourselves.

JOHN HOLT

THE LIVES OF CHILDREN:

The Story of the
First Street School

* 1 *

There is no need to add to the criticism of our public schools. The critique is extensive and can hardly be improved on. The processes of learning and teaching, too, have been exhaustively studied. One thinks of the books of Paul Goodman, John Holt, Greene and Ryan, Nat Hentoff, James Herndon, Jonathan Kozol, Herbert Kohl; and of such researches as those of Bruner and Piaget; and of Joseph Featherstone's important *Report*. The question now is what to do. In the pages that follow, I would like to describe one unfamiliar approach to the problems which by now have become familiar. And since "the crisis of the schools" consists in reality of a great many crises in the lives of children, I shall try to make the children of the First Street School the real subject of this book. There were twenty-three black, white, and Puerto Rican in almost equal proportions, all from low-income families in New York's Lower East Side. About half were on welfare. About half, too, had come to us from the public schools with severe learning and behavior problems.

Four things about the First Street School were unusual: first, its small size and low teacher/pupil ratio; second, the fact that this luxurious intimacy, which is ordinarily very expensive, cost about the same per child as the $850 annual operating costs of the public schools; third, our reversal of conventional structure, for where the public school conceives of itself merely as a place of instruction, and puts severe restraints on the relationships between persons, we conceived of ourselves as an environment for growth, and accepted the relationships between the children and ourselves as being the very heart of the school; and fourth, the kind of freedom experienced by teachers and pupils alike.

Freedom is an abstract and terribly elusive word. I hope that a context of examples will make its meaning clear. The question is not really one of authority, though it is usually argued in that form. When adults give up authority, the freedom of children is not necessarily increased. Freedom is not motion in a vacuum, but motion in a continuum. If we want to know what freedom is, we must discover what the continuum is. "The principle," Dewey remarks, "is not what justifies an activity, for the principle is but another name for the continuity of the activity." We might say something similar of freedom: it is another name for the fullness and final shape of activities. We experience the activities, not the freedom. The mother of a child in a public school told me that he kept complaining, "They never let me *finish* anything!" We might say of the child that he lacked important freedoms, but his own expression is closer to the experience: activities important to him remained unfulfilled. Our concern for freedom is our concern for fulfillment—of activities we deem important and of persons we know are unique. To give freedom means to stand out of the way of the formative powers possessed by others.

Before telling more of the school, I must say that I was

a partisan of libertarian values even before working there. I had read of the schools of A. S. Neill and Leo Tolstoy. I had worked in the past with severely disturbed children, and had come to respect the integrity of the organic processes of growth, which given the proper environment are the one source of change in individual lives. And so I was biased from the start and cannot claim the indifference of a neutral observer. Events at school did, however, time and again, confirm the beliefs I already held—which, I suppose, leaves me still a partisan, though convinced twice over. Yet if I can prove nothing at all in a scientific sense, there is still a power of persuasion in the events themselves, and I can certainly hope that our experience will arouse an experimental interest in other parents and teachers.

But there is something else that I would like to convey, too, and this is simply a sense of the lives of those who were involved—the jumble of persons and real events which did in fact constitute our school. The closer one comes to the facts of life, the less exemplary they seem, but the more human and the richer. Something of our time in history and our place in the world belongs to Vicente screaming in the hallway, and José opening the blade of a ten-inch knife—even more than to Vicente's subsequent learning to cooperate and José to read. So, too, with other apparently small details: the fantasy life and savagery of the older boys, the serenity and rationality of the younger ones, teachers' moments of doubt and defeat. Learning, in its essentials, is not a distinct and separate process. It is a function of growth. We took it quite seriously in this light, and found ourselves getting more and more involved in individual lives. It seems likely to me that the actual features of this involvement may prove useful to other people. At the same time, I would like to try to account for the fact that almost all of our children improved markedly, and some few spectacularly. We were obviously doing something right, and I would like to hazard a few guesses at what it might have been. All instruction was individual, and that was obviously a factor. The improvement I am speaking of, however, was not simply a matter of learning, but of radical changes in character. Where Vicente had been withdrawn and destructive, he became an eager participant in group activities and ceased destroying everything he touched. Both Eléna and Maxine had been thieves and were incredibly rebellious. After several months they could be trusted and had become imaginative and responsible contributors at school meetings. Such changes as these are not accomplished by instruction. They proceed from broad environmental causes. Here again, details which may seem irrelevant to the business of a school will give the reader an idea of what these causes may have been. A better way of saying this is that the business of a school is not, or should not be, mere instruction, but the life of the child.

This is especially important under such conditions as we experience today. Life in our country is chaotic and corrosive, and the time of childhood for many millions is difficult and harsh. It will not be an easy matter to bring our berserk technocracy under control, but we *can* control the environment of the schools. It is a relatively small environment and has always been structured by deliberation. If, as parents, we were to take as our concern not the instruction of our children, but the lives of our children, we would find that our schools could be used in a powerfully regenerative way. Against all that is shoddy and violent and treacherous and emotionally impoverished in American life, we might propose conven-

tions which were rational and straightforward, rich both
in feeling and thought, and which treated individuals with
a respect we do little more at present than proclaim from
our public rostrums. We might cease thinking of school
as a place, and learn to believe that it is basically relationships: between children and adults, adults and adults,
children and other children. The four walls and the principal's office would cease to loom so hugely as the essential ingredients.

It is worth mentioning here that, with two exceptions,
the parents of the children at First Street were not liber-
tarians. They thought that they believed in compulsion,
and rewards and punishments, and formal discipline, and
report cards, and homework, and elaborate school facilities. They looked rather askance at our noisy classrooms
and informal relations. If they persisted in sending us
their children, it was not because they agreed with our
methods, but because they were desperate. As the months
went by, however, and the children who had been truants
now attended eagerly, and those who had been failing
now began to learn, the parents drew their own conclu-
sions. By the end of the first year there was a high
morale among them, and great devotion to the school.

We had no administrators. We were small and didn't
need them. The parents found that, after all, they approved of this. They themselves could judge the competence of the teachers, and so could their children—by
the specific act of learning. The parents' past experience of
administrators had been uniformly upsetting—and the
proof, of course, was in the pudding: the children were
happier and *were* learning. As for the children, they never
missed them.

We did not give report cards. We knew each child,

knew his capacities and his problems, and the vagaries of his growth. This knowledge could not be recorded on little cards. The parents found—again—that they approved of this. It diminished the blind anxieties of life, for grades had never meant much to them anyway except some dim sense of *problem*, or some dim reassurance that things were all right. When they wanted to know how their children were doing, they simply asked the teachers.

We didn't give tests, at least not of the competitive kind. It was important to be aware of what the children knew, but more important to be aware of *how* each child knew what he knew. We could learn nothing about Maxine by testing Eléna. And so there was no comparative testing at all. The children never missed those invidious comparisons, and the teachers were spared the absurdity of ranking dozens of personalities on one uniform scale.

Our housing was modest. The children came to school in play-torn clothes. Their families were poor. A torn dress, torn pants, frequent cleanings—there were expenses they could not afford. Yet how can children play without getting dirty? Our uncleanliness standard was just right. It looked awful and suited everyone.

We treated the children with consideration and justice. I don't mean that we never got angry and never yelled at them (nor they at us). I mean that we took seriously the pride of life that belongs to the young—even to the very young. We did not coerce them in violation of their proper independence. Parents and children both found that they approved very much of this.

Now I would like to describe the school, or more correctly, the children and teachers. I shall try to bring out in detail three important things:

1) That the proper concern of a primary school is not

education in a narrow sense, and still less preparation for later life, but the present lives of the children—a point made repeatedly by John Dewey, and very poorly understood by many of his followers.

2) That when the conventional routines of a school are abolished (the military discipline, the schedules, the punishments and rewards, the standardization), what arises is neither a vacuum nor chaos, but rather a new order, based first on relationships between adults and children, and children and their peers, but based ultimately on such truths of the human condition as these: that the mind does not function separately from the emotions, but thought partakes of feeling and feeling of thought; that there is no such thing as knowledge *per se*, knowledge in a vacuum, but rather all knowledge is possessed and must be expressed by individuals; that the human voices preserved in books belong to the real features of the world, and that children are so powerfully attracted to this world that the very motion of their curiosity comes through to us as a form of love; that an active moral life cannot be evolved except where people are free to express their feelings and act upon the insights of conscience.

3) That running a primary school—*provided it be small*—is an extremely simple thing. It goes without saying that the teachers must be competent (which does not necessarily mean passing courses in a teacher's college). Given this *sine qua non*, there is nothing mysterious. The present quagmire of public education is entirely the result of unworkable centralization and the lust for control that permeates every bureaucratic institution.

In saying this, I do not mean that the work in a free school is easy. On the contrary, teachers find it taxing.

But they find it rewarding, too—quite unlike the endless round of frustrations experienced by those at work in the present system.

We were located on Sixth Street in Manhattan, just a few steps east of Second Avenue, where we rented classrooms, art and shop rooms, and a gymnasium in the old Emanu-El Midtown Y. We took up about a third of the building, and since we were sharing it with others, we could not decorate it, change it, abuse it, explore its nooks and corners, or shout in its hallways as we might have liked. We kept the name of our original location—the First Street School—in which we could have done these things, but which hadn't met the city's fire laws.

Our experience with racial problems is one of the things I want to describe, so I will make racial identifications wherever necessary. Let me say immediately that nothing could be more different from the present ideological uses of the word "black" than the simple indicative speech of children. No child comes into this world with racial hatred. It is foreign even to five- and six-year-olds. In their experience, however, color is one of the attractive properties of an extremely attractive world. One of our teachers, Gloria Aranoff, was Negro. If I were writing a political article, I would say black, as I suppose she herself would. Her young pupils, however, would not. In fact, they could not describe her at all. They were too close, and she too particular, too wholly unlike anyone else. Yet it was obvious that they found her color admirable. To sit near her was to come into an aura of color, a warm, dark-brown glow that was very pleasant, in the way that good health and physical radiance always is. Her tots were always climbing onto her lap. Black, to a young child, means just that: black. Negroes are not black and "whites" are not white. Our older boys, however, were racists. José (just turned thirteen), though he was fond of Gloria, would have said, "She's black," as he said of Michael Hasty, who was as light as himself, "He's black." Twelve-year-old Willard, who was learning to say with pride, "I'm black," identified José by nationality: "a fuckin' spic." These two bloodied each other's noses time and again, and I shall describe some of their fights a bit later. It is worth mentioning here that by the end of the year they could be seen at the school picnics with their arms around each other's shoulders. What had happened was simply this: the real concerns of young boys had gradually welled up within each one, and had finally overflowed the barriers of racism. They had discovered each other—and had discovered themselves—in more richly human terms. On the last day of school, coming back from an outing, I delivered various children to their homes. Finally only Willard and José were left in the microbus. They were talking by now with forced animation. When Willard jumped out at his corner, he turned to José with a tight-faced grin and said, "See you on the block, man," and José, stammering somewhat, repeated, "See you on the block." I was struck by this exchange, for the fact was that their neighborhoods were far apart. As I maneuvered the bus back into traffic, I saw José's face in the mirror. He had begun to weep. He cried for ten minutes. He knew very well that he would not be seeing Willard. There had been a new ease in their lives, a gaiety and spontaneity they had rarely experienced, and José especially (since he had lost all their fights) had won through to it with great pain and courage. Now it would all be lost, for the racial pressures would be decisive once they were on the streets again. And of course he was crying because school was over. It had been a haven. He had had protectors and friends, and had gradually given up pretending that he knew karate, hated niggers, and could vanquish cops.

Not many boys in the public schools could have surmounted their racism as José and Willard did. Racism feeds on anxiety. It is supported by fantasy. When children are herded together in great numbers and are treated as ciphers in some huge, indifferent sum, the anxiety of anonymity absolutely forces them into protective alliances. They reach out for some identity to fill the void of self, however inadequate and fantasy-ridden that identity may be. Yet the power they achieve by banding together—though it may be crippling to growth—is not illusory; it is real.

What I have just said is really the whole of what we learned about racism at our school. The very young wouldn't have it. The older ones were stuck with it, but some few worked through. We teachers never preached tolerance, desegregation, integration, or anything else. Our small, face-to-face community diminished anxiety, eliminated fantasy and estrangement, and supported ego growth; and step by step, at least in school, racism fell away.

For the twenty-three children there were three full-time teachers, one part-time (myself), and several others who came at scheduled periods for singing, dancing, and music.

Public school teachers, with their 30 to 1 ratios, will be aware that we have entered the realm of sheer luxury. One of the things that will bear repeating, however, is that this luxury was purchased at a cost per child a good bit lower than that of the public system, for the similarity of operating costs does not reflect the huge capital investment of the public schools or the great difference in the quality of service. Not that our families paid tuition (hardly anyone did); I mean simply that our money was not drained away by vast administrative costs, bookkeeping, elaborate buildings, maintenance, enforcement personnel, and vandalism (to say nothing of the costs hidden in those institutions which in a larger sense must be seen as adjuncts to the schools: houses of correction, prisons, narcotic wards, and welfare).

Our teacher/pupil ratio varied according to need. Gloria handled up to eleven children, ages five to eight. At least half of her children were just starting school, and were beautifully "motivated," as the educationists say. Motivated, of course, means eager, alive, curious, responsive, trusting, persistent; and it is not as good a word as any of these. They were capable of forming relationships and of pursuing real interests. Every child who came to us after several years in the public schools came with problems.

Susan Goodman, who taught the next group, ages eight to ten, usually had six or seven in her room. Two of these were difficult and required a great deal of attention. They got the attention, and they were the two (Maxine and Eléna) who of all the children in the school made the most spectacular progress academically. In a year and a half, Eléna, who was ten, went from first-grade work to advanced fourth; and let me hasten to say that Susan, like the other teachers, followed Rousseau's old policy of *losing time*. ("The most useful rule of education is this: do not save time, but lose it.") Eléna's lessons were very brief and were often skipped.

The remaining children, boys to the age of thirteen, had come to us in serious trouble of one kind or another. Several carried knives, all had been truants, José could not read, Willard was scheduled for a 600 school, Stanley was a vandal and thief and was on his way to Youth House. They were characterized, one and all, by an anxiety that amounted to desperation. It became clear to us very quickly to what an extent they had been formed by abuse and neglect. Family life was a factor for several, but all had had disastrous experiences in school, and with authorities outside of school, and with the racism of our society as a whole, and with poverty and the routine violence of violent streets. They were destined for environments of maximum control—prison in one form or another. How they fared in our setting of freedom may be interesting.

Some pupils, as Dr. Elliott Shapiro points out (Nat Hentoff's *Our Children Are Dying* is about Elliott Shapiro and the children of Harlem), require a one-to-one relationship. I worked with José on just that basis. At other times I took the boys in a group, or Mabel Chrystie (now Dennison) did, or they were divided between the two of us.

Even in so routine a matter as forming groups, the advantages of smallness are evident. We all knew the children fairly well and were able to match teacher with child. Gloria had had a great deal of experience with younger children, Mabel with specialized tutoring in the city system and with problem children in a free school setting. I had worked with severely disturbed children; and Susan Goodman, who had never taught before, came from a family of teachers and naturally asked for the children predisposed to studies.

Yet the final composition of the groups reflected the contributions of the children themselves. They, too, had a hand. And here is an excellent example of the kind of structuring that arises when the wishes of the children are respected. Two of our most difficult pupils, Maxine and Vicente, actually placed themselves; and the truth is that we teachers could not have improved upon their solutions. I would like to describe this in detail, and contrast our procedure with that of the public school from which nine-year-old Maxine had come to us under threat of expulsion.

Where the public school had dealt with her problems largely by disciplinary action, we were in a position to take them quite simply as the facts of her life. She was a typically "rebellious child," and it was interesting to observe that almost all her disruptive behavior was a way of asking for something she really needed. In effect, she kept saying, "Deal with all of me! Deal with my life!"

She was a rosy, robust, active girl, with bright black eyes and a great deal of wit and awareness in her face. Her intelligence was obvious to everyone, and it was clear that her threatened expulsion had nothing to do with lack of ability, though she was also far behind in her work. She was precocious sexually, and for the first few months at First Street was "obsessed by sex"—as her mother described her behavior at home. She provoked "sexual" advances from the older boys.

I've put the word sexual in quotation marks because there was a great deal of excitement in her behavior, yet it was hardly sexual in the mature sense of the word. The sexuality normal to her age—still diffuse, and permeating the excitement of play as élan rather than eroticism—had been complicated by the fact that she was both more infantile than her age-mates and more advanced. She was infantile in her extreme dependence on adults and her insecurity among sibling rivals. She was advanced physically and intellectually and in her vivid sense of her own powers. Thus she was able to manipulate situations, but never to her own advantage. Nor could she ask directly for what she wanted, for no matter what she wanted, it brought her into conflict with herself. As was true of many of the older children, sex was terribly confused in her mind with violence and contempt. Add to this a profound ignorance of the simple facts of birth and the body, and that her mother had remarried, and that another baby was on the way, and you have the picture of a difficult and highly charged little girl.

Let us imagine Maxine in a regular classroom. (And let me say here that *every* child is plagued by apparently special problems and unmet needs.) She is quite capable of concentrating for short periods of time. She learns rapidly and well. But the lesson goes on and on . . . and the wooden chair is burning her energetic little fanny. She feels herself vanishing in this swarm of children, who are not only constrained to ignore her but constitute a very regiment of rivals interposed between herself and the teacher, her one source of security. The deep confusions of her life are knocking at her forehead—and who better to turn to than a teacher? She does it indirectly. She runs across the room and hugs her favorite boy, and then punches him, and then yells at the teacher, who is now yelling at her, "Do you have a boyfriend? Does he lay on top of you? Do babies really come out of the . . . out of the . . ."—she wants to say the magic word . . . and she does say it—"*cunt.*" It invokes a whole world of power, heat, and confusion. Obviously it is powerful: it makes the grownups jump. But pleasure, fertility, and violence are all mixed up here, and she wants desperately to sort them out. And there is her new daddy, and something he has done to her mother. And there is the forthcoming rival.

All these are the facts of her life. If we say that they do not belong in a classroom, we are saying that Maxine does not belong in a classroom. If we say that she must wait, then we must also say how long, for the next classroom will be just like this one, and so will the one after that.

"I have a new daddy. He loves me just as much as my old daddy. Do you believe that?"

She was too vigorous—and too desperate—to suppress all this. Inevitably she clashed with her teachers. Let us suppose they were fine ones. Under the conditions that prevail in the public schools, they could not possibly have responded to her needs. Nor could they demonstrate, in their own behavior, that the discipline they called for represented their own loyalty to rational imperatives. On the contrary, it was only too evident that in accepting their jobs they had given away their integrity, for the truth was that they could not make moral judgments and implement them. All that was left was the naked conflict of wills, and Maxine entered this conflict all sails to the wind. She paid a heavy price. Yet two aspects of her behavior were profoundly self-protective. First, she did not abandon her animal and psychic needs (nor did she suspend her skeptical judgment of adults); and second, she drove unremittingly toward the kind of encounter that leads to true relation. In short, she placed her life smack in the center of her relations with adults.

Now what is so precious about a curriculum (which no one assimilates anyway), or a schedule of classes (which piles boredom upon failure and failure upon boredom) that these things should supersede the actual needs of the child?

In a small class in a small school, Maxine's needs can be accepted. Nor is a teacher who is capable of real encounter thrown into such abject embarrassment by fundamental questions. What painful and stupid mysteries, what misconceptions and notions of ugliness form in the minds of children because adults are so spinelessly disloyal to the pleasures which vivify their own lives, or contrariwise, send them aching and complaining of their lack to psychoanalysts!

Maxine's need to know about sex was real. She asked real questions and got real answers, answers which reassured her and helped take sex out of the nightmare world and place it among other quite ordinary, though not always so pleasant, human realities. More important than the teachers' answers was her freedom to provoke and play with the boys, for she always ventured something extreme, which precisely because she ventured it, left the fantasy world and took the reassuring forms of reality. The limits we placed on this will be evident later. At times we had to control her, at times protect her. Yet the freedom she experienced was considerable.

Maxine was no easier to deal with at First Street than she had been at the public school. She was difficult. The difference was this: by accepting her needs precisely as needs, we diminished them; in supporting her powers, in all their uniqueness, we allowed them to grow. Difficult as this was, it was extremely rewarding. By the end of the year Maxine had changed spectacularly, especially with regard to a problem that was perhaps more important than her sexual confusion. This was the problem of relating to her peers. Here again, her own disruptive behavior often held the clue to correct action. Surely it meant something if, during a lesson, she began to fret, or shout, or tease. Perhaps she had had enough. Fine. She was free to drop the lesson, free to leave the room. Perhaps her insecurity had overwhelmed her. Often she said: "I'm going up and see Gloria." The answer was positive: "Go ahead."

Which brings us back to the question of forming the

groups. Maxine had been assigned to Susan's. She reassigned herself when the need arose. Her reasons were excellent. Gloria was the warmest and most motherly of the teachers. Her children were the youngest in the school. Maxine could relax among them and give rein to the infant who still lived within her. She was a different girl in this group, cooperative and even affectionate. She was especially friendly toward little Laura, five and a half, and treated her with a consideration we would not have thought possible. Yet presently she would grow bored. What were her *real* classmates doing? What were they up to? Back she would go to Susan's room, and for several minutes, perhaps ten or fifteen, would plunge into a book or a worksheet of math. This may seem like too brief an effort—a mere fifteen minutes of concentration. But these minutes were worth hours of passive listening, and worth years of rebellious conflict. At the end of the year Maxine was reading three years beyond her age level. Which is only to say that for the first time in her life she was using the intelligence she so obviously possessed.

We could not have devised a more constructive way of scheduling Maxine than the way she devised for herself simply by expressing her wishes. But these wishes would not have been acted upon if we teachers had not already been convinced that the preferences of children lie close to their actual needs.

The other child who scheduled himself was Vicente, a diminutive, panicky, intelligent Puerto Rican boy of nine. He, too, had great difficulties with his peers. He was even more infantile than Maxine, and his home life, like hers, held serious problems. He was the child of a love affair during a long break in the family, which was later patched up. Now his mother alternately coddled and abused him, and he was terribly confused about his two fathers. He

was a good-looking child, curly-headed, snub-nosed, beautifully coordinated. When he first came to us, he was violent and frightened. He could not take part in games, or
in singing or dancing, or play in any way with other children. He could not abide lessons, and had been threatened
with expulsion at the public school. His forehead was
wrinkled with anxiety, and he never spoke in a normal
voice but screamed or shouted. He hardly ever walked
either, but ran; and the image of Vicente that stands out
in my memory is of his racing down the stairs to get to
the gym, his eyes shining like a squirrel's, his mouth wide
open, screaming at the top of his lungs.

He was assigned to Susan's group because of his age and
his obvious intelligence. But the children in this group
were capable of working, and he was not. They were
capable of relating to their teacher, and he was not—
except from the vantage point of an infantile tantrum. No
one could say better than he when the pressure grew to
be too much, and no one could say better what his next
move should be. Like Maxine, he went to Gloria's group,
and like her, found relative peace among the five- and six-
year-old children. And it was sweet-natured Laura he be-
friended, too. It may sound odd to speak of a five-and-a-
half-year-old girl as being "accepting," but she was. She
was gentle and warm, and these qualities carried outward
to other children. Her shyness never made her hang back,
rather she pressed forward, blushing slightly, ready to
smile, her eyes lifted in mixed appraisal and appeal.

But this was not the end of Vicente's visiting. Babyish
as he was, he put enormous pressure on himself to act
the little man, and he wanted desperately to be accepted
by the older boys. If Gloria's group was an oasis, Mabel's
and my own were the future—a future Vicente turned

into the present with really admirable determination and courage.

And so he "belonged" to all three groups. Each gave him something that he needed. And it may be that the children of these groups gave him far more than the teachers. His progress, like Maxine's, was spectacular. This is not to say that he stopped screaming, but that in addition to screaming he also began to talk. Toward the end of the year he could be seen sitting quietly beside a teacher reading from a book. He learned to play, and to take part in games, and to wait for his turn, and to show loyalty to teammates. He learned to face failure and to trust some few adults. Things of this kind go to form the background out of which the experience of learning arises. In supporting Vicente's growth, we made it possible for him to learn. If we had simply tried to *teach* him, he would still be hurling toys at the wall and striking the other children.

The richness of experience that was available to Vicente and Maxine was the result of the smallness of our school and of the face-to-face quality of our relations. And of course it was the result of the kind of freedom we offered. But let me replace the word "freedom" with more specific terms: 1) we trusted that some true organic bond existed between the wishes of the children and their actual needs, and 2) we acceded to their wishes (though certainly not to all of them), and thus encouraged their childish desiring to take on the qualities of decision-making.

To some persons it may sound odd to speak of richness of experience when there were only twenty-three children and very little in the way of educational gadgets. Yet this is exactly the case. The huge school does not create diversity of experience; it creates anonymity and anxiety, and an impersonal quality of *show* and *look*. For the children it is like walking through a department store, looking at a thousand things but touching nothing. Among twenty-three children, under conditions of freedom and respect, there is a true abundance of experience. It is experience in depth, and it leads to decisive change.

But how does a teacher, deprived of the familiar disciplinary routines, maintain order in his classroom? The answer is, he does not. Nor should he. What we call order, in this context, does not deserve that name at all; it is not a coherent relationship of parts to a whole, but a simple suppression of vital differences. Nor does the removal of the suppression lead to chaos, but to cyclical alternations of individual and group interests, of which the former are noisy (though rarely irrational), and the latter quiet. Not that real crises will never occur, or important refusals on the part of the children; but for the most familiar kinds of unruliness, the observation holds. The principle of true order lies in the persons themselves.

The usual complaints of teachers are that the children talk among themselves and pay no attention to the teacher; that they interfere with the attention given by others; that they nag at the teacher and sabotage his efforts; that they fight over some object, a pencil, a book, a candy bar. In crowded classrooms, things of this sort, countered by efforts to stifle them, are endlessly disturbing. Even in smaller classrooms they prove to be difficult if the teacher is much given to formal discipline.

Here are some incidents that occurred at First Street.

Dolores, age nine, and Eléna, age ten, both Puerto Rican, begin talking to each other during the lesson in arithmetic, paying no attention to Susan, their teacher. To make matters worse, several of the children begin listening to them. Instead of calling the class to order, however, Susan also cocks an ear. Eléna is talking about her older sister, who is eighteen. Their mother had bought a voodoo charm, and the charm had been stolen. Dodie, a Negro girl of nine, enters the conversation, saying in a low voice, "Voodoo! It don't mean nuthin'!" "What kind of a charm?" says Susan. "A charm against *men!*" says Eléna. And now the whole class begins to discuss it. Rudella, a Negro girl of nine, says, in her broad, slow way, "Phooey! I bet she stole it herself. I know somebody I'd use that thing on." Susan agrees with Dodie that voodoo probably doesn't work, "though maybe it has a psychological effect." "Yeah," says Eléna, "it makes you afraid." The discussion lasts ten or twelve minutes, and then all return to arithmetic.

José used to burst into song, or jump up and do dance steps during our sessions in reading. This had nothing to do with exuberance; it was compulsive and frantic. But it was essential that he do it. The effort he was putting into his work aroused an intolerable anxiety. He needed to boil it off and feel the vigor of his body so as to reassure himself that he was "all there."

Eléna and Maxine are howling and screaming, and pushing and punching, the one with endlessly voluble Caribbean fury, the other with the wide-open, full-throttle voice of New York emergencies, cab drivers in a traffic jam, bargain-day shoppers at Kleins. Each claims possession of a piece of red corduroy cloth, a queen's gown in their theatrical game, now in its fourth day. Children and teachers alike are impressed by their ardor, and by the obvious question of justice, for the gown can hardly belong to both, though both are shouting, "It's mine!" "Where did it come from?" cries the teacher. Eléna repeats, "It's mine!" but Maxine, who now has tears in her eyes, yells, "My mother gave it to me!" "All right, we'll call Maxine's mother and find out." There is immediate silence, broken only by Maxine's voice, much lower (pointing her finger at Eléna): "You'll see, boy." Now fifteen children gather around the telephone, the conclusion of which conference is the teacher's announcement standing up: "It belongs to Maxine. Her mother gave it to her." Eléna hands it over, and Maxine limits her triumph to: "See! I told you, didn't I?" All the other faces have that grave, almost stoical child look of Important Issues Really Settled.

I would like to quote Rousseau again and again: ". . . do not save time, but lose it." If Susan had tried to save time by forbidding the interesting conversation about voodoo, she would first have had a stupid disciplinary problem on her hands, and second (if she succeeded in silencing the children) would have produced that smoldering, fretful resentment with which teachers are so familiar, a resentment that closes the ears and glazes the eyes. How much better it is to meander a bit—or a good bit—letting the free play of minds, adult and child, take its own very lively course! The advantages of this can hardly be overestimated. The children will feel closer to the adults, more secure, more assured of concern and individual care. Too, their own self-interest will lead them into positive relations with the natural authority of adults, and this is much to be desired, for natural authority is a far cry from authority that is merely arbitrary. Its attributes are obvious: adults are larger, are experienced, possess more words, have entered into prior agreements among themselves. When all this takes on a positive instead of a merely negative character, the children see the adults as protectors and as sources of certitude, approval, novelty, skills. In the fact that adults have entered into prior agreements, children intuit a seriousness and a web of relations in the life that surrounds them. If it is a bit mysterious, it is also impressive and somewhat attractive; they see it quite correctly as the way of the world, and they are not indifferent to its benefits and demands.

These two things, taken together—the natural authority of adults and the needs of children—are the great reservoir of the organic structuring that comes into being when arbitrary rules of order are dispensed with.

The child is always finding himself, moving toward himself, as it were, in the near distance. The adult is his ally, his model—and his obstacle (for there are natural conflicts, too, and they must be given their due).

Perhaps I can give the reader some feeling of the atmosphere of the school by describing a fairly typical morning. I mean the very beginning of the day. (And I should start by being more honest: the morning I have in mind was unusually pleasant. What was typical was the simplicity of our routines and the fact that the persons themselves were, by and large, the real business of the day.) I would like to contrast this description with its parallel period in the public schools, as reconstructed by Greene and Ryan in *The Schoolchildren*. My purpose is not to heap criticism on the public schools, but to show what it means to children to begin the day relating on the one hand to institutional routines, and on the other hand to persons they already know and trust.

Here is the start of an institutional day, as Greene and Ryan describe it:

> *I get into 33B just at the bell. Feet thundering by outside.*
> *I get the window down from the top, place a pile of notices*

and junk on desk, unlock back door—but don't make it up front in time. Kicks, sharp poundings—the door's falling open as I reach my desk. The first mass of Ricardo, Jesus, Marshall, Pablo, rolls in. . . . The moment each seat is filled, we begin: salute to the flag, review of days of the week and months of the year. While I take attendance, they review sums in math notebooks. . . . Scrawls from home come next. "You quit make my kid cry, sign, M. Peraro." Some rather sad notes: "Pedro was out with asthma. The heat was off three days, we had to go to my sister's house." . . . Door has slammed open with a pupil bringing a message, "Mr. Zang say, send down lesson plans." "Tell Mr. Zang I spent the weekend making alphabet picture cards. I haven't completed my plans." . . . On through the pile, to the clang and rattle of the room. Milk money, attendance percentage, book room, supply form, PTA notices, gym record, lunch cards, Red Cross, teachers banquet, health folders. Confused Welfare sheet on Pedro . . . (Crash. Messenger.) "Mr. Zang says you fill out dis supply form, and you send down dose healt' cards dis morning, and dese wit' 'em." (Crash. Slam.) The health cards have eaten up time for three weeks. . . . This with extra mimeo'd form from Mr. Spane, the school principal, on "Daily Health and Appearance Check" for teacher to fill out (how many without handkerchiefs, how many ears are dirty, etc.).

I'm occupied, so a fight starts. Three more minutes breaking this up, two to restore order, and monitors are just passing out phonics workbooks when Mr. Spane's morning voice suddenly fills the air above us. It is time for announcements. I have to go into the aisles—the children are talking and laughing freely now, and do so throughout Spane.

"Good morning boys and girls! This is your old friend and principal, Mr. Spane. So sit tall and hearken, all!"

(Pause.) "Well, Mr. Spane made a mistake, boys and girls. He left his glasses at home, and didn't see that the first message was for the teachers."

(Class is now thumbing noses and throwing fist-and-finger signs to the amplifier. "What's he talkin' about? . . .")

"Come on then, teachers, sit tall! . . . etc."

Our own school day began with a companionable milling around in one room, students and teachers still shaking off sleep and exchanging gossip of the night before. Often Gloria and Susan arrived with containers of coffee and that look around the eyes which one inspects so as to guess at the state of the soul. Some few of the children always came to school hungry, and they seized the sandwiches meant for lunch. Munching these, they would talk with other children, or roughhouse, or cluster around the teachers' chairs and reenact television episodes of the night before, or talk of family and neighborhood events. I liked these morning interludes. They were courteous and companionable, and sometimes actually warm. In the description below only a few children are mentioned, but their numbers varied up to twenty-three. I cannot remember that the room became too crowded. They kept running back and forth into the hallway and into the adjacent room. The paragraph is taken from my journal of events at school.

In the morning, as school begins, we tend to sit around for a while in the front room while the kids hang up their coats, all greeting each other and chatting with whomever they please. Tom Gomez has just delivered Maxine and is still outside in the truck he uses for his painting business. José and Eléna, who sometimes ride with him, stand on the window sill and open the top of the window and yell down to him. I join them for a moment and yell down to Tom, who is leaning out from the driver's seat. I kid him about all the breakdowns last Friday when he helped transport us to a picnic. He grins and shouts something back. I can't understand him because of all the yelling in the room, but José, who is used to yelling, interprets for me. A few minutes later I sit down to smoke a cigarette, and five-year-old Laura (almost six) comes over with a roll of masking tape. "Look what I have." She peels a little strip and asks me to break it off for her, which I do. She says, "How come you can break it and I can't?" I say, "Because I have nice big fingernails," meaning the big nail on my thumb, which is the only one I don't bite . . . and I take her hand and look at her fingernails, all bitten to the quick. She laughs and hides her hands. Then I look at the gap in her teeth and ask her if the new teeth are on their way yet, and she shrugs and says, "I don't know," and puts her fingers on another front tooth and wiggles it. "See!" She draws a clockface, almost correctly, on the strip of masking tape and pastes it on my wrist like a wristwatch, saying nothing as she does this. Gloria and I exchange a few words about the Ellison novel she loaned me. At the other end of the room Mabel is opening the lunch provisions because Julio is hungry. She helps him make a sandwich. Vicente asks for a sandwich, too. He usually comes to school without breakfast because his mother works and the older sister who's left in charge either won't or can't make breakfast. Stanley and Willard have asked Mabel if they can make one telephone call, and they are busy doing this. Laura has asked me to tear off several more pieces of masking tape. She draws circles on one of them and holds it up, saying, "What's this?" I say that I don't know, and she informs me that those are peanuts. Gloria says that Susan is home sick, and so she'll take Susan's kids for the day. Eléna complains that there won't be anyone to help her with her arithmetic. I tell her that either Mabel or I will help her. José is strutting and acting tough. He makes a swipe at my head, saying, "Come on, man, you think you tough. Come on, man," and in the very next breath says, "Come on, George, we gonna have the most terrific lesson in the world." Willard has been tinkering with the typewriter. I put some paper in for him and stand there a while. Then I ask him for the typewriter, since it's essential in the lessons with José. He gives it up readily and I promise to return it as soon as we're through.

The milling around usually lasted about twenty minutes and gave way almost imperceptibly to the first activities of the day.

I would like to make clear that in contrasting our own procedures with those of the public schools, I am not trying to criticize the teachers who find themselves embattled in the institutional setting and overburdened to the point of madness. The staggering defeat of teachers as well as children is one of the things made clear in Greene and Ryan's vividly descriptive book. My point is precisely that the intimacy and small scale of our school should be imitated widely, since these things alone make possible the human contact capable of curing the diseases we have been naming with such frequency for the last ten years.

Now that "mini-schools" are being discussed (they have been proposed most cogently by Paul Goodman and Dr. Elliott Shapiro), it's worth saying that that's exactly what we were: the first of the mini-schools. There are other private schools oriented, as we were, toward freedom and organic order, notably the Fifteenth Street School in the city, and the Collaberg School and Lewis Wadhams elsewhere in the state. The children who attend these schools, however, come almost exclusively from middle-class or intellectual homes in which the principles we followed are known through the writings of A. S. Neill, Wilhelm Reich, Paul Goodman, and others. Our students came from the immediate Lower East Side neighborhood of the school. About half of the families were on welfare. The rest were too poor to pay tuition. And so in practice we were a public school, open to whoever in the neighborhood cared to come. The fact that we didn't charge tuition was made possible by a private (nonfoundation) grant sufficient to provide rent, salaries, equipment, lunches, trips, etc., for two years. Lacking this grant, we, too, would have found ourselves drawing exclusively on parents of the middle class. I need hardly say that it was fortunate we had the grant. Not only did we make a great difference in the lives of some few children (and to an important extent in their parents' lives as well), but we had a chance to see the effects of a free school on children who, because they are routinely classified as underprivileged, delinquent, rebellious, etc., are usually treated to heavy doses of manipulation and control.

The existence of the school was due almost entirely to Mabel's work, though Gloria helped a great deal with recruitment and in threading the horrible maze of accreditation. The latter problem, like all problems in the environment of Red Tape, requires doggedness, patience, and fortitude. The other problems—especially recruiting the children—are questions of direct action, no red tape at all, just talking to people face to face. And so I would like to describe here some of the things that Mabel and Gloria did. They were marvelously sensible and direct.

Mabel had worked previously at the Collaberg School as well as at reading clinics in the Lower East Side. She was convinced of the values demonstrated by A. S. Neill at his Summerhill School in England, and she wanted to apply his methods where they had never been found before, namely, among the urban poor. Her idea, however, was to form a "block school," since for New York children the immediate block often provides all that there is of community life. Having chosen the neighborhood and located facilities, Mabel promptly moved in, taking an apartment just a few doors from the school. And then by way of meeting children and parents (that is to say, mothers), she did something so simple that it deserves to be called brilliant. She walked up and down the streets on the hot days of summer, knowing that on every other stoop she'd find a pair, or a trio, or a little gang of young kids wondering what to do with themselves.

"Do you want to go to the beach?"

That was her recruiting speech. She spent the summer taking children to Coney Island and Rockaway and also to nearby parks. Most of the kids were too young to travel alone. Their mothers worked and were grateful that someone was helping out. Many of the relationships formed on these summer trips carried over through the days at school.

Mabel and Gloria both went knocking on doors in the neighborhood, explaining the school in its most important features: that the classes would be small, that a great deal of individual attention would be given, that it would cost nothing, that children of all races could be at home, that lunches would be provided. Handbills were printed in English and Spanish and were delivered to neighborhood doors. Local community centers were consulted, as were several psychologists attached to the public schools. All of these efforts eventually bore fruit. The school opened with a nucleus of nine children, but new pupils kept arriving from all of the sources just mentioned. Inevitably we received a number of children who had been hard to handle.

The first few weeks of school were extremely pleasant. With nine children and four adults, it seemed like a family gathering, or a picnic, or perhaps a clubhouse of some sort. In the range of educational endeavors, it must certainly have represented, for teachers and children alike, an extraordinary luxury. Within this period many of the children's faces took on that glow of eagerness that we associate with childhood. And we launched out immediately on the business of *losing time*. That is to say, we got to know the children really well, held long conversations with them, not on school topics, but on whatever occupied their minds: details of family life, neighborhood events, personal worries and personal interests. And of course I'm describing this from a teacher's point of view. To the children it was probably more important that they got to know us and to know each other. They played a great deal among themselves, and we went on many outings. José Portillo was present at this time, as was his sister Eléna, and the relationship I established with him was absolutely essential to our later lessons in reading. He was thirteen years old, and after five years in the public schools still could not read, though he was of normal intelligence.

When new children applied for admission, they first visited for several days so we could size each other up. As things turned out, we accepted everyone, except one pathetic little boy who had obviously suffered brain damage and could not have taken his place among normal children. It was not exactly that we had an open-door policy, but simply that we felt confident we could get results. We were correct in all cases but one, and in this instance we made a serious error, which I shall describe later.

Within three months we had twenty children, and the school was in full swing. I was impressed immediately by something that remained a constant source of wonder. This was the rapidity with which the children availed themselves of the relationships and freedoms we offered them. Everything in their prior experience of school had prepared them to depend on orders from above, yet they needed no time at all to test our sincerity and begin making use of their new opportunities.

I worked with the older boys in the morning, gave special sessions to José, held a long play period in the gym, and if an outing were planned for the afternoon, often took part in that, too. Usually, however, I hung around through the lunch period and then went home. Sitting in my own kitchen, slowly drinking the coffee I had wanted all morning, and with the hubbub dying in my ears, I noted down in a journal whatever had impressed me that day at school. Occasionally I mentioned matters of instruction. More often I wrote of the emotional problems that made learning so difficult for certain of the children. Most frequently I simply described the children in their relationships with each other and with the teachers. My chief reason for this was, of course, personal: it was what interested me. But in addition, just this aspect of school is usually missing from educational writings. We read of statistics and percentages, and are told that learning is the result of teaching, which it never is and never was. We hear of new trends in curriculum and in the training of teachers, and of developments in programmed instruction —of everything, in short, but the one true object of all this activity: the children themselves. This is the real reason that in spite of the enormous expenditures of money and effort, so little progress has been made. Our own experience was quite the opposite. The children called upon us as persons, and we responded as persons. School was not a parenthesis inserted within life, but was actually an intensified part of life. It was just this, of course, that made the job so wearing for the teachers. But it was just this, too, that was the one source of every good thing that happened.

It is worth mentioning here that Mabel, Gloria, and I all lived within a few blocks of the school. Susan lived ten minutes away in the West Village. Our homes became adjuncts to the school, especially Gloria's and Mabel's. And the children who lived nearby were invariably delighted when they ran across us in the street. Often when I went shopping, I would go up Michael Hasty's block. He was a slender, high-strung, extremely worried little boy from a broken home and a mixed marriage. He would

shout my name and leave his ball game, and often accompanied by a younger playmate, would walk beside
me for a block or two, chattering excitedly. I would see
José in the street, too, and during part of the year, when
things were going badly for him at school, he came to my
apartment for reading lessons. Gloria frequently had visitors. Michael Hasty would stand shyly in the hall and refuse to come in. Eléna, José's ten-year-old sister, would
visit for hours. She and Dolores would occasionally travel
crosstown and call on Susan Goodman. Mabel's apartment was wide open to the children. It was filled with
schoolbooks and art equipment, and the young girls especially went back and forth a great deal. Sometimes they
cooked there, and for a while, in the mornings, a group
of them prepared our lunches and wrapped them to bring
back to school.

Given this continuity, this intermixing of our lives, the
subjects of the classroom began to look like what they
really are: the knowledge of adults. Too, the children had
acquired allies and havens, and this is no small thing in
the hostile streets of New York.

* 2 *

I've been surprised by the way the children have identified with each other and have become a group. Relationships have sprung up where I never would have expected them—ferocious Vicente (almost ten) with little Laura, who is quiet and sweet. The change in Vicente is probably the greatest of these recent weeks. At first he kept very much to himself, ate lunch alone and wouldn't take part in games, except to attack and destroy. He still screams, but the violent temper fits and the harsh attacks on the other children have diminished. He's forming some sort of relationship with me, also with José and Kenzo. He's beginning to play in the gym a bit, and has permitted himself to show some small interest in the lessons. Like the other Puerto Rican boys, he is underdeveloped and seems far more childish than his actual years. At the same time, he tries to act tougher and more knowledgeable than he could possibly be. He has no real defenses. Failure of any kind is an excruciating experience—and he suffers a great deal of failure.

José, who at first couldn't concentrate for more than five minutes, now sits with me for as long as an hour of reading and conversation. His concentration still breaks down in almost panic confusion. His eyelids flutter, he looks around with spasmodic little movements of his head, doesn't *see* anything, makes wild guesses at the words. These guesses are almost always an attempt to say that the new word is actually one of the words he already knows, as if he were trying to tell me that he *does* know something. Both he and Vicente are so used to an atmosphere of testing, and of comparisons that invariably humiliate them, that neither can yet quite realize that he is not being asked to perform. José, however, is responding to encouragement. Inwardly, he keeps comparing himself to others. More correctly, he is simply convinced that he is stupid and is doomed to failure. But he's beginning to understand that we don't give grades here, and that his lessons are really *his*.

José, oddly enough, is more accessible than Kenzo, who for a nine-year-old is both large and sophisticated, but is something of a hipster.

We've been playing an excellent game in the gym. I turn out the lights. We've masked the windows, and the gym is thrown into the blackest darkness. Vicente and José run and hide, and I go find them in the dark. Those two, who act so tough ordinarily, invariably hold hands when the lights go out; and whenever I draw near them in the dark, they begin to titter and squeal, half-frightened, half-pleased, like five-year-olds. We played this several days, sometimes with variations: if I caught one of them, he had to help me catch the other. When I caught Vicente, he clutched my hand and said, "Hold my hand! Hold my hand!" Dodie and Rudella, the nine-year-old Negro girls, played one day. Dodie was very lively and swift, venturing to run in the dark, yet when I came near her once, catching her by surprise, she got quite frightened and yelled, "Oh, mama!" before taking to her heels and making her getaway. Rudella made a point of getting caught immediately. Then she'd cling to me, holding my sweater or my hand. The last time we played this game, a whole crowd joined in: Eléna, Dodie, Rudella, Maxine, José, Vicente, Kenzo—even little Laura for a while. I had made paper disks that glowed in the dark, and everyone carried one so that will-o'-the-wisps were floating everywhere. I had thought that these disks might help prevent collisions, but the game was so hugely exciting, and there was so much running back and forth, that soon enough there were two collisions—Vicente and Laura, head to head, and Eléna against the wall, resulting in a bloody lip.

12/22/64

I wanted to take José and Vicente out to do some reading in the street—store signs, street signs, etc. Kenzo raised such a fuss that I took him, too, against my better judgment. He reads better than they do, and they can't stand the competition. I made a strict rule that each take his turn, otherwise (I knew) Kenzo would be answering all the time. Kenzo read a sign—LICENSED PLUMBER—not without difficulty; and then José failed to read FOR RENT. Kenzo cried gloatingly, "I see what you mean!" A few minutes later he was whispering the "answers" to José and Vicente, trying to con everyone. José and Vicente, and I, too, heartily wished he wasn't there.

12/23/64

We all went ice skating at the Wollman rink in Central Park.

Leaving the school, Susan, Mabel, and I went with the young ones in a scattered herd, the boys racing on ahead to the bus stop. On the bus, the little ones sat together in the back, but José, Vicente, and Julio (visiting—a Puerto Rican boy of twelve) sat up in the middle of the bus on both sides of the aisle. They were noisy and excited, immediately opened their windows wide and leaned out, Vicente tooting at the cars and trucks on his recorder, playing shrill, ear-splitting notes. He obeyed me, however, when I asked him to keep his head in. We got off at Sixty-fourth and walked a couple of blocks up Madison before turning toward the park. The kids were noticeably affected by all the signs of wealth, the fancy stores, and the stolid, well-dressed passers-by. They became especially noisy and vulgar—mother-fuckin' *this* and shit-man *that*—and got that glassy-eyed look, flushed and feverish, which means that the world has become a blur of images and they are taking in very little. Yet their responses to the window displays were certainly expressive, transmuting into low vulgarity the high vulgarity of Madison Avenue. I can't say that I like either, but I prefer the former. There was a mannikin in black panties and bra, and José immediately yelled, "Pussy!" and reached out his hand. He expressed enthusiasm for sex and contempt for the window display, not a bad combination. The display itself, with its hairless crotch and its disgusting archness, expressed contempt for the body, coyly appealing, at the same time, to the most spineless kind of prurience. All the wealth of this street is the same that appears on these kids' television sets at night. They shuttle from the fantasies of their living rooms to the daytime fact that they haven't got a chance.

We skated for about two hours. Mabel, as usual, went around without zest and occasionally seemed awkward.

But when I asked her if she could do anything fancy, she grinned and said, "Sure," and executed a swift backward circle, coming to a sudden halt on her toes. She threw me a look of triumph Buster Keaton would have admired: it conveyed absolutely nothing. Then she resumed her manner and seemed awkward again.

All the kids wanted to be skated with and to hold hands. Maxine, as usual, made a number of friendly enemies by breaking the rules, skating into the roped-off areas, etc. But she wasn't as bad as the previous time; and I marvel continually at how we adults manage to bore ourselves with our rules and regulations, and how we perk up when someone comes along with enough consideration to break them.

Kenzo met us at the rink, since he lives nearby. He is Japanese-American, extremely good-looking, very suave. He seems to have an image just back of his forehead made up equally of James Bond and Jazz Musician. There is a good bit of loneliness and anxiety under this show of sufficiency. He rarely lets himself seem like nine years old.

He buddied up with some strange boys, white boys on vacation, and took sides against his Puerto Rican classmates. He wanted money not only for his own lunch, but to treat his new friends as well. I gave him lunch money. After the skating, he and his new friends climbed a little hill and pelted us with snowballs as we straggled across the park.

Walking crosstown to the Lexington Avenue subway, José, Julio, and Vicente became quite ugly, yelling insults to the well-dressed people, shaking the trash baskets, flaunting themselves in the paths of cars and cabs. They became a little calmer when we got back to the East Side, but once in the school again they behaved angrily (except for José), slamming toys around, screaming, bullying the little ones. This reached a pitch when Julio struck Laura viciously in the belly with a football. I hustled him out of the room rather roughly, and shook him and said we didn't allow that by any means. When I went back, Vicente was screaming and punching another of the little ones, so I hustled him out of the room and told him to sit by himself until he cooled off. Now all the teachers had arrived, so I hustled myself out of the room and on out of the school to the corner delicatessen, where I sat by myself until I cooled off. I'd had a bellyful of that wretched ugliness.

And of course the remarkable thing is not that they are so often ugly—there is terrible deprivation at work here, and the class and racial ugliness aimed at them exceeds what they themselves are capable of—but that they are sometimes sweet-natured and gentle. Still, I know of no other way of working but to show my feelings as they arise. I can trust myself to be fair, and they can trust me not to hit them. So they have to contend with my feelings as I contend with theirs. I finished my coffee and went back.

The day ended with a perfectly horrible "party" in the auditorium, me playing rock-and-roll piano and trying to organize a game of musical chairs, José and Julio plugging in the jukebox I had unplugged, Maxine pulling and pulling the draw curtains on the stage, Vicente dancing on top of the piano and then dashing backstage and working the loudspeaker in such a way as to break it—such howling, screaming, and crashing as to drive anyone crazy—in the midst of which Jimmy Mosley wandered in, looking for Mabel. I said, "Jimmy, we're playing musical chairs, take a chair." He said, "You ought to see the look on your face, George."

Later I realized how mistaken I had been in trying to organize that particular game in that particular room, with its so exciting array of gadgets. Too, just those children are the ones who find it so hard to structure their own excitement. This comes up all the time in the reading lessons with José. The sheer excitement of understanding —the closure of a whole form—is too much for him. Routinely, I make way for his excitement and help him structure it as it arises. Why had I thought of musical chairs? I know. Years ago, working with the severely disturbed children at Forum School, I had put that game to a number of therapeutic uses. And I had thought of it today. Obviously it was myself I was trying to calm.

1/4/65

Back from Christmas vacation, everyone a little glazed, relationships interrupted by too long a break.

Mabel said that she had heard a horrible story from Maxine—that Eléna and José (my own favorites) had been burned in a fire and that José was in the hospital in danger of his life. I found Maxine and asked her what she had heard.

"They got caught in a fire. José is in the hospital. He got burned very bad. Maybe he'll die. You know what? Jerry Lewis stayed at my house. Yeah, for real. Don't you believe that? He's not staying *all* the time, but he's going to come a little bit every day. Don't you know who Jerry Lewis is?"

I asked her where she had heard the story about José and Eléna, and she said that her father had told her. She was obviously in a lying mood, but I couldn't tell whether to believe her or not. There are a great many fires in that neighborhood. Too, it was late, and neither José nor Eléna, both of whom enjoy the school, had arrived.

Mabel and I took Julio and walked over to Avenue A to settle the question for ourselves. We met Mrs. Portillo in the hall and she took us upstairs. As she opened the door, I could see José jumping out of a folding bed in his shorts. Eléna scampered across the room in her slip. Mrs. Portillo stepped inside and closed the door, and we waited in the hall while they put away the bed and got dressed.

Both Eléna and José were pleased that we had come to enquire about them. José had pants on now, but no shirt (the room was very warm), and he sat on the sofa beside his mother. Eléna had put on a blouse, but she hadn't yet adjusted her skirt over the petticoats. She greeted Mabel happily, but wouldn't so much as look at me until she got her skirt in place. Then she grinned and said she wanted to come to school, and made cat claws at me. "I'm goin' to kill you, George," referring to her tiger-prowling gambits in tag-in-the-dark. She sat in a chair by the windows, which were covered with cheap but fairly attractive flowery drapes. The room was tidy and well kept. There was a religious picture on one wall, and beside it a tinted photograph of a handsome, somewhat babyish Puerto Rican man. On the opposite wall another tinted photograph showed an elderly woman in a hospital bed, a younger woman standing beside her.

Eléna's older sister, a slender, attractive girl of eighteen (she looked younger, like all these kids), sat curled on the sofa on one side of Mrs. Portillo. José and Julio sat on her other side.

Mrs. Portillo is like a figure out of folklore, some Papuan divinity-matriarch. She weighs two hundred pounds, at least, and not much of it is belly. She's tall, enormously broad-shouldered and deep-chested, with huge breasts aimed out like ritual cannons by a brassiere you could carry pumpkins in. The effect is not exactly one of stateliness, but of a massive, powerful, barbaric calm, animated from under the surface by a disposition to good humor and a calm authority that is both grave and conniving.

She leaned forward with her elbows on her knees, and puffing on the cigarette I had given her, spoke without any hestitation (translated by her eldest daughter) the little string of lies and inconsistencies which added up to the fact that she intended to keep the kids home until the welfare investigator could be informed that they had no coats to go to school in. Both kids, I knew, had coats. Susan had given José a very good one, down-quilted, and I asked him where it was.

"It's all dirty, man, it's no good to wear. I fell down in it. It's all broken here and here . . ."

There was some mention, too, of the truant officer. Mrs. Portillo wanted him to be informed that the kids were staying home. He would then make a report and put pressure on her, and she in turn could add the weight of his complaints to her own complaints to the investigator.

She handed Mabel an official welfare card and asked her to copy out the name and telephone number of the investigator. She asked Mabel to call the investigator and urge her to hurry up.

While she conducted this business, Mrs. Portillo appeared stolid and unconcerned about her children, who chattered around her. She never responded to them, except to request translations from the girl. When I asked her a question, she conferred with her translator and phrased short, ambiguous replies, watching her daughter as she delivered them, but not looking at me.

José's older brother came into the room, a slender, good-looking boy in his late teens, dressed in slacks and a white shirt. A plastic automatic was tucked into his shirt pocket, the handle projecting out. José looked up at him and then at me. "You better watch out for him, George. Nobody can push him around." The older boy grinned shyly and waved his arm at José. José noticed that I was winking—the tic in my right eye when I'm tired (I'd had no sleep the night before)—and he began to tease me about it, winking at me solemnly and making comments in Spanish that made everyone laugh. Mrs. Portillo had finished her business, and now she joined in the laughter and began responding to the children with good humor. I could see what a tower of strength she was, and how José and Eléna have been able to preserve some kind of graciousness in spite of the poverty and violence of their neighborhood.

The kids wanted to come back to school with us, but they understood that they were essential to her plot. Neither Mabel nor I let on that we understood her plan. Their struggle with poverty takes this form, among others. The family is without a father. All we can hope is that she'll get results quickly. Unfortunately, this very day was the day of the walkout strike of most of New York's 12,500 welfare workers.

We told the kids at school, especially Dodie and Rudella, who are fond of Eléna (the mother in all their games), that Eléna was all right, there hadn't been a fire. Both of the young Negro girls had been upset by Maxine's story, but now hearing the truth, they moved not a muscle in their faces.

At lunchtime Maxine was terribly excited. She ran around poking, yelling, passing out torn bits of paper and calling them alternately "candy" and "kackie." She swayed back and forth at the blackboard, covering it with streaks of chalk and chanting wildly, "Kackie, booby, kackie, doody, my daddy, my mommie, my daddy doodie, bookie kackie . . ." Her mother, Jewish, is married to her second husband, a husky, good-natured Puerto Rican Negro, and is pregnant with his child. He is Maxine's stepfather.

Maxine sat in the wastebasket and then tilted herself out on the floor and crawled like a baby. I asked her to get back in the basket and said I should deliver her like a regular baby. She complied immediately. The kids were very interested. I asked Maxine to make baby sounds in the basket. She did. I said, "Do you want to come out, little baby?" "Waaaa, raaaaa . . . yes." So I delivered her and she crawled on the floor like a baby. I said "Oh, look at the new baby! How are you, new baby?" She said, "Gooby, gooky, gobbledy kackie." "What's your name, new baby?" "My name is Baby Kackie." So I called her Baby Kackie and we played baby games awhile. She made a point of being very messy with her food. After a few minutes of this, the frenzy melted away from her and her eyes became clear. This is a good line to take with her, since she's imaginative and bright. I suggested to Susan that she do some Baby Kackie painting with Maxine during art class—anything and everything to do with birth and the body.

1/5/65

Neither Eléna nor José came today. Vicente showed up. He had been ill yesterday. He's less frantic than when he started, and has begun to be friendly with me and to want my attention, though he he still refuses anything that looks like a lesson. He was peaceful for quite a while this morning, sat with me and talked coherently and in good context, though like Maxine he started out with a long yarn (which I at first believed), making up in fantasy for the disappointment of Christmas. He said he had gone to Puerto Rico for the holidays in an Astro-Vision TWA jet, and that it had television for each row of seats, and that when you weren't watching television you could listen to music with "a thing like the doctor has." He drew a picture of the interior of the plane, and another picture of the plane in flight. He said the plane traveled very quietly and smoothly because the engines were in the back. He told me that the truant officer caught him in Puerto Rico and wouldn't believe that he lived in New York and so took him around to all the schools in Puerto Rico, and at each school they said, "He's not ours." I asked him where his mother was, and he said he had traveled alone—unable to keep from smiling now—"They let you do that, you know. Oh, man, everyday on that plane I ordered hot dogs and soda pop."

I wanted him to write part of the story just below the pictures he had drawn, but he refused and began clamoring to go to gym.

When Vicente first came to school, he was incapable of participating in games. Ordinary roughhouse always affected him as a personal affront, and he would stop the game and scream until he had "gotten even." He is able to play much longer now and take a little more in stride, but is still very infantile. He and Julio and I played football. One centered me the ball and ran out for a pass and the other tried to block the pass. Once, when Vicente was in the field and was waiting to block my pass to Julio, he began screaming because Julio and I went into a huddle. "No plans!" he screamed. "No plans!" He walked away and we had to drop our "plans" in order to entice him back.

During a lesson, or simply in conversation, the Puerto Rican boys look for clues when they are asked a question. They are unable to read, but the intelligence with which they search for clues would more than suffice them for learning. They scan your face, notice your gestures, take sidelong glances at whoever else is present. They recapitulate the entire trend of questioning (very accurately, too), trying to dope out what answer you *want* . . . all this in place of reading the word or of saying outright, "I don't know."

1/7/65

José and Eléna came back today, obviously happy to be in school. I spent an hour with José, talking and going through the twenty or so words he is able to read. The confusion he suffers because of the two languages, English and Spanish, was quite apparent, for instance, when I tried to show him the similarities between *a*, *an*, and *and*. He pointed to *a* and said, "I can say that in Spanish . . . *ah*."

If my own Spanish were better, and if I knew the colloquialisms of the streets, I would teach him to read through Spanish. All his "gut-words" are in that language.

I'm spending more time now teaching him the correct pronunciation of English words. He'll pay close attention to the movements of my mouth when I say them, but when I point to the written word, he has to force himself to look. It's interesting to notice that his awareness of my sound production has improved his ability to *hear* certain English sounds he formerly did not know existed.

During the lesson José cut up the bulb of a syringe. With the split in it, it looked exactly like a woman's hips and ass. He showed it to me, saying only, "Look." I said, "It looks exactly like a woman's ass." He roared with laughter, in which there was a ringing note of release. He widened the split so that he could make alternately a fat woman and a skinny one.

Eléna asked me to read with her after I had finished with José. She brought a storybook and sat down beside me and read it through. When the words were easy, she read with the animation appropriate to the story; when the words were difficult, she struggled with them and lost the story. She's learning very rapidly and knows how to grapple with a strange word.

Vicente was jealous of the attention I gave José. He refused to have a lesson with me . . . and in general, all day long, was stand-offish. He joined the games in the gym, but otherwise kept very much to himself.

We played dodge ball and then tag-in-the-dark. Whoever was "it" carried the rubber soccer ball. I had coated it with luminescent paint so that it glowed in the dark, as if the full moon were chasing some invisible object through the night. The usual scampering and outcries— and when the lights were turned on unexpectedly, it was touching to see five or six kids stretched out in a line, each holding a hand or an arm or leg of the one in front, and the first in line holding fast to Mabel's skirts.

Kenzo is making some kind of breakthrough. For weeks now he has been acting the self-sufficient hipster, giving the appearance, say, of a sophisticated fourteen-year-old, where in fact he is only nine, though large. He has always squabbled a great deal about the rules of dodge ball, always with the tone of I-know-it-better-than-anyone-here. But today he haggled and haggled about one of the rules, and said at last that he was only nine years old and needed the protection of the rules. It was a really significant kind of self-exposure and was the first genuine exchange he's had with me, speaking directly in his own behalf and not just trying to manipulate the situation from the outside. It affected the other boys, too. Rules had always been a question of general agreement, and they had always outvoted him. This time they granted him his interpretation.

Kenzo has taken a shine to nine-year-old Dolores, who is Puerto Rican, and who, like himself, is very good-looking. She wears her hair long and glamorous, is shy but responsive, somewhat provocative and flirtatious. Kenzo tries to pull the zipper in back of her white slacks. She punches him. He steals her ring. She yells and chases him.

Barney, the folk singer, came today, as he does regularly three times a week, with his guitar and autoharp. It was a marvelous session and the best possible demonstration of what the freedom in the school is all about. He came at the end of lunch period, and lunch itself was unusually pleasant today. There was the usual roaming around and shouting, everyone sitting where he or she liked and changing seats often, sometimes to sit by favorite teachers and sometimes to sit by friends and sometimes to sit alone. Maxine and José are up on their feet every two minutes, doing dance steps. José expands his chest and makes like a wrestler; Maxine flaunts her fanny.

The children have come to know each other and to understand, with great finesse, where they stand in their various relationships. If Maxine steals Rudella's cookies, Rudella will pout with such incredibly sustained, immobile dignity that sooner or later everything will come to a halt until her grievance is taken care of. If Maxine drinks Dodie's soda pop, she can get away with it if she doesn't take too much. Dodie will gape at her with mingled anger and fascination (Maxine is so unladylike), but then Dodie's lively spirit will flare up and she'll make more of a fuss than Maxine can handle. If Maxine takes something of Eléna's, Eléna will pull and push until Maxine is on the floor, at which point Eléna will bawl her out and kick her in the rear four or five times, moderating the force of her kick very nicely, not enough to hurt but a jolt sufficient to drive home the rapid warnings and curses, usually shouted in Spanish. This simple anger, followed (as it always is) by forgiveness, is so much more civilizing, in the end, than a teacher's homilies enforced by discipline from above.

The shouting, etc., was relatively softened today, and the thing that struck me most was the smiling faces of the young ones. All the five- and six-year-olds were simply looking around with smiles of pleasure, and sometimes wandering back and forth, interested in everything and calmly smiling.

After most of the food was consumed, everything became very noisy and active. José began juggling with apples, and Maxine tried first to imitate him and then to interfere with him. (The pained look on Mabel's face every time an apple crashed on the floor—her almost religious feeling about food.) Gloria, Susan, and I were all just trying to relax, i.e., there was never any pressing reason to interfere with the growing pandemonium. Which is to say that no one was becoming hysterical or being injured. And all that noise, when you really listen to it, turns out to be a boiling mixture of very specific meanings and relations. Kenzo steals Dolores' lunch box. Dolores yells for it, but is also pleased. Kenzo inveigles José into helping him hide it, and the two boys rush from the room, followed by Dolores. Now there is a great squabbling in the hall. Dolores can't find it. Kenzo comes skipping into the room, whizzes past me, flicks my hair with his hand, and with a beaming face shouts the one word, "Cooperation!" Maxine runs about among the boys, shouting and pushing, but her position as Sex Queen has been usurped by Dolores, who didn't even want it; and Maxine gives up the boys for a while and goes to sit beside her friend Laura, the sweet-natured charmer of five. Then Maxine takes Laura out to the hall, and almost all the children are in the hall or running from room to room, and the shouting has reached a tremendous pitch; at which point Barney arrives . . . and that great volume of energy, without losing its head of steam, modulates into a series of shouts—"Barney is here! Barney is here!" —and several of the kids, especially the young ones, come back into the room and cluster around him. The older kids are still shouting in the hall. Mabel tells them it's time for singing and comes into the room herself. Barney is greeting all the children and forming the chairs into a circle. The yelling continues in the hall. José runs into the room, runs out again. Dolores runs in, gets interested and stays. Suddenly the shouting is all over and the kids are sitting in a great circle, swinging their legs and chattering. Some have doubled up in the chairs and are leaning against one another, the little girls especially, and Eléna, who mothers them with real affection. Barney asks several of the children what verses they would like to sing of the "Michael" song. Maxine has the verses on the tip of her tongue and immediately jumps into the center of the circle, and flaunting herself more or less in Twist style, shouts out the verses so loudly that no one can hear what Barney is saying. The corners of her lips are turned up and she keeps one eye cocked on Barney. And so Barney is forced to concentrate on Maxine for a while. But several of the children join in on Barney's side. "Come on, Maxine!" "Hey, Maxine!" "Shut up, Maxine!"

And so the verses are parceled out. Barney strums the guitar. All are smiling and wiggling and swinging their legs against the chairs. José jumps up and does a dance step and sits down again. Dodie is supposed to sing the first verse, but she is bashful, and while she sits there blushing, Maxine hollers out the verse and jumps into the center of the ring again. Dodie's big smile turns into a big frown. Now she refuses absolutely to sing the verse. But it's time for the chorus anyway, and everyone knows the words . . . and they sing them with marvelous, full-throated voices, retaining all the zest of their scampering and squabbling in the hallway. When Maxine is invited now to stand in the center and sing her own verse, she suddenly becomes bashful. But she leans against the desk and sings it and everyone listens. Then the thunderous chorus again, and the song goes straight through now with the greatest animation and pleasure. When it's over, Maxine asks Barney to play "Glory, Glory, Hallelujah," adding, "It's a very sad song." "That's funny," says Barney, "the one I know is not sad." "Oh, yes," says Maxine, and she begins to howl, "Glooooory, gloooory, halle-luuuuuuuuuuujah," just as it might be howled at the Volunteers of America. Barney accompanies her, and soon all the kids join in. Now Maxine has become inspired. She jumps into the center of the ring and brings on gales of laughter by her stylization. She puts one hand on her hip, looks utterly bored, turns her head to one side, and speaks the words "Glory, glory," abruptly and dryly, like a stock clerk reading inventory; then grinning wildly and waving her arms, she jumps up and down and yells, "Hal-lelujah!" Then abruptly bored again, "Glory, glory," and jumping again, "Hallelujah!" The teachers, especially, are howling with laughter. When this is over, Hannah, a ten-year-old white girl who is thoughtful and quiet, tells

Barney she knows a song. Barney asks her what it is . . .
and Dodie says she knows it, too. Barney asks them to
sing it together. But Dodie is sitting all the way across
the room and is too bashful to walk through the center
of the circle. So José shouts, "You have to bring her!" and
he goes over and pushes her chair back through the circle, Dodie grinning and blushing and enjoying the ride.
So Barney plays, and Hannah and Dodie, in timid voices,
sing the song. Here again everyone listens. Now comes
a Catalan folk song, sung in French, with lots of hand
gestures—the sea, the mountains, the sun, the hill, the
wineskin—with a shouted chorus of "Olé!" Everyone
makes the gestures and roars the olé with gusto. Julio
outlines a woman's curves instead of the full circle of the
sun, and winks at José. Laura has come running across
the room and is sitting in my lap. Whenever toro, the
bull, is named in the song and everyone makes horns,
Laura, holding her fingers at her head, charges all the
way across the circle and gores Barney very gently in
the knee, then runs back smiling to sit in my lap until
toro is shouted again. This song has a dancing rhythm,
and Maxine leaps into the center and makes up a kind of
folk dance, throwing out her legs and hopping. The next
song is Spanish, a real dance song, and suddenly José and
Eléna and Julio are out in the center dancing a very
graceful approximation of the hat dance, their hands behind their backs and their bodies swaying with the music.
Several of the children join them, and since the floor is
crowded with dancers now, Barney swings into a lively
Twist number, and soon everyone is doing the Twist. José
and Kenzo are both very good at it, and they pair off and
do some fancy steps. Even little Laura is doing the Twist,
which she varies from time to time by putting her fingers
at her head and charging into me. Rudella is carried out

of her reserve and does a few fancy steps (leaving out all
the simple ones) that she probably saw her older brothers
and sisters doing at home. She goes around in a circle
with one arm held high and loose. Dodie, too, is carried
away. She executes a step and tries to end it with a full-
extension split on the floor. She gets stuck in the split and
stays there a few moments, looking around with a long
face. Then she gets up and tries it again. Everyone is
dancing, even the teachers. Barney is singing and strum-
ming. Kenzo and José look happier than I have ever seen
them, and Eléna, who very frequently is joyous, looks
joyous, twisting and whirling in her big Christmas boots.

Only Vicente has been unable to participate. He leaves
the room for extended intervals. Mabel goes with him and
they play in the gym.

After the dancing, the older children gather around
Barney and he gives each one a little lesson on the guitar,
one or two chords, and a little lesson on the autoharp.
José and Julio are especially interested, pay close attention, and put themselves into it.

Now Susan and Gloria have opened the art room upstairs . . . and the drift-to-the-next-thing begins.

I should mention that I took José aside at the end of
the dancing and asked him if he knew some of the words
to the songs I had heard in Mexico. He was familiar with
all of them, since they are regular features of the Puerto
Rican culture in New York. I sang some of the verses and
asked him to check me on the words and supply some
that I had never learned. He was delighted by the fact
that I knew them and could sing them in Spanish. His
face was bright and exuberant, as always when I am able
to put something in Spanish.

1/12/65

Today was José's birthday—thirteen. I said to him
(he'd been lying to us for weeks), "You've been fourteen
for a couple of months, and now you're thirteen. Con-
gratulations." He roared with laughter. An excellent day
for him. We sat down and I gave him his notebook and
asked him to go through it and read what he wanted to.
He went from page to page with great energy, tapping
the words with his finger and rattling them off. Gradually
he has come to realize that his mistakes are not being
held against him and that he is not being graded all the
time.

Julio had a metal toy, a naked woman facing a naked
man with a big erection; you move a lever and he fucks
her. I laughed when he and José showed me. They ran
around and showed the other teachers, but wouldn't let
the little kids see, and wouldn't let the girls see. But after
they had aroused the curiosity of the girls—especially
Eléna and Dolores—they teased them with it later. And
once, during a squabble between Maxine and José, Julio
came galloping up working the lever of his toy, shouting,
"To the rescue! To the rescue!"

José has been bullying Julio, who is larger and stronger
than he, but who cringes and whines. During tag-in-the-
dark, José thought Julio had put his arms around his sister Eléna, and so he punched him several times on the
arm, warning him, "Keep your hands off my sister, man.
I'll kill you."

The long sessions in the dark, the kids holding each
other and sitting side by side, or in a heap in "jail" on
one of the mats, have become less giggly, less scary, more

erotic . . . and more calming. Kenzo and Eléna have eyes for each other. Eléna knows it, but won't let on.

The day ended with a birthday party for José. He was very pleased with his gifts—a big sketch pad and some good watercolors and oil crayons. He has already shown some talent for drawing. He wanted to go right up to the art room and use the stuff instead of singing with Barney. I went with him and got things set up, showed him how to squeeze out small dabs of color, wet the brush, etc., then left.

1/14/65

José hadn't forgotten that I'd promised to take him and Vicente on a special trip to the Museum of Natural History. I tried to talk him into putting it off until Monday, but he insisted, and so we went.

Vicente was groggy and unusually quiet, not depressed but withdrawn, a kind of bright-eyed, quiet anxiety. He said he hadn't fallen asleep until five a.m., and when I asked him why, he said that he had been talking to himself. I asked him if he had had any breakfast, and he said, "No." As soon as we got outside, he took my hand. Every half block he said, "Wait," and pulled up his socks. He and José and I had breakfast at the corner luncheonette, and then we walked to Ninth Street to get the bus. But it was bitterly cold and Vicente was shivering in his thin coat, so we decided to take a cab. I stood out in the street, looking for one. José said, "I'll get one," and ran off around the corner on Tenth Street . . . and sure enough showed up in the back seat of a cab, grinning and very pleased with himself. We got out at the subway on Sixth Avenue. Here José and Vicente asked to be given their tokens. Vicente stepped ahead of me into the turn-stile, and when he saw me put in my token, he ducked under and ran . . . not much of a duck, either, as his head is not much higher than the crossbars. José ducked under the adjacent turnstile and started to run, but a cop standing by the change booth yelled at him and he had to go out the exit gate, with his shame-faced grin, and come back in, putting his token in the slot.

José had been to the Museum of Natural History be-fore, and he led the way from the subway. We arrived just as it was opening.

Vicente had come to life finally, but now, going from exhibit to exhibit, the dinosaurs first, he became over-excited and ran from one to another, crying, "Look at this! Look at this!"—running on before he himself could see anything. I made no effort to slow him down, since I knew we'd be coming back again and he might just as well get acquainted in his own frenetic way. The moment he saw the sales desk at the entrance, he began asking me, as always, to buy him something.

José saw much more than Vicente, and from time to time I was able to extend his contact: "Can you find a bird in this one?" (The African room, with painted back-grounds.) Once he started off down a long corridor. I called him back and asked him to read the sign over the door at the end of it. He gestured impatiently and con-tinued down the corridor, only to find that the door was locked. When he came back, I pointed to the sign again. "What does it say, man?" he asked. I said, "It says *closed*." He laughed, but he also blushed and looked away.

José wanted to go to the planetarium. Vicente had be-come withdrawn again and said he wasn't feeling well and wanted to go home. So they talked it over in Spanish —a reasonable, quiet conversation—and we went to the

planetarium. I had never been there. It was swarming
with groups and long lines of schoolchildren, and we
found ourselves in the runway to a ticket cage, but there
was no cashier. Before I could turn my head to see where
she was, José and Vicente had ducked under the stile,
José calling back to me, "Go under! Go under!"—which
I couldn't resist; and so under I went, and we wandered
into the downstairs auditorium, our illegal mobility in
striking contrast to the lines and regiments of schoolkids
with teachers riding herd. Some of the young teachers
were lively and sweet-natured and seemed to have good
contact with their charges; other were sharp and frantic.
We found seats. Soon the auditorium was filled, and the
high-pitched chattering of all the children sounded just
like a flock of birds, a level, fluttering, vibrating sound,
almost metallic, almost musical. Overhead the earth and
the planets moved around the sun. There was a great, soft
cry of excitement—the usual response of children to the
sudden dark.

We were the first to leave after the performance, and
the first to enter the upstairs auditorium, where the big
show takes place, constellations projected on the curved
ceiling, very beautiful and enthralling. The illusion of the
nighttime sky was so perfect that many of the children
looked around in wonderment. And when the lecturer
mentioned the relative movement of earth and stars,
and the stars began to move, it was evident that many of
the children thought that they themselves were moving.

The lecture, unfortunately, was a poor one, rather gar-
bled and abstract. The lecturer began talking of the animals in the sky, without making it clear that their outlines could not be seen in the stars. Vicente, hearing him
say, "Lion . . . scorpion . . . ," kept asking me, "Where?
Where? I don't see it," and José, faking it, would say, "I

see it." Vicente leaned his head against my shoulder all the way through. Right behind me a wizened, frantic teacher kept hissing and yelling at her kids, who in fact were not noisy. The lecturer had become obscure and the kids were talking among themselves. In front of me a youngish, good-looking, elaborately coiffured teacher managed her kids with a queenly, narcissistic air, not without warmth.

We ate in the cafeteria—a hot dog and soda pop for Vicente—and ran into my friend Phil Smith, with his new beard. He was doing research for Harry Jackson's historical paintings. Then back to the subway. José borrowed my pencil. As he walked past the big advertising posters, he said something to each one—"You stink," "Fuck you," "Shit"—and when there was a pretty girl on the poster, he leaned over and kissed her. Then he drew some mustaches with my pencil, me standing there embarrassed, and like most other adults, with their embarrassed smiles, wanting to do the very same thing, for we feel instinctively that this public space is really our own and has been sold out from under us. Once again they both ducked under the turnstiles. I feel, fundamentally, that they *should,* or rather, that there should be no turnstiles. Yet how can I approve behavior that will get them in trouble? They are children, not revolutionaries. I give them their tokens and insist that they pay. They duck under and run. I haven't got it in me to bawl them out—or to ask for the tokens back again, taking pennies from the poor. And so I shake my head in stupid embarrassment and put my token in the slot.

We went to the art room when we got back. All the girls were working very contentedly. Rudella looked up when we came in and said, "Hey, George, take these boys outa here. We don't want 'em."

Rudella has loosened up a great deal. In fact, she has become prettier. She swings in with the others now, cursing occasionally in her broad, slow, imitative way. She had been priggish before and envious of the others' freedom. She has many brothers at home, whom she characterizes as bad and enviably free, while she characterizes herself as good and woefully bored.

We held our staff meeting at Rappaports, where years before, after some of the Living Theatre productions, a kind-hearted waiter had passed out free bagels to the bohemian theater folk.

Susan told me about her evening with Dolores and Eléna. She had invited them to dinner, had taken them to the bank with her, and on a visit to *The Village Voice*, for which she used to write. She cooked supper at her apartment, the girls helping, and then they sat around and talked girl talk until ten o'clock, including an explanation of contraceptives and the physiology of birth, about which both girls had been confused and curious. Susan told Eléna that, contrary to what she believed, a girl did not *have* to get married at the age of eighteen.

Eléna was afraid of going home alone, and Susan discovered that Mrs. Portillo always insisted on her being accompanied—and not without reason, given the neighborhood they live in. Susan took her in a cab, and they met José on the way, who was just setting out to get her.

Susan told me that Dodie finally stood up to Maxine, and in fact beat her up. All this demoting that Maxine has suffered in her power relations with the children will actually have a calming effect on her, since she suffers a great deal from her own ability to manipulate others, i.e., she rarely has the security of limits she can trust. And these are real limits she's encountering, not the front-line skirmishes of uniform discipline. Maxine's mother has given birth to another girl.

Gloria often argues with me at these staff meetings, though I rarely argue with her. There's something in this of "the narcissism of petty differences." She becomes impatient if I psychologize or make any reference to A. S. Neill. She doesn't want to be thought of as a Summerhillian. Yet Gloria is inevitably so considerate of each child, taking differences into account and measuring her response accordingly, that the distance between her and Neill is not very great. And Neill, of course, is not a Summerhillian, but the headmaster of Summerhill and a rectitudinous old Scot. There is no such thing as "freedom," but only the relations between persons. Gloria is so direct and gently strong in these relations that each child is getting just about what he needs. She's firm with Maxine and permissive with Laura. She reads to the little ones a lot, and often the older kids drop in to listen. She has ten just now, all going at different speeds and using different books. When she goes shopping for books, the whole class goes with her, and they consult back and forth about which books to buy. She often settles conflicts in the same way (just like Neill), gathering the kids together to hear both sides, after which they give their reactions. All study is voluntary, but she's firm about the quiet period being quiet. She seems to think that Mabel and I give the older boys too much rein, and we, in turn, think that she does not appreciate the peculiarities of their needs. Gloria, for instance, has seven-year-olds who know more than José, who is thirteen. Our problem is to give, first, elbowroom, and then nourishment, to a *self* that has been thoroughly crushed by its experience of America.

Susan described the conversation of several of her kids.

Caroline, a girl of seven, blond and blue-eyed, is called
The American Girl by Eléna and Dolores, who don't
make the same distinction about Maxine. And so what
American means here is not "white," but the style that
Caroline, quite without knowing it, exemplifies. She is
pretty and friendly, relatively inhibited, a little patroniz-
ing (again, without knowing it, but probably imitating
her parents), a bit too clean, a bit too soft-spoken, a bit
too disapproving. Well-scrubbed, prettied-up, sheltered,
sweet-natured—and everything about her is dulled and
aborted: feeling, thought, humor, sexuality. Nothing at
all comes out loud and clear.

1/18/65

José, Vicente, and I came down to the gym after our
lessons and found that the girls were playing in the large
back room, where there are shower stalls and a bathroom.
It was an elaborate, pomp-filled, but very vague game
about kings and queens, crimes and punishments. Eléna
and Dolores were the dominating spirits of the game,
since both are imaginative and lively and sweet-natured
(no order-wrecking hostility). But especially Eléna ener-
gizes these games. Even the older boys will listen to her,
and it's not simply that she's fearless; their obedience is
based just as much upon the fact that she is fair, always
wants something rational or interesting, and rarely demands more than her rights.

Kenzo came down, and at first the three boys invaded
the game as three free-lance raiders, but soon—since the
girls lumped them all together in their howls of indigna-
tion—they became a group, and in no time at all their
group was assimilated into the game.

They had all found sticks in the closet, which had been left open by mistake (the sticks were tent poles), and so there was a great deal of swordplay, and lots of yelling because everyone was getting hit on the knuckles.

No one can withstand Eléna when it comes to dueling. She charges in with great energy and speed, and is far less concerned about getting injured than the boys are.

The castle was a pile of mats at the far end of the room. A little doll's crib stood in the castle, and Maxine —with a new baby at home—immediately threw herself into the crib and lay there with the glazed look of acting-out-something-special. She had been in the crib quite a while before Eléna announced that the queen was having a baby. It was this announcement that led to the marriage of the king and queen.

José, who is always throwing out his chest and acting like a strong man, became Hercules, and as soon as he acquired this identity, the girls were able to appeal to him for help. Kenzo and Vicente, his former comrades, were ganging up on Dolores, going from swordplay to wrestling, and she screamed, "Hercules! Hercules! Save me!" and Hercules promptly went over and throttled her attackers. A few minutes later he joined her attackers and they stormed the castle. Eléna defended the castle, the treasure of which was now the queen's baby. She held the boys at bay while Rudella ran up behind them and gingerly, but daringly, hit each one in the rear with her sword. Now Dolores, too, rushed to the defense of the castle.

I was watching all this from the other end of the room, holding a few sweaters. Dodie, of all the kids, played the freest and strangest role. She would dash into the fun and do nothing but get in trouble. No matter whom she approached, she was attacked and driven away, and she kept running and hiding behind me. I asked her if she was one of the guards of the castle. She said, "No, I'm a killer."

I had written an innocuous, humorous little play the night before, simple enough for the kids to do, but as I stood there watching this scene of mayhem and crime, of lofty though terribly aborted speeches—e.g., "My lord, I command you . . . uh . . . ah . . . my lord . . . Hey! You're not supposed to hit *me!*" "The monarch has given orders . . . uh . . . Cut off their heads!"—I wondered what in the world I had been thinking of.

Eléna, performing the marriage ceremony: "Do you take this woman to be your lawful woman?"

During lunch we talked about the game and talked about getting costumes and making a "real castle" of cardboard. The girls especially were tremendously excited by all this, and soon we were talking of staging a play. I found it exciting myself and began thinking of props and plots.

Kenzo and Vicente went out together to eat lunch at the corner luncheonette. Vicente was very excited about this, and when they came back, his face was beaming and proud. He came over to me, smiling happily, with an unusually open look, and started telling me all about it. I was responding to him warmly, and just at the moment that he became aware of it, he reversed his tracks and began begging me to give him money for lunch. I take it this way: by his constant begging he is asking to be taken care of, and deeper still, to be loved. But he is afraid of being dependent and exposed. And so by this nagging and begging he expresses both the need and the fear, and at the same time attempts to control the response of the adult. When he found himself talking to me with genuine spontaneity, revealing his pleasure so frankly that it amounted to an admission of trust, he became panicky and reverted to his customary attempts at control. Thus my policy in general is to set firm limits for him, but within those limits to put very little pressure on him.

The pubescent boys are hardly *in* their bodies, certainly not as the younger ones are. The body at this age, in spite of tremendous energy and physicality, seems almost to be a fantasy object, though perhaps it is the Self of which this should be said. I imagine the Self floating above the body, like the cloud above the boat in Ryder's painting.

1/19/65

I carried some old draperies to school, large enough to make tents for the castle game, and some old pieces of corduroy, red and black, and some safety pins and gummed tape for making the cardboard castle. Mabel, in the meantime, had brought over some huge pieces of cardboard.

Great excitement. It was hard to organize anything. José helped me carry the cardboard down to the gym, then Vicente and Julio helped me put the castle together with masking tape and pins. The other kids—and for the most part Vicente and Julio, too—kept horsing around and took no interest whatever in making the castle. And I realized that the image in my mind was from my own childhood, and that these boys, who cannot feel safe on the street unless they carry knives, have no such images in their minds. Nor can they make anything that requires the slightest patience. The moment anything goes wrong, Vicente scatters the material like an angry baby. (He did finish a shoe box in shop with Mabel, but a moment later took the hammer and destroyed it.) It was clear, too, that they could not accommodate their game to the flimsiness of the castle (five feet high). The girls perhaps *could* have, but not the boys. I saw that it was a waste of time, that it would be wrecked in three minutes. It took even less than that. Maxine crawled in and promptly smashed it over. By this time no one cared. It simply hadn't touched their imaginations. And the chief reason, of course, was that I myself had ruined things by taking such an active role. Left to their own devices, they would certainly have used the cardboard. It would not have resembled the castle in *my* mind, but would have been the castle of *their* game, adapted exactly to their energies, interests, and insufficiencies. The correct way to amplify their games is simply to give them new and unexpected props and say nothing. The fabrics I brought down made a difference; they became robes of state.

José's older brother and sister were visiting to see the play. Both are sweet-natured, like Eléna, rough but affectionate with each other, and good at playing together. I was impressed by the way Ernesto treated the younger children, showing them the consideration of an adult, yet enjoying himself in an easy, direct way, with none of the embarrassment or self-conceit so typical of American adolescents in this kind of situation.

Finally the girls showed up for the play—Eléna, Dodie, Rudella, Dolores—all in robes and crowns, Rudella with a tall black witch's hat. At first there was a melee as the boys attacked them, but Eléna cursed and cajoled—"*Déjalo! Déjalo!* I'll kill you, man! *Si lo haces otra vez* . . . Julio! *Déjalo!* José! Be nice, be nice . . ."—and soon was commanding the boys to fight to the death like gladiators while the girls held a courtly dance. There was a royal wedding, too, and then everyone danced together in the style of the minuet.

But it was chaotic today, incredibly noisy and hard to get things going. Vicente, Maxine, José, Julio—all the trouble coming from these. It was a relief to get out of there.

1/20/65

After all the turbulence of yesterday, today was calm and productive. A good lesson with José, he paying close attention and going over the words from previous lessons. It's hard to know what new words to introduce to him. The truth is that reading is almost superfluous in the kind of life he has worked out for himself, or has been driven to. Our own relationship is the best base we have to work from.

José had a toy, salvaged from the street, and he wanted to take the cogwheels out of it, so he carried it upstairs to the shop room, which I opened for him. While he worked there alone, I read with Vicente—the first lesson he has been willing to have with me. He said, "I read with Gloria," and I said, "That's fine. You can read with me, too, if you want to." He went and got his reader, one of the Look-See books which I find so sterile, but which are well laid out. He insisted that he be allowed to skip pages and finish the book before really finishing it. I told him he could read however he liked, and he proceeded to read, adopting a soft, babyish voice and reading well on about the second-grade level, much ahead of José, who is almost four years older.

Still much excitement about the castle game. They are all concerned with heroes and legendary figures, which they make use of without much sense of the legends. Hercules is simply strong and brave and wears a lion's skin.

Samson, Tarzan, Superman—strong and brave, variations only in styles and powers: Superman can fly, Tarzan can talk to the animals. For the girls: Cleopatra, queens, angels—again, beauty and power.

When I was trying to explain to José the difference between Atlas and Ajax, he jumped up and sang the television commercial for Ajax the Foaming Cleanser. He did not quite know what to think when I told him that Atlas was not a real man and did not *really* lift the world onto his shoulders.

Eléna, all excited, was jabbering with Dolores during lunch, telling her what kind of clothing Hercules wears: the lion skin that leaves his breasts bare. She outlined it on her own body, giggling when she mentioned that his nipples were exposed. She spoke in Spanish to Dolores and in English to me. She didn't know the English word for nipples, and so with a laugh she reached out and tweaked my nipple, grinning into my face and blushing a little. The American girls, in general, do not have such an easy approach to their own (and other people's) bodies.

1/26/65

José home with a fever. I mentioned it to Maxine. "He's home with a fever?" she said. "It's good for him!" "Why?" "Because he fucks people an' kisses 'em an' makes 'em cry, an' he must be gettin' sick an' tired o' that!"

Maxine met me at the door when I arrived. She was friendly and calm, took my hand, walked with me up the stairs. Ten minutes later, surrounded by her rivals, she began shoving and yelling and grabbing. Mabel had emptied a box of magnets on the desk in the front room, and all the kids were gathered there, playing with the magnets. There were a number of magnets and Maxine had one, like everybody else, but she suddenly grabbed a handful, snatching them from the other kids and pushing Laura, who began to cry. What had been a peaceful scene, lively interest, etc., was transformed into howling chaos. I tried to make Maxine give the magnets back and play with her own. She was playing with none now, but was clutching them all to her belly. She refused and fought with me and kicked me in the shins. I got angry and took them from her and shook her by the shoulders. She cursed me and fought back; and so I took her into the next room, where we wouldn't be observed (for I didn't want to embarrass her), and for the first time turned her over my knee and spanked her, all the while marveling at her solid, powerful little body, and at my own gasping and panting. She sulked and yelled at me for a while. "I'm going to tell my daddy and he'll beat you up!" "No he won't. He'll agree with me." "He'll beat you up! You'll see, boy!" Then very quickly she grew peaceful, and in some important way she had been reassured by the spanking, which probably meant to her that she could, after all, have some of the privileges of infancy, privileges meaning limits for which she herself need not be responsible. I went to the art room with her later and we worked at the same table for half an hour, very peacefully and with friendly conversation back and forth. She said: "Are you still mad at me?" And I: "No, I'm not mad at you anymore." She: "Help me make a star for my crown. I never can draw them right." She was painting a paper crown, to be a queen's daughter in the castle game.

José's absence gave Julio more room for his sneaky malevolence; it left Vicente without a protector and ally; it took away the restraints on certain of Kenzo's desires:

to act tough, to make advances (in his fashion) toward Eléna. But Kenzo and Eléna had anyway been baiting and annoying each other in Susan's class for several days, and today it boiled over in the gym. They began fighting. Kenzo is stronger and knows judo. Eléna wouldn't give up. He got her down on the floor. Then Julio, in his wretched way, sidled up and threw the volleyball against Eléna's face. Eléna thought Kenzo had slapped her. She was both enraged and deeply insulted. She grabbed his hair with both hands. She was kneeling on the floor, her face hidden. Kenzo was squatting in front of her trying to pull away. She wouldn't raise her face from the floor, and I could see that her chest was shaking with sobs. She didn't want anyone to see her tears, and she wouldn't let go of his hair. Kenzo apologized to her. I tried to separate them, and I explained to her that Kenzo had not slapped her. But she was truly not in her senses. Her fists were closed like iron balls on his hair, which is long. I didn't want to humiliate her further by overpowering her, and I hoped that Kenzo's apologies would have some effect. But she held on and held on. She was not coherent. Other kids tried to pile on. I held them back and tried again to get her to quit. Again no response. Suddenly Kenzo became panicky. He is fearful of his body (or body image) and is somewhat narcissistic, and probably he feared that his hair would come out by the roots. He punched her three times in the back—very hard, swift punches, much harder and more expert than I would have guessed he could throw. She screamed and arched her back and let go of his hair. She cried for the next half hour. Various people comforted her. Kenzo was frightened. I told him only that he should not have hit her that hard. It was all an ugly error, and wouldn't have happened if it were not for Julio. Eléna was worried about her back, and so Susan took her to the doctor, who said she was okay, though bruised. Kenzo, by this time, was very worried about José's revenge, for it was certain that he would do something when he came back. We teachers were worried, too.

1/27/65

José returned—and Kenzo, to no one's surprise, was absent.

I took José and Vicente to the Statue of Liberty, as I had promised. Both were in high spirits. Vicente asked me to sit beside him on the bus. "Hey, man, look this way, look this way now, keep looking. . . . There! That's where my gran'mother lives! You see those green curtains?" He showed me where his father lived, too, but he is an illegitimate child and I didn't know which father he meant. There was the usual contrast between the boys' eager scrutiny of the street, leaning out the windows, bouncing around, etc., and we poor stolid adults sitting sadly, as if the bus were a pneumatic tube on the way to the graveyard. These kids encounter much hostility from adults—shopkeepers, guards, cops, and people in general—but many unexpected kindnesses, too.

We waited an hour for the boat to the Statue of Liberty —potato chips and coffee in the lunch house, crackerjacks for Vicente. He looked eagerly for his prize—paper stickers, little pennants. He glued them on the cover of the notebook I carry. Also gave me a lot of crackerjacks. Mabel had loaned him an old-fashioned pocket watch. He couldn't tell time, and he resisted my efforts to explain, so I stopped explaining. A little later he asked me how to read the hands. What he can bear to listen to, he picks up immediately. He kept pulling the watch out every five minutes and announcing the time. José made a face of disgust and said, "Man, you keep pulling out that watch all the time."

They ran up the gangplank to the boat, and José comically saluted the attendant and shouted, "Coming aboard, sir!" The man gave a startled twitch and said, "Yeah, all right, all right."

Both were disappointed by the Statue of Liberty, as they are disappointed by everything. José later said it was "cheap." As always, a frantic first encounter, a kind of hectic glance, racing around to see where it ends; then complete withdrawal, no curiosity, no questions. (Though José did absorb my correction—that we got it from France and not England—and referred to it again much later.)

A lot of schoolkids were on the boat, but many tourists, too, including some Castilian Mexicans who spoke Spanish and did not look Puerto Rican. Both Vicente and José were very interested in their appearance and the unusual accent.

José ran out on deck and tested the wind by spitting, and laughed to see it blown back at him, as I had told him it would be.

José spoke of the vengeance he intended to take on Kenzo. I tried to dissuade him.

José: "Sure, I'll get him, man. What you think? He hit my sister, didn't he?"

But Kenzo wasn't there when we got back.

* 3 *

Perhaps after these excerpts from the journal, something of our intimate, informal style may be apparent. What may not be so obvious is that there was any connection between this style and the advances in learning made by the children. And here we come to one of the really damaging myths of education, namely, that learning is the result of teaching; that the progress of the child bears a direct relation to methods of instruction and internal relationships of curriculum. Nothing could be farther from the truth. Naturally we want good teachers. Naturally we want a coherent curriculum (we need not impose it in standardized forms). But to cite these as the effective causes of learning is wrong. The causes are in the child. When we consider the powers of mind of a healthy eight-year-old—the avidity of the senses, the finesse and energy of observation, the effortless concentration, the vivacious memory—we realize immediately that these powers possess true magnitude in the general scale of things. Beside them, the subject matter of primary education can hardly be regarded as a difficult task. Yet the routine assumption of school professionals is that somehow or other learning is difficult.

Why is it, then, that so many children fail? Let me put it bluntly: it is because our system of public education is a horrendous, life-destroying mess. The destruction is primary. The faculties themselves, the powers of mind, are nipped in the bud, or are held inoperative, which eventually comes to the same thing.

There is no such thing as learning except (as Dewey tells us) in the continuum of experience. But this continuum cannot survive in the classroom unless there is reality of encounter between the adults and the children. The teachers must be themselves, and not play roles. They must teach the children, and not teach "subjects." The child, after all, is avid to acquire what he takes to be the necessities of life, and the teacher must not answer him with mere professionalism and gimmickry. The continuum of experience and reality of encounter are destroyed in the public schools (and most private ones) by the very methods which form the institution itself—the top-down organization, the regimentation, the faceless encounters, the empty professionalism, and so on.

Eléna and Maxine suddenly began assimilating schoolwork at a fantastic rate. Their lessons were brief and few, yet in a year and a half both girls covered more than three years' work. Maxine, who had been behind in everything, was reading three years beyond her age level. But the truth is that there was nothing unusual in this, though certainly it seems to be rare. I mean that the girls found it *easy*. José gradually reversed his long-standing habit of total failure. He began to learn. His progress was slow, but his experience was much like that of the girls. I mean that he discovered—just barely glimpsed—the easiness of learning. And invariably, when he glimpsed it, a very particular laughter bubbled out of him, expressing release.

The experience of learning is an experience of wholeness. The child feels the unity of his own powers and the continuum of persons. His parents, his friends, his teachers, and the vague human shapes of his future form one world for him, and he feels the adequacy and reality of his powers within this world. Anything short of this wholeness is not true learning. Children who store up facts and parrot the answers (as John Holt has described in *How Children Fail*) invariably suffer a great deal of anxiety. If they are joined to the continuum of persons, it is not by the exercise of their powers, but by the suppression of their needs. Rebellious children are more loyal to their instincts, but they suffer the insecurity of conflict with the persons who form the continuum of life.

The really crucial things at First Street were these: that we eliminated—to the best of our ability—the obstacles which impede the natural growth of mind; that we based everything on reality of encounter between teacher and child; and that we did what we could (not enough, by far) to restore something of the continuum of experience within which every child must achieve his growth. It is not remarkable that under these circumstances the children came to life. They had been terribly bored, after all, by the experience of failure. For books *are* interesting; numbers are, and painting, and facts about the world.

Let me put this in more specific terms by saying a few words about José. At the same time, I would like to show that what are widely regarded as "learning problems" are very often simply problems of school administration.

José had failed in everything. After five years in the public schools, he could not read, could not do sums, and had no knowledge even of the most rudimentary history or geography. He was described to us as *having* "poor motivation," *lacking* "reading skills," and (again) *having* "a reading problem."

Now what are these *entities* he possessed and lacked? Is there any such thing as "a reading problem," or "motivation," or "reading skills"?

To say "reading problem" is to draw a little circle around José and specify its contents: syllables, spelling, grammar, etc.

Since we are talking about a real boy, we are talking about real books, too, and real teachers and real classrooms. And real boys, after all, do not read syllables but words; and words, even printed words, have the property of voice; and voices do not exist in a void, but in very clearly indicated social classes.

By what process did José and his schoolbook come together? Is this process part of his reading problem?

Who asks him to read the book? *Someone* asks him. In what sort of voice and for what purpose, and with what concern or lack of concern for the outcome?

And who wrote the book? For whom did they write it? Was it written for José? Can José actually partake of the life the book seems to offer?

And what of José's failure to read? We cannot stop at the fact that he draws a blank. How does he do it? What does he do? It is impossible, after all, for him to sit there *not listening*. He is sitting there doing something. Is he daydreaming? If so, of what? Aren't these particular daydreams part of José's reading problem? Did the teacher ask him what he was thinking of? Is his failure to ask part of José's reading problem?

Printed words are an extension of speech. To read is to move outward toward the world by means of speech.

Reading is conversing. But what if this larger world is frightening and insulting? Should we, or should we not, include fear and insult in José's reading problem?

And is there a faculty in the mind devoted to the perception and recollection of *abc?* Or is there just one intelligence, modified by pleasure, pain, hope, etc. Obviously José has little skill in reading, but as I have just indicated, reading is no small matter of syllables and words. Then reading skills are no small matter either. They, too, include his typical relations with adults, with other children, and with himself; for he is fiercely divided within himself, and this conflict lies at the very heart of his reading problem.

José's reading problem is José. Or to put it another way, there is no such thing as a reading problem. José hates books, schools, and teachers, and among a hundred other insufficiencies—*all of a piece*—he cannot read. Is this a reading problem?

A reading problem, in short, is not a fact of life, but a fact of school administration. It does not describe José, but describes the action performed by the school, i.e., the action of ignoring everything about José except his response to printed letters.

Let us do the obvious thing for a change, and take a look at José. This little glimpse of his behavior is what a visitor might have seen during José's early months at the First Street School.

He is standing in the hallway talking to Vicente and Julio. I am sitting alone in the classroom, in one of the student's chairs. There is a piece of paper in front of me, and on it a sentence of five words. The words appear again below the sentence in three columns so that each word is repeated a number of times. Now since José came to us with a reading problem, let us see what relation we can find between these one dozen syllables and the extraordinary behavior he exhibits.

He had been talking animatedly in the hall. Now as he comes to join me, his face contracts spasmodically and the large gestures of his arms are reduced to almost nothing. There is no one near him, and he is absolutely free to refuse the lesson, yet he begins to squirm from side to side as if someone were leading him by the arm. He hitches up his pants, thrusts out his lower lip, and fixes his eyes on the floor. His forehead is lumpy and wrinkled like that of a man suffering physical pain. His eyes have glazed over. Suddenly he shakes himself, lifts his head, and squares his shoulders. But his eyes are still glassy. He yawns abruptly and throws himself into the chair beside me, sprawling on the tip of his spine. But now he turns to me and smiles his typical smile, an outrageous bluff, yet brave and attractive. "Okay, man—let's go." I point to the sentence and he rattles it off, for his memory is not bad and he recalls it clearly from the day before. When I ask him to read the same words in the columns below, however, he repeats the sentence angrily and jabs at the columns with his finger, for he had not read the sentence at all but had simply remembered it. He guffaws and blushes. Now he sits up alertly and crouches over the paper, scanning it for clues: smudges, random pencil marks, his own doodles from the day before. He throws me sagacious glances, trying to interpret the various expressions on my face. He is trying to reconstruct in his mind *the entire sequence* of yesterday's lesson, so that the written words will serve as clues to the spoken ones, and by repeating the spoken ones he will be able to seem to read. The intellectual energy—and the acumen—he puts into this enterprise would more than suffice for learning to read. It is worth mentioning here that whenever he comes upon the written word "I," he is thrown into confusion, though in conversation he experiences no such difficulty.

Now what are José's problems? One of them, certainly, is the fact that he cannot read. But this problem is obviously caused by other, more fundamental problems; indeed, his failure to read should not be described as a problem at all, but a symptom. We need only look at José to see what his problems are: shame, fear, resentment, rejection of others and of himself, anxiety, self-contempt, loneliness. None of these were caused by the difficulty of reading printed words—a fact all the more evident if I mention here that José, when he came to this country at the age of seven, had been able to read Spanish and had regularly read to his mother (who cannot read) the post cards they received from the literate father who had remained in Puerto Rico. For five years he had sat in the classrooms of the public schools literally growing stupider by the year. He had failed at everything (not just reading) and had been promoted from one grade to another in order to make room for the children who were more or less doomed to follow in his footsteps.

Obviously not all of José's problems originated in school. But given the intimacy and freedom of the environment at First Street, his school-induced behavior was easy to observe. He could not believe, for instance, that anything contained in books, or mentioned in classrooms, belonged by rights to himself, or even belonged to the world at large, as trees and lampposts belong quite simply to the world we all live in. He believed, on the contrary, that things dealt with in school belonged somehow to school, or were administered by some far-reaching bureaucratic arm. There had been no indication that he could share in them, but rather that he would be measured against them and be found wanting. Nor did he believe that he was entitled to personal consideration, but felt rather that if he wanted to speak, either to a classmate or to a teacher, or wanted to stand up and move his arms and legs, or even wanted to urinate, he must do it more or less in defiance of authority. During his first weeks at our school he was belligerent about the most innocuous things. Outside of school he had learned many games, as all children do, unaware that they are engaged in "the process of learning." Inside the school this ability deserted him. Nor had it ever occured to him that one might deliberately go about the business of learning something, for he had never witnessed the whole forms of learning. What he had seen was reciting, copying, answering questions, taking tests—and these, alas, do not add up to learning. Nor could he see any connection between school and his life at home and in the streets. If he had heard our liberal educators confessing manfully, "We are not getting through to them," he would have winced with shame and anger at that little dichotomy "we/them," for he had been exposed to it in a hundred different forms.

One would not say that he had been schooled at all, but rather that for five years he had been indoctrinated in the contempt of persons, for contempt of persons had been the supreme fact demonstrated in the classrooms, and referred alike to teachers, parents, and children. For all practical purposes, José's inability to learn consisted precisely of his school-induced behavior.

It can be stated axiomatically that the schoolchild's chief expense of energy is self-defense against the environment. When this culminates in impairment of growth—and it almost always does—it is quite hopeless to reverse the trend by teaching phonics instead of Look-Say. The environment itself must be changed.

When I used to sit beside José and watch him struggling with printed words, I was always struck by the fact that he had such difficulty in even *seeing* them. I knew from medical reports that his eyes were all right. It was clear that his physical difficulties were the sign of a terrible conflict. On the one hand he did not *want* to see the words, did not want to focus his eyes on them, bend his head to them, and hold his head in place. On the other hand he wanted to learn to read again, and so he forced himself to perform these actions. But the conflict was visible. It was as if a barrier of smoked glass had been interposed between himself and the words: he moved his head here and there, squinted, widened his eyes, passed his hand across his forehead. The barrier, of course, consisted of the chronic emotions I have already mentioned: resentment, shame, self-contempt, etc. But how does one remove such a barrier? Obviously it cannot be done just in one little corner of a boy's life at school. It must be done throughout his life at school. Nor can these chronic emotions be removed as if they were cysts, tumors, or splinters. Resentment can only be made to yield by supporting the growth of trust and by multiplying incidents of satisfaction; shame, similarly, will not vanish except as self-respect takes its place. Nor will embarrassment go away simply by proving to the child that there is no need for embarrassment; it must be replaced by confidence and by a more generous regard for other persons. It need hardly be said that when these transformations take place, the child's ability to learn, like his ability to play and to relate positively to his peers and elders, will increase spectacularly. But what conditions in the life at school will support these so desirable changes? Obviously they cannot be taught. Nor will better methods of instruction lead to them, or better textbooks.

When, after ten minutes of a reading lesson, José said to me that he wanted to go to the gym, and I said, "Okay," a little revolution began in his soul. His teacher respected his wishes! This meant, did it not, that the teacher took him seriously as a person? It became easier for José to take himself seriously as a person. And when he cursed, bullied, fought with classmates, and the teachers responded only with their own emotions, not ever with formal punishment, demerits, detention, etc., did it not mean that they were encountering him precisely as he was, and that in order to face them he did not first have to suppress everything but his good behavior? He could stand on his own two feet; they could stand on theirs. His anxiety diminished, and his resentment—and his confusion.

The gradual changes in José's temperament proceeded from the whole of our life at school, not from miniscule special programs designed expressly for José's academic problems. And not the least important feature of this life (it was quite possibly the most important) was the effect of the other children on him. I mean that when adults stand out of the way so children can develop among themselves the full riches of their natural relationships, their effect on one another is positively curative. Children's opportunities for doing this are appallingly rare. Their school life is dominated by adults, and after school there is no place to go. The streets, again, are dominated by adults, and sometimes by a juvenile violence which in itself is an expression of anxiety.

In writing these words I cannot help but compare the streets of our cities with my own environment as a child in the late-Depression small-town suburbs of Pittsburgh. There were woods all around us, and fields and vacant lots. And American parents had not yet grown so anxious about their children—or about themselves. When school let out, and on Saturdays and Sundays, our parents rarely knew where we were. I am speaking of the ages of eight, nine, and ten. We were roaming in little gangs, or playing in the woods, the alleys, the fields. Except at mealtimes we were not forced to accommodate ourselves to the wishes of adults. In the New York of today, and the world of today—with its anxieties, its plague of officials and officialdom, its rat race of careers, its curse of all-pervading politics, which seduces even intelligent minds into regarding abstractions as if they were concrete—the life of a child is difficult indeed.

Perhaps the single most important thing we offered the children at First Street was hours and hours of *un*supervised play. By unsupervised I mean that we teachers took no part at all, but stood to one side and held sweaters. We were not referees, or courts of last resort. Indeed, on several occasions with the older boys, I *averted* violence simply by stepping out of the gymnasium! We provided some measure of safety in the event of injury, and we kept people out. It was a luxury these children had rarely experienced.

I would like to return to this subject later, and say in some detail why it is and how it is that children, left to their own devices, have a positively curative effect on one another. This is the kind of statement that many professionals look upon askance and identify as Romantic, as much as to say that the sphere of the world rides upon the tortoise of their own careers. Many teachers and parents, however, will recognize in this assertion one of the loveliest and most meaningful of the facts of life. Would growth be possible—indeed, would there be a world at all —if the intake of the young were restricted to those things deliberately offered them by adults? Consider, too, how shocking it would be if for two minutes we adults could reexperience the powers of mind—the concentration, the memory, the energy for detail, to say nothing of the physical élan—we possessed at the age of ten. Our vanity in relation to the young most certainly would not survive.

Here are two little incidents that occurred at school. They are typical of the thousands which supported the development of self-respect, confidence, trust, and regard for other persons. The same events, by the same token, diminished shame, embarrassment, self-contempt, hostility, and distrust of others. As a by-product of all this, the barrier was lifted which had formerly clouded the children's experience of all things, including studies.

Rudella, the Negro girl of nine, took offense at some harsh words that were addressed to her in Susan's class. Because of her shyness, she found it difficult to speak up for herself; but she was not, on that account, forced to sulk and swallow her pride. She put on her coat and announced that she was "leavin' this place." She said that she wasn't coming back, meaning forever, but implying *all day*. And so she departed, enjoying an exit every bit as good as a Triumphant Entrance. She went to the candy store on the corner and bought herself a chocolate soda. One might well imagine that as the soda dwindled, forever dwindled to a day; and that when the soda vanished, the day seemed very long. Perhaps she reflected that she had departed triumphantly and with great dignity, and that her classmates were well aware of her pride. In any event she suddenly appeared in the doorway of the classroom, taking off her coat, angrily warning her teacher that that sorry event had better not happen again. Her teacher smiled, and one of her classmates said vivaciously, "Here's Rudella!"

When Kenzo injured Eléna, he knew that José, following the code of *machismo* so important to Puerto Rican men, would take revenge in order to restore the family honor. José was almost three years older than Kenzo, and Kenzo had good reason to be frightened. Kenzo was large for his age and was well coordinated; also, for his age, he was expert in judo. In a straight-out fight he might beat José, but in fact—and Kenzo knew it—José was indomitable. He simply would not give up. And he would not forgive. If he lost with his fists, he would resort to a knife. Perhaps he would not *use* the knife, but then again he might. And he would lay in wait after school. José was accustomed to the violence of the local streets. Kenzo had been raised far more gently, by a bohemian father and an artistic mother. He was not by temperament a fighter.

Such thoughts as these must certainly have passed through Kenzo's mind. But if José would not give up and would not forgive, there was still one thing he *would* do: like all boys, he would gradually (that is to say, *swiftly* by adult standards) forget. And so Kenzo stayed out of school for three days, a Friday and a Monday and Tuesday, thus interposing five whole days between the event and his next confrontation with José. When he returned, he was prepared to placate José, and he brought with him a little gift.

The outcome of this adventure will appear in the next installment of the journal. For the moment, I would like to point out that Kenzo knew he would not be forced to come to school. We would not mark him absent and would not punish him on his return.

How abject he would have been if in spite of his fears and his quite accurate estimation of the danger, an unfeeling coalition of adults had forced him to attend! Was he not entitled to be frightened? And by what right could we have forced him to expose himself to danger when we could not offer protection, especially in the hours after school? It meant a great deal to him that we accepted his own solution. His young-boy feeling of helplessness was diminished, as was his resentment of adults and of authority in general—a resentment so routinely engendered by the unwilling submissions of childhood.

The effect on José was significant. He found himself dealing directly with the fact of Kenzo's absence. Adult intervention at this point would have raised an absolutely spurious smoke screen of "ethical issues," which in their blindness to the real facts would not have been ethical at all. More important, the pronouncements of authorities would have convinced José that he was outside the law. I did explain to him that Kenzo could not really be blamed for hitting Eléna; and I expressed my own dislike of violence. Aside from this, we adults did not try to "settle" an isue that belonged to the children. And José did not at all feel outside the law, but quietly conjured with the fact that he himself was the cause of Kenzo's absence. It was a little flattering to be so feared, but it was a little depressing, too. What did Kenzo think of him, really? Were his occasional overtures of friendliness simply the result of fear?

I think I need hardly stress that such freedoms as I have just described did much to restore the children's self-esteem and natural pride. What may not be so obvious is that freedom also allows moral considerations to enter actively into the life at school. The question of right action can never be raised at all unless feelings are expressed and respected. There is no such thing as a moral action without a moral feeling. Even "the sense of duty" —which often omits compassion—involves feelings, and usually very deep ones. Lacking feeling, there is nothing but precept, and precept is nearly valueless. Nor can the feelings that belong to right action—doubt, shame, guilt, compassion, love, the sense of justice—be isolated from other feelings and cultivated like hothouse flowers. They literally belong to all the other feelings. The evolving self knows itself through feeling. When emotion in general is suppressed, the "finer feelings" are suppressed as well.

It is worth mentioning here, too, that when children are allowed to work out their ethical problems, adults no longer appear to them as mere figures of authority. They are removed from the central position of actors and become interested observers, in which position they appear as the elders of the community rather than the heads of organizations. Where the pronouncements of authorities are often repugnant and damaging to children, the opinions of elders are just as often respected, and are sometimes eagerly sought. Here again the natural authority of adults is thrown into optimal relations with the needs of children.

I keep remarking on the growth of children. I should say also that under conditions such as I have been describing, teachers, too, can be seen to grow. It is no small thing to enter into sustained face-to-face relations with a number of children. They are not great encouragers of vanity, conceit, capriciousness, or any of the other self-illusions to which we adults are all too prone. Once the barrier of force is removed between the age-groups, the adult is drawn inevitably toward simplicity, directness, and honesty.

There were many other incidents—literally thousands —in which the growth of the self could be observed in direct relation to the conventions we followed. Some have been mentioned in the journal and more will appear in forthcoming excerpts. My point in describing them is a simple one: we cannot raise children to be free men by treating them like little robots; we cannot produce adult democrats by putting children in lock step and placing all decisions in the hands of authorities. Nor can we enhance the moral prestige of school by basing the entire institution on the act of force which compels attendance.

So many adults these days live in a world of words—the half-real tale of the newspapers, the half-real images of television—that they do not realize, it does not sink in, that compulsory attendance is not merely a law which somehow enforces itself, but is ultimately an act of force: a grown man, earning his living as a cop of some kind, puts his left hand and his right on the arm of some kid (usually a disturbed one) and takes him away to a prison for the young—Youth House. I am describing the fate of hundreds of confirmed truants. The existence of Youth House, and of the truant officer, was of hot concern to two of our boys. They understood very well the meaning of compulsory attendance, and understanding it, they had not attended. We abolished that act of force, and these chronic truants could hardly be driven from the school. We did try to drive them out on several occasions—I mean seduce them out, inveigle them out, urge them out. We wanted them to take their bikes and go exploring the city instead of wasting another springtime day in school. But their opinion of the city was such that they preferred not to go—an ironic limitation on our hopes for freedom.

* 4 *

Alfred North Whitehead, in his *Aims of Education*, tells us that one of the greatest of intellectual tasks is routinely performed by infants under the aegis of mother and father.

The first intellectual task which confronts an infant is the acquirement of spoken language. What an appalling task, the correlation of meanings with sounds. It requires an analysis of ideas and an analysis of sounds. We all know that an infant does it, and that the miracle of his achievement is explicable. But so are all miracles, and yet to the wise they remain miracles.

All parents have observed this process. All know that they have contributed to it. Few indeed, however, will insist that it was they who *taught* their children to talk. Here again we find evidence that instruction, of itself, is not the highroad to learning.

What is it about the environment of the home that so marvelously supports this great intellectual task of infancy? I would like to pursue this for a moment, and then raise the question of transposing these environmental qualities into the overall structure of school.

Crying is the earliest "speech." Though it is wordless, it possesses in prototype many of the attributes of true speech: it is both expressive and practical, it effects immediate environmental change, it is directed to someone, and it is accompanied by facial expressions and "gestures." All these will be regularized, mastered by the infant long before the advent of words.

Two features of the growth of this mastery are striking:

1) The infant's use of gestures, facial expressions, and sounds is at every stage of his progress the true medium of his being-with-others. There is no point at which parents or other children fail to respond because the infant's mastery is incomplete. Nor do they respond as if it *were* complete. The infant, quite simply, is one of us, is of the world precisely as the person he already is. His ability to change and structure his own environment is minimal, but it is real: we take his needs and wishes seriously, and we take seriously his effect upon us. This is not a process of intuition, but transpires in the medium he is learning and in which we have already learned, the medium of sounds, facial expressions, and gestures.

2) His experimental and self-delighting play with sounds—as when he is sitting alone on the floor, handling toys and babbling to himself—is never supervised and is rarely interfered with. Parents who have listened to this babbling never fail to notice the gradual advent of new families of sounds, but though this pleases them, they do not on this account reward the infant. The play goes on as before, absolutely freely.

The infant, in short, is born into an already existing continuum of experience. The continuum is the medium within which his learning occurs. In the ordinary home the continuum is one of maximum relation. From the infant's point of view—even though he be often frustrated —the ratio of effort and effect is high indeed. There are no breaks in the continuum in the sense that important demands meet no response. (When this does occur, we read of it in case histories of autism and schizophrenia.) Volition, too, is maximized: nor does being alone, inventing, playing, following mere whim, in any way threaten the security of the continuum.

The role of imitation in all this is essential to any theory of learning. The extent and nature of it are often misunderstood. An infant of, say, fourteen months, not yet in possession of many words, will often enter vivaciously into the conversation of his parents, will look from face to face, join in the laughter, and "speak up" in sounds which are far from being words, but which are spoken with very definite facial expressions and in rising and falling tones. These will often be accompanied by hand gestures obviously copied from the parents. The infant seems to be imitating grown-up speech. But *is* this what he is doing? Parents are perhaps deceived because the sight is inevitably so charming, all that display of participation, with so little content. They forget that among their own motives the desire to charm, to enliven, to make a merry noise, is not insignificant. And they overestimate the content of what they themselves have said, for the truth is that the music of our ordinary conversations is of equal importance with the words. It is a kind of touching: our eyes "touch," our facial expressions play back and forth, tones answer tones. We experience even the silences in a physical, structural way; they, too, are a species of contact. In short, the physical part of everyday speech is just as important as the "mental" . . . and precisely this physical part has already, to an impressive extent, been mastered by the fourteen-month-old child. Too, when we raise the question of imitation, we tend to forget that the whole forms of our own speech consist actually of a great many parts, all of them very intricate: sounds, rhythms, accents, tones, breathing patterns, facial expressions, gestures. When even a small number of these are present in an infant's "speech," we are already far beyond the stage of mere imitation.

But in truth there never was such a stage. The infant is surrounded by the life of the home, not by instructors or persons posing as models. Everything that he observes, every gesture, every word, is observed not only as action but as a truly instrumental form. And this indeed, this whole life of the form, is what he seeks to master. It is what he learns. No parent has ever heard an infant abstracting the separate parts of speech and practicing them. It simply does not happen. Even in those moments that we might think of as instruction—when, for example, we are bending over the baby, saying "wa-ter" to correct his saying "waddah"—our inevitable élan is that of a game; and in any event, as every parent knows, the moment this élan vanishes and mere instruction takes over, the infant will abruptly cease to cooperate. It is not only that he is unable to conceptualize, but that we have removed the instrumentality he has all along been studying. He no longer recognizes the sounds as a *word;* and indeed, at this moment, they are not a word in the true sense, but a conceptual device of pedagogy.

When we see the infant in action, then, it is impossible to say that any given expression or gesture is an imitation. What we mean is that we recognize its source. The fact that we observe it at all indicates that it has already been assimilated, or is well on the way. We are observing it in use.

A true description of an infant "talking" with its parents, then, must make clear that he is actually taking part. It is not make-believe or imitation, but true social sharing in the degree to which he is capable. We need only reduce this complex actuality to the relative simplicity of imitation to see at once what sort of loss he would suffer. The vivacity, the keen interest, the immediate sharing in the on-going intercourse of others, and above all, the environmental effect—all these would vanish. His experience would be reduced to the dimensions of a chore, like that of an actor preparing a part. But in fact we cannot conceive of experience reduced to such dimensions. The infant, in short, is not imitating but doing. The doing is for real. It advances him into the world. It brings its own rewards in pleasure, attention, approval, and endless practical benefits.

This very distinction between imitating and doing lies at the heart of John Dewey's thoughts on education. It is the root meaning of "learning by doing," words which for many years now have been little more than a catchphrase signifying the filling-in of blanks in prepackaged experiments. Dewey's strength lies in his profound understanding of the whole forms of experience: the unity, in growth, of *self*, *world*, and *mind*. It was because of his perception of this unity that he insisted that school be based in the community and not in the Board of Education. (Another of the disastrous myths of the educationists is that we have already availed ourselves of the thought of Dewey. Nothing could be further from the truth.)

These things, then, for the growing child, are maximized in the environment of the home: relationship, participation, freedom of movement, and freedom of volition with respect to the objects of attention. Knowledge is gained in immediately instrumental forms. The gain is accompanied by use and pleasure. The parents do not pose as models, but are living their lives, so that from the point of view of the infant the model is life itself.

Before comparing this optimum environment with the usual environment of school, I would like to give another example from the home, one more deliberately educative, and one again with which most parents are familiar.

Let us imagine a mother reading a bedtime story to a child of five. And let us apply Dewey's wholistic terms, bearing in mind that normal learning is not a function merely of intelligence, or of the growth of the self, but that self, mind, and world belong together as one fact. In Dewey's formulation, mind *is* the on-going, significant organization of self and world.

We can judge the expansion of self and world by the rapt expression on the face of the child, the partly open mouth and the eyes which seem to be dreaming, but which dart upward at any error or omission, for the story has been read before a dozen times. Where does the story take place? Where does it happen in the present? Obviously in the mind of the child, characterized at this moment by imagination, feeling, discernment, wonderment, and delight. And in the voice of the mother, for all the unfolding events are events of her voice, characteristic inflections of description and surprise. And in the literary form itself, which might be described with some justice as the voice of the author.

The continuum of persons is obvious and close. The child is expanding into the world quite literally through the mother. But here the increment of *world*, so to speak, is another voice, that of the author, made durable in its subservience to literary form. Because of the form itself, there hover in the distance, as it were, still other forms and paradigms of life, intuitions of persons and events, of places in the world, of estrangement and companionship. The whole is supported by security and love.

There is no need to stress the fact that from the point of view of learning, these are optimum conditions. I would like to dwell on just two aspects of these conditions, and they might be described, not too fancifully, as *possession* and *freedom of passage*. The former refers to the child's relation to ideas and objects of perception, the latter to his relations with persons already associated with such forms.

Both the mother, in reading the story, and the author, in achieving it, are *giving* without any proprietory consciousness. The child has an unquestioned right to all that transpires; it is of his world in the way that all apprehendable forms are of it. We can hardly distinguish between his delight in the new forms and his appropriation of them. Nothing interferes with his taking them into himself, and vice versa, expanding into them. His apprehension of the new forms, their consolidation in his thoughts and feelings, is his growth . . . and these movements of his whole being are unimpeded by the actions of the adults. Certainly there is effort on his part, but it is experienced as fulfilling action. The effort does not include self-defense against the environment. Nor is it accidental that he is blessedly unaware of himself. This follows from the fact that he is already accepted, already included, by his mother's act of giving and by the absolute offer inherent in the literary form.

If we wished to retard his learning and complicate his growth, we could do it by the following steps: 1) turn his attention back upon himself by letting him know that he is being observed, measured, and compared with others; 2) destroy his innate sense of his own peerage among sensible forms by insisting that they are to be apprehended in standardized ways and that their uses are effectively controlled by others; 3) make his passage among persons dependent upon the measurements to which he has been subjected; 4) apply physical coercion to his freedom to move, to express his feelings, to act upon his doubts, to give or refuse his attention—all of which will convince him that learning is an act of disembodied will or of passive attention, neither of which he can find within himself; 5) present him with new forms in a rigidly preordained order and quantity, so that he will give up utterly the hope of the organic structure which proceeds outward from his own great attraction to the world.

We need not extend this list. It is obvious that I am describing the ordinary school. The results of such methods, *in extremis,* can be seen in the behavior of José as he sits beside me for a lesson. His attention is so centered in himself—in his fear of failure, his resentment, his self-contempt—that quite literally he cannot see what is under his nose. The words on the paper, the words of the teachers, books, pictures, events of the past—all these belong to school, not to the world at large, and certainly not, by prior right, to himself. His passage among persons— among teachers and schoolmates both, and among the human voices of books, films, etc.—is blocked and made painful by his sense of his "place," that is, by the measurements through which he must identify himself: that he has failed all subjects, is last in the class, is older than his classmates, and has a reading problem. He is under coercion of all kinds and no longer knows what it means to express his own wishes simply and hopefully, or to *give* his attention, or to take seriously his doubts and special needs. As for the organic unity of self, mind, and world, he is so fragmented, so invaded by an environment too much for his feeble defenses, that by any serious standard he must be described in terms of crisis.

I've been using the words "reality of encounter," "continuum of persons," and "relation." All these are vital aspects of environment. When a teacher conceives of his task as mere instruction, the accomplishment of a lesson, and when he addresses himself to his pupils as to containers of varying capacities into which the information must be poured, he is creating conditions which are fatal to growth. Testing, grading, seating arrangements according to the teacher's convenience, predigested textbooks, public address systems, guarded corridors and closed rooms, attendance records, punishments, truant officers—all this belongs to an environment of coercion and control. Such an environment has not consulted the needs of normal growth, or the special needs of those whose growth has already been impaired.

If the environment of the home is optimal for the great tasks of learning that belong to the early years, it is no longer so by the age of four or five. A larger community is essential, a larger body of peers, and perhaps persons of special talents. Yet in order to obtain these, it is not necessary to abandon utterly the environmental qualities that proved so marvelously supportive to the first tasks of learning, those remarkable feats which, in Whitehead's words, "to the wise remain miracles." Obviously we cannot make our schools into "second homes." Nor would it be desirable, for children are not born into families alone, but into nature and civilization as well. It would be crippling to delay the child's progress into the whole.

We can, however, pay attention to the salient features of our only known excellent environment; and by experimentation we can discover which of its aspects can be carried over into the environment of school. This was precisely our opportunity at First Street. We made much of freedom of choice and freedom of movement; and of reality of encounter between teachers and students; and of the continuum of persons, by which we understood that parents, teachers, friends, neighbors, the life of the streets, form all one substance in the experience of the child. We abolished tests and grades and Lesson Plans. We abolished Superiors, too—all that petty and disgusting pecking order of the school bureaucracy which contributes nothing to the wisdom of teachers and still less to the growth of the child. We abolished homework (unless asked for); we abolished the category of truant. We abolished, in short, all of the things which constitute a merely external order; and in doing this, we laid bare the deeper motivations and powers which contribute to what might be called "internal order," i.e., a structuring of activities based upon the child's innate desire to learn, and upon such things as I have already described: the needs of children, the natural authority of adults, the power of moral suasion (the foundations of which are laid in the home), and the deep attachment and interest which adults inevitably feel toward the lives of children. This last—the motivation of teachers—tends to be lost sight of in the present low-grade careerism of the teaching profession. Yet many adults do find themselves and expend their love in precisely this function. Their own motivation is one of the most reliable sources of organic order.

* 5 *

In our own time, the most important example of freedom in education has been A. S. Neill's Summerhill School in England. It is a residence school—a community, really—and its laws and customs are worked out by all participants. In spite of the great popularity of Neill's book, *Summerhill: A Radical Approach to Child-Rearing*, the school itself still has an undeserved reputation for anarchy. Its distinctiveness lies actually not in the absence of regulations, but in the kinds of regulations it makes use of and in its manner of arriving at them. There is a General School Meeting every Saturday night. All questions pertaining to the life of the community are discussed here and are settled by vote. Where certain kinds of rules (e.g., bedtime regulations for the young) tend to survive in one basic form, others are changed frequently or refined. Penalties are extremely specific. One lonely boy, for example, was cured of stealing when his fellows voted to give him money for each offense.

But there is no need to describe Summerhill here. Interested persons will have read the book, which in its paperback edition was a long-term best seller in this country. I would like to quote from John Holt's description of the school, however, as it appeared in the *Bulletin* of the Summerhill Society, U.S.A., in 1965:

> It was the young children, six, seven, and eight, who made the strongest impression on me. The older children, though free, seemed not to have had their freedom long enough to be able to relax with it and take it for granted. The little ones were quite different. Occasionally, very rarely, in a particularly happy family, I have seen little children who have seemed wholly secure, at ease, natural, and happy. But never before this meeting had I seen so many of them in one place, least of all in a school. They were joyous, spontaneous, unaffected. I wondered why this should be, and at the party I thought I saw why. More times than I could count, I would see a little child come up to a big one, and with a word, or a gesture, or a clutch of the hand, claim his attention. I never saw one rebuffed, or treated anything but lovingly. The big kids were always picking them up, hugging them, swinging them around, dancing with them, carrying them on their shoulders. For the little children, Summerhill was a world full of big people, all of whom could be enjoyed, trusted, and counted on. It was like living in an enormous family, but without the rivalries and jealousies that too often plague our too small and too possessive families. . . .
>
> One of the rules is that bedtime in the cottage, where the little kids live, is at 8:30. Further down the page I read another rule, obviously passed under pressure of necessity: "All kissing good-night involving cottagers must be over by 8:30."

The two issues most frequently discussed by persons who are interested in Summerhill—either for or against —are its sexual mores and the children's freedom to stay away from classes.

In sexual matters, Neill's point of view is a simple one: the evils of repression can be avoided. We are not *sexual* beings, but human beings. Sexuality cannot be excluded from our lives; neither will it dominate our lives under conditions of freedom. Neill detests pornography, prurience, and priggishness. To be antisex is to be antilife.

In short, sex is not treated as an evil at Summerhill. In fact—so I infer from Neill's pages, and so I gather from talks with Summerhill alumnae—it is not much "treated" at all. The boys and girls are let alone. One might say that Nature takes its course, but the fact is that Nature always takes its course. I doubt if there is any more sex at Summerhill than at American high schools, but certainly the air is cleaner than ours, the lives of the students freer of cant and hypocrisy and lame-duck psychology.

Neill speaks often of the "free child," and in many respects his book is intended as a manual of child-rearing. The idea of sexual freedom is not a Neillian idea. We hear it instead from the mouths of his critics and of some few disciples he himself has declared he wished he did not possess. One of Neill's great virtues is that he keeps his eyes on persons. We tend to do the opposite here in America, and lose ourselves among issues. The distinction is crucial in practice, and is worth going into in some detail.

The phrase "sexual freedom," like almost every phrase involving the word freedom, is a polemical abstraction. Its background is a long series of heated arguments. When we turn from these arguments to the phenomena of lives, we see immediately that what we call "freedom" is not ours to give, and what we call "sexuality" cannot be defined by kissing, caressing, and making love. I have listened to arguments about sexual freedom at conferences sponsored by the Summerhill Society in New York. They were often touching, almost always excited and urgent. Adults cannot speak of this issue except in tones of longing, regret, resentment, anxiety, bitterness. One finds housewives in the audience who seem to be speaking of their children, but whose tones and facial expressions are saying, "I am yearning for love! Absolve me of my sexual guilt!"; and others who, in effect, cry bitterly, "I was denied it, and by God I won't grant it to anyone else!" Some speak with sadness and regret, and soon find themselves reassuring the anxious ones. Both band together and attack the authoritarians in their midst. I have observed all this when adolescent students were also present. One had only to look at their faces to understand the truth: they preferred the dignity of being let alone, but come what may, they would certainly fuck. Nor were they interested in sexual freedom, but in Jane and Harriet, LeRoy and Dick. Love, after all, is love. It may tolerate poets, but *spokesmen* are anathema, whether they're *for* or *against*.

Yet these young persons were extremely interested in the arguments. There was something they shared immediately with the adults.

Aside from regret for the past, and the anxious fear of regret itself, the adults were not speaking (either pro or con) of the actual behavior of particular young persons. They were speaking of their own willingness to sanction sexuality, or their desire to confine it. Nor were the young who were present worried very much that their own pleasures would be denied them. They would outwit the adults, as always. They would climb out windows and down rainspouts; they would tell lies, etc. Yet they, too,

were extremely interested, and their interest was similarly in the question of sanction.

Sanction is not a matter of *what happens*, but of methods of control and ideals of life: what sort of world must
we build? The young understand this question with great
immediacy. And they want a great deal more than sexual
freedom. They want *wholeness*. They do not want to lie
and evade and suffer guilt, but to affirm themselves in
the largest possible harmony of self and society, passion
and intellect, duty and pleasure. They want the esteem
of their elders, and they cannot help but want the excitement that rises so imperiously in their own experience.
They know very well, too, that where sanction is involved,
the attitudes of a few teachers are mere grains on a sandy
shore. The problem begins in infancy and runs through
the whole of society. Mere slogans and attitudes are of
little value, and there is a terrible, naive hubris in the
behavior of a teacher who believes that he can sanction
sexuality by conferring freedom. He can no more sanction
it than sanction the law of gravity. All he can do is cease
to attempt to control the young. Beyond this he can ally
himself with the student's quest for wholeness. Here the
teacher's own quest for wholeness is extremely valuable.
Life being what it is, there is no man who can stand before the young and acclaim himself an exemplar of liberated energies. The "do as I do" cannot be put in this
form, for if he boasts of sexual freedom, the young will
wonder about the propaganda: why does he boast? Why
is so much energy devoted precisely to polemics? A good
example of this attitude can be found in the writings of
Henry Miller, which carry a heavy theme of sexual and
self-liberation. One observes, however, that the liberated
self constructs a peculiar and hermetic environment, one
of proselytizing: endless rhapsodies on liberation, preach-

ing freedom in order to retain the illusion of it. The loss
is obvious: it is the world. Euphoria, in this context,
might be defined as anxiety masquerading as pride.

In life, as in art, the healing truth is the whole truth.
The libertarian teacher cannot give freedom. He can only
cease to control. He cannot sanction sexuality. He can
only seek to allay guilt. He cannot eradicate sexual embarrassment either in himself or in his students by an act
of will, but he *can* identify embarrassment as a problem,
just as he can hold forth a human ideal in which hatred
of the body, distrust of emotion, and repugnance toward
sex will find no part. At best, the libertarian can demonstrate reason, faith, generosity, and hope struggling
against the damages he himself has already sustained and
which he hopes to mitigate in the lives of his students.
This is a far cry from the banner-waving of sexual freedom. Let me give an example to make this more plain.

I visited a school ostensibly modeled on Summerhill,
but in fact (so I believe) not much like it. I noticed two
teen-agers who were pathologically depressed. I learned
that they were suffering severe conflicts with their parents. I was informed, too, that their parents were small-
minded, narrow, repressive, status-seeking petit bour-
geois; which is to say that the suffering of the two students had been invested with a programmatic, radical
meaning: their detestation of their parents appeared as
a form of loyalty to the school. The two students, in short,
were in a hopeless quandary, being tugged in opposite
directions by self-interested adults. To make matters
worse, the tugging at school was largely *sub rosa*, implicit
rather than overt, and the foreground was filled by "freedom," that is, by lack of contact, lack of guidance, lack
of structure, lack of everything that children experiencing

such disorders absolutely require. Let me hasten to say that such lacks as these cannot be filled by rules and regulations. They must be filled by persons, and not just any persons, but those capable of true encounter and decently motivated for work with the young. The problem at this school was that the director himself regarded staff and students less as people than as events in his own protracted crusade against middle-class America. The faculty, too, consisted of True Believers, and I had never before seen such a listless, resentful bunch, or heard the words "creativity" and "spontaneity" bandied about quiet so often.

When the young are experiencing conflicts within themselves, it is disastrous for the teacher to "take sides"; and no vice is more prevalent among teachers than taking sides against the parents. What the student needs is not an ally in one quarter of his own psychic economy—which tends to perpetuate his conflict precisely as conflict—but an ally in the world. This is what I mean by supporting his quest for wholeness. It is the difference between saying, "You are right to detest your parents," and saying, "You are obviously suffering because you detest your parents." It is the difference between saying, "Transcend your sexual guilt! Be free!" and saying, "Let us take your guilt seriously. How do you experience it?" I am not suggesting that every teacher be a psychotherapist. I am insisting that every teacher put himself in relation with the person before him, and not with one portion of that person's conflicts. Just to the extent that a teacher will do this, he will recognize, too, that sexuality permeates everything. It cannot be set aside and given special treatment. When, in the classroom, the child is allowed to speak freely and experience the creative unity of feelings, hunches, thoughts, humor, etc., we are in fact supporting a positive sexuality. When we create conditions which do away with shame and self-contempt, we are supporting a positive sexuality. And so on.

The notion of sexual freedom, in short, is another of many symptoms of the massive sickness of our world. It is not an idea we can use, but an idea that needs to be dissolved until its atoms come to rest again in the phenomena of life. It would be helpful, too, to recognize that sexuality is a world phenomenon, not merely an individual one. There is an ecology of the emotions. No better example can be found than that of the hippies of New York's East Village. They are remarkably good-looking and sweet-natured young people. They believe earnestly in sexual freedom and the beauty of the human body. And they act upon their beliefs. But alas! alas! the erotic élan of youth simply isn't there. And all their modest or desperate bravery, and their earnest believing, cannot put it there. The conditions of their lives are decisive. Their lot is anxious, insecure, badly nourished, cut off from the future, alienated from the past, anonymous in the present. They are haunted by the bomb and deadened by crises of identity. Where will the joy of life come from? Another example, showing again the meager role of opinion where such broad, primitive phenomena as sexuality are involved: I attended a showing at an avant-garde film house, and after the main course a little divertissement was thrown on the screen for laughs, one of those all-girl-orchestra shorts of the early 1930's, two dozen marimba players in low-cut gowns and long-enduring smiles. Members of the audience (not all, for I think some must have felt as I did) laughed complacently at their provincial style and the bouncy banality of their music. None of that meant much to me. I was absolutely astonished at the sensual appearance of those girls. Their smiles were in fact naive smiles of pleasure, their eyes were bright, their faces vivacious, their arms and shoulders softly rounded and relaxed, and there was something melting and fluid in the way their torsos rode upon their hips. Would any one of them have come out for sexual freedom? One might well suppose that they had few attitudes at all, and if asked would simply affirm for the moment the most conventional—and by our standards, retrograde—morality. But that was prewar America, not yet so hugely organized, rich in space and time, the future undarkened by the bomb or the present by unending war, hot and cold. I need not list the differences. Flesh and psyche were simply better off, and they certainly looked it. The lights went on and the girls in the audience stood up, adjusting their plastic coats and mini-skirts. Some were still smiling. All most likely were digesting the Pill they had taken that morning. And how put-upon they looked! I do not mean that they were spiritless. Not at all. There was something strong in them, something admirable. But the verve and color was all in their clothes. Their eyes were lightless or fixed, their faces drawn tight by lines of strain. Tension showed in their throats and the unyielding motions of their gaits. Some, no doubt, had a style in bed, as they had a style in clothes and a style in cars. They would quite routinely speak in affirmation of sex, and confess to the psychotherapist that the issue was not sex but meaning, joy, life, passion, love, and describe a nightmare of growing cold, not unrelated to the style of being "cool." As for the therapist, he will have heard the identical story, in essence, a thousand times. These tales are not produced by family strife alone, or by America destroying itself in isolation. They are the landscape of the modern world.

If we want to release and sustain and civilize, in the

true sense, the sexuality of the young, we can begin by putting sexuality back into the person. It is the whole child we are interested in. We can increase his security, treat him with justice and consideration, respect his pride of life, value the independence of his spirit, be his ally in a world that needs to be changed. We can do nothing —more directly than this—about his sexuality.

The practice at Summerhill is a case in point. The security of the individual, his constructive role in the community, the absence of punishment and coercion, the student's responsible awareness of other lives—these things taken together promote a healthy, positive sexuality for the same reason that they promote unusual courtesy (many visitors have remarked on this) and vigorous self-reliance: the whole person is encouraged to flourish. If many problems still remain, it is not surprising, since Summerhill is a small part of a large and troubled world.

Nor is it odd that some few of Neill's disciples should have distorted his meaning. This happens inevitably to every innovator, which is another way of saying that Neill is not a Summerhillian, any more than Freud was a Freudian, or Reich a Reichian. Pioneers of this kind emerge into history in severe conflict with the value systems of their youth. In their own persons they represent profound resolutions of conflicting experience. Their conflicts, however, tend to become background. I mean that their chief appearance in the writing is a stylistic one. Freud, for example, was adopted as the patron saint of the French surrealists, but after an interview with Breton, refused to take seriously their use of his insights. They had not understood him. For one thing they had paid no attention to the meaning of his style—his reverence for reason and for ordinary virtue—but had seized upon the revelation of the Unconscious as if it were the key to the whole of life. Reich, similarly, believed in the self-regulation of the organism. But by regulation he meant its harmony in a world which included rationality and duty. Just so, the character of Neill was not formed in a Summerhillian universe, but in a difficult world containing both traditional and revolutionary values. This world is present at Summerhill in the person of Neill, which is to say that many of its values are present by active demonstration, though they may not be much spoken of: values of rectitude, courage, patience, duty, pragmatic common sense. These are much in evidence, too, in Neill's writing, which helps to account, I think, for its popularity in this country, surfeited as we are with the voiceless "objectivity" of our hordes of Experts. If some few of Neill's disciples have minimized these things, it is because they have seized impatiently upon certain insights, namely, those which justify their own anger at a world that has injured them.

Summerhill is our chief point of reference, too, when the question of compulsory attendance comes up. This is an issue much discussed by libertarian teachers, and is one that will become important on a larger scale if the present liberalizing tendency in education should ever really alter our public schools. Should we compel attendance, or not? Neill tells us that at Summerhill the children are in no way pressured into attending classes. Unfortunately he does not tell us enough about what they do in the meantime. Some few purists that I have observed have bent over backwards on this issue, creating a kind of vacuum between themselves and their students in order to give the students' volition enough room to mature. This, it seems to me, is an error. It arises, in good part, from posing the problem in terms of attendance and compulsion.

But the whole issue, as we know it in this country, testifies to a really peculiar anxiety and lack of faith on the part of adults. Would children really abandon school if they were no longer compelled to attend? Or, more properly, would the acquisition of skills and knowledge and the participation in large-scale social life with their peers suddenly lose all attractiveness? The idea of *school*—not perhaps in its present bureaucratized form—is one of the most powerful social inventions that we possess. It rests squarely on the deepest of necessities and draws on motives we could not disavow even if we wished to. Teaching is one of the few natural functions of adults. Vis-à-vis the young, we simply cannot escape it. Too, our legitimate demand of the young—that in one style or another they be worthy inheritors of our world—is deeply respected by the young themselves. They form their notions of selfhood, individual pride, citizenship, etc., in precisely the terms that we put forward, converting our demands into goals and even into ideas of glory. I cannot believe all this is so feeble that we need to rest the function of education upon acts of compulsion, with all the damage this entails.

If compulsion is damaging and unwise, its antithesis— a vacuum of free choice—is unreal. And in fact we cannot deal with the problem in these terms, for the real question is not, What shall we do about classes? but, What shall we do about our relationships with the young? How shall we deepen them, enliven them, make them freer, more amiable, and at the same time more serious? How shall we broaden the area of mutual experience? If these things can be done, the question of school attendance, or classroom attendance, will take a simpler and more logical form, will lie closer to the fact that classroom instruction is, after all, a *method* (one among many) and deserves to be criticized in terms of its efficiency. It is not the be-all and end-all of a child's existence. Let me put this in terms of our experience at the First Street School.

It was not the case that there was a lesson available and that José, for example, was free to go or not to go. The first facts were otherwise. By first facts I mean the context within which the possibility of *any* lesson unavoidably arose.

1) He was thirteen years old and had behind him six years of the most abysmal failure. He did his best to hide his mortification, but it was obvious that he suffered because of his inability to learn. He was afraid to make another attempt, and at the same time, he wanted to.

2) We established a relationship. This was not difficult, for I liked him, though liking him would not have been essential. We spent several weeks getting to know each other, roughly three hours a day of conversations, games in the gym, outings, etc. We lived in the same neighborhood and saw each other on the streets. He knew me as George, not as "teacher."

3) He understood immediately that our school was different, that the teachers were present for reasons of their own and that the kind of concern they evinced was unusual, for there were no progress reports, or teacher ratings, or supervisors. Yet this concern, which appeared so unusual in a school setting, was identical with the everyday concern of his relatives and grown-up neighbors, who often asked him about his schoolwork and were obviously serious when they expressed their hopes for his future.

4) He understood that I had interests of my own, a life of my own that could not be defined by the word "teacher." And he knew that he, though not a large part of my life, was nevertheless a part of it.

Now given this background, what must José have thought about my wanting to teach him to read? For I did want to, and I made no bones about it. He saw that I considered it far more important than many of the fleeting feelings he expressed or exhibited.

The fact is, he took it for granted. It was the right and proper relationship, not of teacher and student, but of adult and child, for his relatives wanted him to read, and so did his neighbors; and if it were not for the dreadful pressures of life in the slums, among which are the public institutions and the general hatred thereof, many of them could have taught him. But the idea occurred to no one, least of all José.

And so I did not wait for José to decide for himself. When I thought the time was ripe, I insisted that we begin our lessons. My insistence carried a great deal of weight with him, since for reasons of his own he respected me. Too, his volition, in any event, could arise only from a background in which I myself already figured, with my own interests and my own manifestation of an adult concern he was accustomed to everywhere but in school. He did *not* feel that his own motives were no concern of mine. No child feels this. This belongs to the hang-ups of adolescence and the neuroses of the hippies. To a child, the motives of adults belong quite simply to the environment. They are like icebergs or attractive islands: one navigates between or heads straight for them. The child's own motives are similarly projected outward; they become occasions for dissimulation or closer contact. It is because of this that both affection and straight-out conflict come so easily. They come inevitably, and they belong, both together, to the teaching-learning experience.

My own demands, then, were an important part of José's experience. They were not simply the demands of a teacher, nor of an adult, but belonged to my own way of caring about José. And he sensed this. There was something he prized in the fact that I made demands on him. This became all the more evident once he realized that I wasn't simply processing him, that is, grading, measuring, etc. And when he learned that he *could* refuse—could refuse altogether, could terminate the lesson, could change its direction, could insist on something else—our mutual interest in his development was taken quite for granted. We became collaborators in the business of life.

Obviously, if I had tried to compel him, none of this would have been possible. And if I had made no demand —had simply waited for him to come to class—I would in some sense have been false to my own motives, my own engagement in the life of the school and the community. In his eyes I would have lost immediacy, would have lost reality, as it were, for I would have seemed more and more like *just* a teacher. What he prized, after all, was this: that an adult, with a life of his own, was willing to teach him.

How odd it is to have to say this! What a vast perversion of the natural relations of children and adults has been worked by our bureaucratized system of public education! It was important to José that I was not just a teacher, but a writer as well, that I was interested in painting and had friends who were artists, that I took part in civil rights demonstrations. To the extent that he sensed my life stretching out beyond him into (for him) the unknown, my meaning as an adult was enhanced, and the things I already knew and might teach him gained the luster they really possess in life. This is true for every teacher, every student. No teacher is just a teacher, no student just a student. The life meaning which joins them is the *sine qua non* for the process of education, yet precisely this is destroyed in the public schools because everything is standardized and the persons are made to vanish into their roles. This is exactly Sartre's definition of inauthenticity. I am reminded here, too, of how often John Dewey and, in our own time, Paul Goodman and Elliott Shapiro have urged the direct use of the community. The world *as it exists* is what the young are hungry for; and we give them road maps, mere diagrams of the world at a distance.

What I have just described of my relations with José might also be said of Mabel, Gloria, and Susan in their relations with the other children. Gloria and Susan were perhaps more demanding than Mabel and I. Nevertheless, all of the children could refuse. They needed a good reason to do it, and they had to stand up to the adults. But they discovered that good reasons were respected. Boredom, for instance, is a good reason. The beautiful days of spring are good reasons. An ardent desire for something else is a good reason. Anxiety is a good reason. So is a headache or a toothache. And there are many things which if they arise during the course of a lesson, deserve and must be given full precedence, such things as considerations of justice, self-respect, friendship. We and the children, in short, were in an on-going experience of attraction and repulsion, of cooperation and conflict. Out of this flexible and many-faceted encounter, the actual structure of our time together evolved. The essential thing was the absence of compulsion. For every child there was always *a way out* and *a way in,* and—most important—a Bill of Personal Rights equal to that of the teachers. The children *could* win, not by availing themselves of an empty foreground of "freedom," but by encountering the adults head-on. It was a noisy school, as should be, though often, as should be, an electrically quiet one.

It is so easy to underestimate the importance of conflict that I would like to stress for a moment that it is both inevitable and desirable—I mean desirable in a developmental sense, for it certainly hurts a teacher's ears and frays his nerves. I am referring, of course, to the noisy conflicts, the kinds that *do* arise and that only rarely have a parliamentary outcome. It boils down to this: that two strong motives exist side by side and are innately, not antagonistic, but incongruous. The one is that we adults are entitled to demand much of our children, and in fact lose immediacy as persons when we cease to do so. The other is that the children are entitled to demand that they be treated as individuals, since that is what they are. The rub is this: that we press our demands, inevitably, in a far more generalized way than is quite fitting for any particular child. And there is nothing in this process that is self-correcting. We must rely upon the children to correct us. They'll do it in their own interests, however, not in ours. In fact, they'll throw us off, perhaps with much yelling and jumping, like a man in a pair of shoes that pinch his feet. Let any teacher think back over the course of a month and ask himself how often this has occurred; and ask himself, too, if he would knowingly eliminate it, however much he might like to in the interests of his nerves. These mutual adjustments occur steadily in a broad, broad stream, and we notice everything about them—their noise, duration, obduracy, etc.—everything but the fact that their additive shape is beautifully rational and exceeds anything we might invent by the exercise of our wits.

I must admit that I have mentioned conflict just here because I have always been annoyed by the way some Summerhillians speak of love, of "giving love," or "creating an atmosphere of love." I have noticed, not infrequently, that the "love" of such enthusiasts is actually inhibited aggression. But this is by the way. The point itself is worth making: we cannot give love to children. If we do feel love, it will be for some particular child, or some few; and we will not give *it*, but give ourselves, because we are much more in the love than it is in us. What we *can* give to all children is attention, forbearance, patience, care, and above all justice. This last is certainly a form of love; it is—precisely—love in a form that *can* be given, given without distinction to all, since just this is the anatomy of justice: it is the self-conscious, thoroughly generalized human love of humankind. This can be seen negatively in the fact that where a child (past infancy) can survive, grow, and if not flourish, do well enough in an environment that is largely without love, his development in an environment that is largely without justice will be profoundly disturbed. The absence of justice demands a generalized suspicion of others and alters the sense of reality down to its very roots. The environments I have just referred to are not hypothetical but institutional. The former is an orphanage I had a chance to observe; the latter is Youth House.

I have said nothing of the times when the children don't want to go to class. What happens then? But there are no such times, any more than there are times when we adults cross the street because we don't want to stay on the same side, or go to a ball game because we don't want to stay in the house. Often at First Street the children knew fairly well what they wanted to do instead of sit in class: a trip, a picnic, a project of some sort. But usually they did not quite know what it was, though a lesson was clearly not it. Some dim figure of what they wanted —perhaps of what they needed—was present in their minds and they could not quite see it or name it. And isn't it traditionally the role of adults to help them discover what will truly engage them? It is part of a teacher's job, then, to help his students find out what to do instead of sitting in class. Here is an example. The five older boys had passed through a period of strife (largely racial) and had suddenly become united, almost as a gang. The warm weather had arrived. They were restless, hated the idea of lessons, ran out of the school, ran back, milled around in the hall, went out again and sat on the front steps, moping ferociously. They didn't know what to do. We suggested that they go out on bikes. That wasn't quite right. And they didn't want dodge ball or games in the park. They didn't want a supervised trip either. It became apparent that something real was lurking in their minds, something they vaguely agreed upon or vaguely sensed was important. What was it? Mabel intuited what it was: they wanted to do something *together*, some shared and purposeful activity that would confirm their new relationships. She suggested they make a pool table—and that was it! They trooped off to the lumberyard and bought a big piece of plywood, and strips for the sides, and some foam rubber, and green felt, and glue, and a coping saw to make the holes, and a file to smooth them. They worked at their table almost a week and it came out surprisingly well, and they used it when it was finished. And it was evident all along that this table was an embryonic clubhouse—exactly what they needed.

At the risk of repeating myself, let me stress again that we cannot, as teachers, define our relations with children in terms of lessons, or even school. School itself is merely one feature of the on-going relationship between children and adults. Or rather, it should be. Our society, as it is, is dreadfully closed to children, dreadfully compartmentalized. And between home and school there is no provision at present but the truant officer.

In comparison with residence schools in the country, we were fortunate in having the city all around us. I am not thinking so much of the activities that were available as of the fact that in our relationships with the students we were not so unremittingly confined to our roles as teachers, as if to say that classes and lessons were all that we shared with them. We shared the world with them, and this brought lessons, and school itself, into a much healthier and more realistic perspective.

* 6 *

José's revenge never took place. Kenzo came in
quietly, poised between flight and tears. José ignored him. Whether this truce could have lasted
all day, it was impossible to tell, for two new boys arrived that morning who so obviously looked like trouble
that both José and Kenzo, to say nothing of the teachers,
began immediately to size them up.

They were eleven-year-olds, but tougher, stronger, and
more hardened by the slums than any of ours (who, to
this point, were all Puerto Ricans and had behind them
—however far behind—the softening influence of sub-
tropical village life). The new arrivals were Stanley, an
Italian-Jewish boy, and Willard, a Negro, broad-shouldered and steely, very large for his years.

We left the school en masse to see the Paper Bag Players at the Henry Street Playhouse.

Stanley and Willard, who have known each other for
several years, sat together in the back of the bus, with
excited faces and contemptuous smiles. Stanley held Willard by the arm and talked rapidly into his ear, indicating
different boys by movements of his eyes. Willard, who

was about to be sent to a 600 school (in which he did not belong), followed his glance a bit slowly. His broad smile gave off some little quantity of plain humor.

Stanley is an operator, a juvenile con man who deprives himself of everything he needs. He is intelligent, athletic, sometimes charming, more often vicious, a liar and thief, unstable and desperate. His hair and eyes are black and bright, his mouth both pugnacious and infantile. He has the double-jointed, curved-back thumbs I've noticed before on agile, headstrong, eccentrically gifted persons.

The theater was filled with children from the public schools. The Paper Bag Players were humorous and inventive. Their essential quality is a kind of bland delight. As usual I watched the audience; they were mostly under ten. There were many Puerto Rican and Negro girls here, enjoying it immensely and following everything with such intelligence and verve that I couldn't help wondering how many would end in factories or on welfare, and what would become of those bright, bright faces, so ready for life. Dodie, Rudella, Eléna, Hannah, Maxine—a whole line of ours sat together, stretching their necks like everyone else. From time to time they leaned their heads together, whispering and pointing. I located Stanley and Willard, who again sat apart from the rest of us. Stanley seemed like a little thug, as if he had modeled himself on some television notion of Al Capone; and then his face would change, and a very appealing, high-spirited, desperate child would appear. He was scornful of the antics on the stage and kept whispering to Willard, who sometimes seemed annoyed with him, yet bent his head and listened.

We had visitors at lunch, one of the teachers and several of the children from the Collaberg School, near Bear Mountain. We sat in a large circle eating leisurely, with

a great deal of talking back and forth. Suddenly an outcry went up. José and Willard fell to the floor, pummeling
each other and cursing. José's blows were few, and Willard punished him viciously. José kicked to get free, and
they rolled back and forth so violently that I was afraid
they'd hit some of the little ones. One of the Collaberg
kids, a boy of thirteen, was so terrified that he hid in the
closet and then ran from the room crying. I managed to
separate them. I was astonished at Willard's strength. I
put them in separate rooms, insisting that they cool off.
When I got back to the main room, Stanley was rolling
on the floor with Julio, hitting him in the ribs and screaming. I sent Stanley and Willard downstairs with their
coats. We teachers conferred and then sent them home
for the day.

José was shaken by the fight. It was clear to him, too,
that if these boys came to school, his privileged place as
the oldest boy would be changed to a wretched third.
"They're no good, man! Don't let them come to this
school!"—under which sentiments lay the violent racial
contests he had already suffered on the streets.

Kenzo, too, had understood the change in power. He
had sidled up to the new boys with words of flattery and
disparaging comments on his Puerto Rican classmates.

We teachers discussed the new boys at length that afternoon. We decided to down our misgivings and enroll
them. Willard did not belong in a 600 school. Stanley had
been expelled a number of times and was on his way to a
life of crime, though it was especially he who showed so
much promise. Both were in the care of a psychiatric social worker, who had urged us almost plaintively to accept them. "This is the last chance for really meaningful
help." We decided to admit Willard first, and in a couple
of weeks, Stanley.

The kids from the Collaberg School have a sense of being special. Many of them come from intellectual families. The boys wear their hair even longer than the Beatles, and one, Donnie, a blond, wears it so long and is so pink and rosy that it's hard to tell whether he's a boy or a girl. For several minutes Vicente, Julio, and Kenzo stood in a row staring at him, their mouths hanging open.

Watching the Collaberg kids, one senses the intellectual convention of being "outsiders," which is to say that they have many important connections with the mainstream culture. Our kids, especially the Negroes and Puerto Ricans, are truly deprived and are discriminated against, and from the point of view of the general culture might very well be called outsiders. But they would never describe themselves in that way. On the contrary, they make a strong identification with what they take to be the power at the center. The Collabergians talk Volkswagens and Porsches, ours talk Cadillacs.

It's so indicative of José's situation that where he has learned to read such words as "brother," "father," "mother," "dream," he still gets confused when he sees the word "I"!

2/2/65

Our plan to have Willard first, and Stanley later, was upset by the effective conniving of Willard and Stanley. Willard failed to appear. Stanley came instead, all smiles and innocence, explaining that Willard's mother wanted him to stay in the public school. Their tactic was transparent, as were Stanley's lies; but he so obviously wanted to come to the school, and was so obviously on his good behavior, that we had no choice but to admit him. He acted friendly toward the other boys and seemed attentive to the teachers. It was easy to see the qualities that had won the sympathy of his psychologist. Trouble wasn't long abrewing, however.

Several of the girls were still in the gym when the boys went down. Stanley was immediately attracted to Eléna and began to tease her. But where this kind of teasing, with its vein of real cruelty, is routine among Americans, it is relatively rare among Puerto Ricans. Eléna did not know how to take it. To make matters worse, she turned her ankle and began to cry. Stanley mocked her crying, and then—the last straw—even José joined in the teasing. She railed at José in Spanish, pointing her finger, arm extended. He stuck out his lip and wrinkled his nose. Eléna leaped on him and threw him to the floor. Before he could roll over, she clamped her teeth on his chest, on his nipple, and held on while he howled in pain. José wouldn't hit her, and was too firmly captured to escape. He beat his arms against the floor and howled. Finally she let go. But she was still upset and cried some more. Stanley mimicked her crying. His cruelty was too obvious to be ignored. José pushed him. "Don't insult my sister, man!" In a moment they were rolling on the floor. Stanley is much stronger than José, and faster, though not as tall. He dominated him easily, and was aware of it and held back from hurting him. Vicente danced around them and skipped over to where I stood. "Let them fight it out, man!" José was not only losing the fight, but was failing badly in his effort to uphold the family honor. And yet he wasn't failing either, for there was nothing Stanley could do to make him give up. José kept yelling, "Don't do that with my sister, man! I'll get you, man!" Stanley let him up at last. José rushed at him, and down they went again, José on the bottom.

When they got up this time, José was frantic. "I'll get you, man! You'll see! I'll cut you up!" He ran from the gym. Stanley was worried about the knife. I wasn't sure that José had one, or had hidden one, as seemed to be the case. I told Stanley that I would confiscate any knives. I went out into the hall to intercept José. He came running down the stairs, Vicente right behind. Again Vicente screamed at me, "Let them fight it out, man! Don't stop them, man!" His eyes were large, bright, and glazed. It was all a television show. He had no idea that real blood comes out, that real intestines get cut. I stopped José. "I don't have no knife, man!" I looked at both his hands, and felt his pockets. There was no knife. The two boys ran past me. Vicente reached in his pocket and handed José a knife. José opened it, revealing a six-inch blade. Stanley's face went white, then flushed with rage. He picked up one of the metal folding chairs and cried, "I'll kill you, man!"

I stepped in front of José and took his wrist. I was chiefly worried whether he was in or out of his senses. Eléna, with her blind rages, would be truly dangerous with a knife. José was another matter. I looked at him closely. He did not know whether to cry or curse. He was partly frightened himself. Yet the knife was no mere show. It would be hard to say how far he would go if he were driven. He did not struggle, however, when I took the knife out of his hand. By now both boys wanted an honorable way out of their dilemma. They yelled back and forth, and I joined by yelling that Stanley did not know that Eléna was José's sister. Stanley seized on this immediately. The boys kept yelling, but now there was a slight deflection in their accusations and replies, and it was obvious that some essential point had been granted. José went back into the hall. He asked me for his knife. I told him that I'd give the knife to his mother, and that he mustn't ever bring it to school again. At the mention of his mother, he became frightened. He went upstairs. When I came up for lunch, I found him sitting by himself, fuming and blinking away tears. I told him I wouldn't tell his mother, but I would keep the knife for a few days, and he mustn't ever bring it again. He said he didn't want that new kid around the school. He repeated this several times. "He has to go, man!" I said that there were eighteen kids now, and José couldn't make decisions for all of them. Even as I said this, I felt my dishonesty. We hadn't asked the kids at all, and it was clear that not one would vote to accept him. But then not one of them could understand either that if we rejected Stanley, he would soon be in Youth House, and perhaps over the hill forever. We could not run a rescue service and refuse to rescue him.

Later that day Stanley made friendly overtures to José, addressing flattering comments to him and sneaking pieces of candy into his hand.

Both Eléna and her mother have been going to the clinic, Eléna for work on her feet (some kind of warts on the soles), and her mother for some sort of leg trouble which might require hospitalization. Eléna and José are worried. If their mother is hospitalized, they may be forced to stay with relatives in Puerto Rico.

2/3/65

Mabel brought an old typewriter to school. Several of the kids were fascinated and played with it eagerly.

Dodie gave a hilarious imitation of a high-speed typist, her fingers flying everywhere and her face hanging with lordly unconcern over that huge display of energy. José, too, was interested, and so I sat beside him and looked on. Soon enough he said to me, "What should I write?" I suggested the word "see." He located the letters by himself and struck them. We did some more simple words, and then I suggested a sentence I knew he was familiar with. He hunted for the letters and struck them. On this ancient typewriter, due to a defect, you can't see what you've written except by turning up the roller one line, and so you don't know while you're typing whether you're doing it correctly or not. When José needed help, he asked for it. Most of the sentence he was able to do by himself. And now he turned up the roller to see how it had come out, *and for the first time at school let out a gleeful yell of accomplishment!* There was the sentence, and he had written it himself, and it was perfect! He even stamped his feet with glee. And so we kept at it for more than half an hour, and another learning game evolved from it. I took the typewriter and asked him to suggest words to me. After typing them, I cut them out in little pieces and gave them to him and asked him to make sentences by laying them end to end. He did this readily, putting himself into it, though it wasn't easy. He was sufficiently absorbed to accept my postponement of gym, though he had suggested going down after the first part of the lesson.

The boys played dodge ball, and Stanley was eager to show off his speed. Same with tag-in-the-dark: Stanley dominated the game. José was jealous but not unfriendly.

Maxine came into the gym for a while during the dodge-ball game, and in her provocative voice yelled obscenities at the boys and turned her back to them and flaunted her ass. Stanley caught her and wrestled her to the floor. Maxine's shouts of protest were richly mixed with laughter. José came to where I stood at the far end of the gym and insisted that I call Stanley off. He was furious and jealous. I pointed out that Maxine was laughing and therefore wasn't frightened, as some days previous she had been frightened and I had intervened. "She's no good!" said José, who if Stanley hadn't been there, would have been wrestling with her and giggling. After a few minutes I made Maxine leave the gym. José followed her to the door, called her a whore, and kicked her in the rear.

Later in the day both Kenzo and Vicente expressed their dislike of Stanley. They're quite aware of the instability of his character and of his viciousness. José said, "He wants to be king."

José's days of playing Hercules are over, all that strutting and throwing out his chest. It's pathetic. He always did it childishly and without viciousness, and got something out of being able to do it. Stanley's presence robs them all of a certain childishness and richness of experience. He shows more promise than any of them, and at the same time is far more deeply disturbed. All the dynamics of petty tyranny are visible in his behavior. He is really a typical strong man, a South American general, a U.S. cop—every strength, every ability, corrupted and frozen in the protection of the desperate infant trapped inside.

2/4/65

Willard, Stanley's pal, came to school today, with a broad, guilty grin: "My mother say I don't get in fights, I can come to school." And so here they are together, just as they planned. Their presence changes things enormously. The school is sharply divided between younger and older, for none of the older boys now dares reveal his childishness by playing with the little ones, and this means an end to the marvelous games, the castles, kings, and queens, gladiators and robbers, in which all participated a few weeks ago. The girls and younger boys still play among themselves, but neither Stanley nor Willard is able to play. The anxiety of these tough guys! How wretched it is! Now Kenzo, Julio, José, and Vicente are caught in that trap, too.

This morning, while Stanley was using the telephone, little Bertrand Kleist, who weighs about fifty pounds and is six years old, but bold and bright, prankishly pulled out the jack. Stanley became enraged and wanted to beat him up, and I had to intervene.

Dodge ball has become a racial struggle. Willard and Stanley square off in their contempt of the Puerto Ricans, and Kenzo joins them fawningly. Just because of this animosity, however, the game is spectacularly alive. José shouts with bravado, "Throw, man, throw!"—offering himself as target. "We beat you easy!" And Willard, who throws strongly, knocks him out on the first shot. José walks to the sidelines, scuffing his feet, *reality* passing like a shadow down his face. But Julio throws strongly, too, and both he and Vicente are more agile and have faster reflexes than either Stanley or Willard . . . and the ball flies back and forth to the accompaniment of insults, jeers, taunts, and shouts of exultation.

Before lessons this morning, José made a great show in front of Willard and Stanley of talking tough to me, throwing back his head and using foul language. As soon as we went to the other room, he reverted to his gentler style, and we had a good lesson. I've been asking Mabel to lock us in the room, not to keep José in but to keep the others out. This is all that's needed now for things to go well, i.e., that he be protected from all comparison with others and from his own terrible sense of failure.

Stanley and Willard stole Maxine's lunch early in the morning and ate it. They were surprised that we didn't punish them, and surprised again at lunchtime to discover that all could eat their fill—there was no limit. Yet it will take them some time to learn that no special glory attaches here to defiance of the teachers. Everything is personal . . . and it's boring (surely) for a lively kid to persist in some generalized attitude when he's faced every day only by an individual, not a System.

José came to my apartment after school today. It was obvious that he felt threatened by the arrival of the new boys and wanted to be reassured that he wouldn't be displaced. I was working on an article. I gave him some paper and paints, and he busied himself in the other room while I typed.

And now that he sees I won't abandon him, he acts especially blustery toward me when they're around, so that they won't take him for a teacher's pet. His blustering is usually a bit comical, since he's quite gentle as a rule, far more childish and sweet-natured than most American boys of that age.

2/5/65

We took the kids sledding this morning, up to the Collaberg School, near Bear Mountain. Mabel used to teach there, and years ago, under its original name—The Barker School—it was the pioneer in this country of the

Summerhill methods. I drove the microbus, and Tom Gomez, Maxine's stepfather, took a gang in his station wagon, which kept breaking down.

The day was enormously successful. The snow, the hills, the trees, and the wide-open sky—all this excited our kids immensely. They burst out of the cars as if hurled by an explosion and ran up the hill, waving their arms and shouting. Several sleds lay in the snow by the schoolhouse. Vicente seized one and flew down the hill—headlong into a ditch. Ah, Experience! As usual there had been nothing in his head but two or three images, no sense of cause and effect, no notion that trees, for instance, might not remove themselves from his path (he almost hit one), or that a ditch, which had no proper place in the Sled-Riding Image, might nevertheless obtrude into it at the bottom of the hill. He got up and shook himself and looked around. One could almost see the images dissolve. Here was a real hill, real snow, real trees, real ditch. His face brightened again and he went racing up the hill.

As usual, too, our boys, so starved for pleasure and possessions and so convinced that every moment demands a struggle, fought for the sleds and refused to take turns. But there were other things to slide on, big pieces of cardboard, some planks, the hull of an old plastic boat. And soon enough the boys were taking turns, giving up their sleds to each other and sliding on these makeshifts in-between. Tom Gomez and I both used a piece of cardboard.

The Collaberg kids joined us, and I was impressed by how good they looked, how lively, yet considerate and gracious. Our kids learned a lot that day. They explored the school buildings, looked at projects in art and science, ate informally in the kitchen, and I'm sure were impressed by the ease and friendliness of it all, to say nothing of the fact that they were invited to share things and did not have to fight for them. If only the rest of their lives could be like this! There was a murder on Julio's block last week, and a drug arrest on José's that made the newspapers.

Riding back, they struck up songs in the microbus, the ones Barney has been teaching them. That is, the younger ones did, and the girls. Willard and Stanley were silent, but their faces were more relaxed than I had ever seen them. They looked almost happy.

2/9/65

As we mill around in the morning, kids hanging up their coats and everyone gabbing, José struts and acts tough. He makes a swipe at my head, saying, "Come on, man, you think you tough. Come on, man," and in the very next breath says, "Come on, George, we gonna have the most terrific lesson in the world."

Mabel locks us in the room again, as she has been doing for several days. It works like a charm. José sits at the desk with the typewriter, puts the paper in, rattles the keys, and says, "Okay, boss, I'm your secretary." And so I dictate words to him, those he can read but can't quite spell: "Look at the book," "I see the dog." This is task-work, quite different in spirit from our work in the note-book. It makes him stretch a bit, yet I'm careful to keep it within his range. He taps his foot excitedly, listens attentively, and types the words with positive eagerness. When he makes a mistake, he feels crushed. Where he used to collapse into apathy, however, now he acts it all out, groaning, blushing, hitting his head. It is as if the least error were the same as total failure. But he recovers from all this and confronts the typewriter again.

Our informal style really and truly works. It's not just the relationship with me that José finds so supportive, but the absence of grades, testing, official goals, etc. He still has no conception of the experience of learning, but he came to us totally flattened and is now alive and willing.

When I spell a word that is hard for him, he turns from the typewriter and scans my face. He tries to remember when I last spelled the word and what he did then. He cannot make the learning process his own, not by trial and error, memory aids, or simple questions; which is to say that he is still trapped in the effort to perform as demanded, though it is now chiefly he alone who makes the demand. He does not ask of himself that he learn, but that he cease failing. When he grows confused, he breaks into snatches of rock-and-roll, thumps his feet, even jumps up and dances around. I never interfere with this. It permits him to extend his confrontation with his own anxiety.

We end with his typing some longer sentences made up of the words with which he is most familiar. He is very careful and types them flawlessly. I tell him it was a good lesson, and he grins and shouts, "Let's go to gym!"

I am convinced that when children (except perhaps for the seriously disturbed ones) remain vicious or violent toward each other, it is because their motives are invaded by those of adults, and they cannot evolve their own better terms of relation. When they're given enough room, their adjustments to each other, and to their own fears and impulses, are marvelously creative and subtle.

When Stanley and Willard first came to school, there was a violent fight. When Stanley came alone, there was another fight, and José pulled a knife. And for several

days, with Stanley and Willard in school together, there
was violence in the air, those two squared off against the
Puerto Ricans. Yesterday some trivial incident occurred,
and the boys decided to "fight it out." At first the fight
was scheduled to take place after school, but then they
decided to have it in the gym. They ran down the stairs
in a flock, Vicente looking back at me and raising his
finger: "Don't you break it up, man!" (He says this,
really, because he still has impulses to run to me for protection, and this is one way he resists them. He has improved enormously. Two months ago he was afraid to
play dodge ball at all, quit at the slightest bump, refused
to follow rules, acted like a resentful infant, spited everyone by stalling whenever he got the ball. Now he plays
with great zest, and in fact—because his reflexes are about
three times faster than anyone else's—has become the star
dodger. He's learning to throw the ball and takes his
knocks very manfully.)

The boys shouted back and forth excitedly—insults,
plans for the fight, threats, boasts, and some kind of cooperative exchange concerning vague outer limits of behavior. They cooperated, too, in getting out the mats and
laying them in a great square. I helped them with this
and then withdrew to the end of the gym, where I sat on
the floor and leaned against the wall.

A great shout went up, a roar, and all five piled into
each other . . . and stopped abruptly to let José take
off his shirt. Stanley and Willard took their shirts off, too.
They were about to clash again when Stanley paused and
took off his shoes, and so Willard and José took their
shoes off, too. The roar went up again and they tangled,
Stanley and Willard against José, Julio, and Vicente. Their
fighting included both punching and wrestling. Vicente,
so much tinier than the others, kept grimacing and gritting

his teeth, fighting a courageous, woefully losing battle.
He wanted to use some of the throws he's been learning
in his judo class, and he kept sidling up to his enemies and
more or less sketching out the throw in the empty air,
receiving a lump on the head at the completion of each
one. Where Stanley and Willard were quite ferocious
with Julio (and less so with José, whose bravery they
respect), they couldn't help but take a shine to Vicente,
and Stanley even complimented him: "Gee, Vicente, you
have a hard head!" There was much cursing, many shouts
of pain—strange shouts, really, for each one had in it a
tinge of protest and flattery. It was in these overtones
that one could sense the fine changes in their relations.
They were saying things for which they had no words, and
the refinement of this communication was extraordinary
and beautiful. It was apparent immediately that the boys
had set some kind of limit to their violence, though they
had not spoken of limits. Rules, codes, acknowledgments
popped up spontaneously and changed swiftly. When
anyone got hurt, he stepped off the mats (it was usually
Julio, holding his head and complaining in a voice which
paid tribute to Willard's strength); and the rule was accepted by all, without having been announced, that no
one could be attacked when he stepped off the mat. Julio
would have preferred to leave the fight altogether, but this
would have invited the contempt of José and Vicente.
Julio, in fact, was able to overcome some of his cowardice,
and he seemed surprised at his own ability to twist and
squirm out of the others' grips. Stanley often attacked
with his fists, quite violently, but in such a heedless,
stumbling rush that he and his retreating opponent fell
quickly to the mats and proceeded to wrestle. It was
clear that the boys took these heedless rushes in a special
light, for they were well aware that Stanley's blows rarely

landed. Stanley was dangerous because he went out of control, but if you could handle those reckless fits, you could handle Stanley. José especially learned to drift back and then pounce when Stanley stumbled, for he always did stumble. Occasionally, as the boys rolled and squirmed, they also punched each other in the ribs. These blows, however, were almost formal and were very subtly adjusted. The loser must prove that he is really struggling, and so in order to ensure himself against the contempt of the victor, he punches him in the ribs. Delivered with just the right force, these punches remain compliments ("I esteem you and want you to think well of me"). They are tributes, too, to the reality of the fight. Delivered a bit harder, they are "unfair." Delivered still harder, they precipitate a bloodletting. And so they are very nicely attuned.

Mabel came down to watch the fight, and we sat together leaning against the wall, simply marveling at the richness of this spectacle. Little Gladys, Julio's six-year-old half-sister—a spry, wry, humorous, very lively and attractive little girl, very Caribbean—came down and watched for a while, laughing delightedly to see her big brother getting beaten up. I sent her away after a few minutes because I knew Julio would beat her up later if he became aware of her pleasure.

For about fifteen minutes the fight was a melee, a pattern of up and down, up and down, for no matter whom Stanley and Willard threw to the mats, there was always one Puerto Rican left over to tug at their feet or jump on top. Soon all the boys had lumps, and by an absolutely unspoken agreement stopped fighting to catch their breath. They wandered around, enemies comparing bruises in very friendly voices and exchanging indirect flattery; e.g., José says to Vicente, in a loud voice, "Man, did you hear his head"—pointing to Julio—"hit the floor!" and Willard, who had accomplished that sound, turns away and grins. And so the boys sit down side by side against the wall, huffing and puffing. They pay no attention to Mabel and me, leaning against our own wall at the end of the gym. They talk for a while about wrestlers and boxers, José Torres and Antonino Rocca, and then they decide to continue their fight in tag-team style, like the wrestlers on television. Where before a simple roar had preceded their clashing, there is now an element of play in their voices as first one and then another imitates some star and calls out his name. The tag-wrestling leads quickly to single combat, for Stanley overwhelms Vicente in a moment, and then the two of them must step off the mat, and so must Julio, and now all three turn and watch the prolonged battle between José and Willard. They are so fascinated, in fact, that they sit down side by side, yelling advice, insults, and encouragement.

Willard is very muscular, with broad shoulders and strong hands, and he easily dominates José, who is older but not so well developed. Yet though he dominates him, he can't quite pin him and can't make him give up. He succeeds—almost—in immobilizing José, whose arms and legs project here and there beneath Willard's dark brown body. Vicente and Julio yell from the sidelines, "Punch him! Shove him off, José!"—together with other practical bits of advice, such as, "Roll over!" José squirms and tugs. His face appears under Willard's armpit. The face looks here and there. It turns it eyes and brings Vicente and Julio into focus, where they are leaning against the wall, yelling, "Shove him! Roll over!" The eyes look at them questioningly for a moment, then widen as if to say, "Can't you *see*?" The mouth makes an expression of disgust. More squirming, and the face disappears. Willard is grinning and trying different holds, but in-between the grins he exerts himself to the utmost and still can't pin José. And so he shouts again and again, "Give up?" and José cries, "You have to kill me!" The decision is in Willard's hands. Soon he lets José up, but punches him on the arm so José won't think he has been let up. Willard shows great tact in his awareness of victory. He smiles openly at José, not a triumphant smile, but a friendly one. Now all the boys come to the mats and round things off with a general melee. José is somewhat abashed by his defeat, but he squares off against Willard, bluffing to the hilt and acting tough. He takes a boxer's stance, with curled fingers and weaving shoulders, saying, "Come on, man, come on." Willard looks at him for a moment. In boxing he could demolish José, and there is no doubt about it. Nothing shows in his smile. He puts up his hands and shadowboxes with José. In fact, they are playing together, and this is the first time.

2/11/65

Again a good lesson with José on the typewriter.

He is still fearful of making mistakes. I wanted to bring this anxiety into the open. I wanted also to get him to see that he himself must do the learning. He wants to learn, or rather, he wants not to fail; but he still doesn't see that learning is his action, not mine. When he began to look for clues, pointing to different letters on the keyboard and watching my face to see if he was touching the right one, I closed my eyes and said banteringly, "I don't know. I can't see." He tricked me into opening my eyes by making a false click on the typewriter, but I closed my eyes again without giving him a reaction he could use. Then I said I'd punch him for every mistake he made. This was such an accurate parody of the pressure he puts on himself that he burst out laughing, and ventured to make a few mistakes. Later, when we were working with letters, he got mixed up between *m* and *n*. I asked him to try to figure out for himself some way of distinguishing between them. He pointed out the differences in their structure, but he was still confused about their names. He had drawn a picture of a bridge on the blackboard. I asked him if he could use *m* in a bridge, and he promptly used two *m*'s for double arches. A moment later I struck an *m* on the typewriter and asked him what it was. He said, "*N*?" So again I asked him to figure something out that would help him learn it. He became angry and nervous, but hit upon the word "*em*barrass." I said, "Good." The important thing was that he had internalized the problem. I had never before seen quite this look on his face. It was dark and angry, but did not look stupid. He scowled still more deeply, and suddenly said, "I hate your guts." I said nothing. He hid his face with a book, and said again, "I hate your guts," adding, "I'm not smiling, either." I said, "Okay." He took the book away and was bubbling with laughter. As always in these situations, it was a laughter of release.

At the Zen restaurant around the corner I ate the Macrobiotic Special: broiled butterfish, lotus root, rice, and vegetables. I got a fishbone caught in my throat. The proprietor heard me coughing and called Sam, the student of Oriental philosophy. He came to my table and asked me to hold out my hand. He massaged the muscles at the base of my thumb; same on the other hand. "Of course," he said, "this won't have a *direct* effect." I agreed with him, since I had not rubbed the fishbone into my hands, but had swallowed it. Nevertheless, the bone went away.

The proprietor had invited the whole school to have lunch there, since his daughter, Dolores, is one of our pupils. The five older boys all sat together in a friendly and surprisingly quiet way. Gloria sat at a big table with the girls. Maxine and Laura, looking very pleased with themselves, sat at a tiny table in the old fireplace, like a minature alcove. I talked with our host afterward in the kitchen. José, Julio, and Vicente went back to school, but Willard and Stanley hung around, listening to our conversation and examining all the utensils, the little heaps of chopped vegetables, the fish filets, the big urn for making tea.

2/16/65

Now that the boys have established more or less friendly relations, they have suddenly become a juvenile gang and are interested only in defying the teachers.

They noticed that some gum and candy machines had been left on the sidewalk overnight. They knew that the store would not open until eleven, and they talked excitedly—egged on by Stanley—of stealing the machines and hiding them in the school. Mabel and I told them they would do no such thing. They shouted defiantly that they *would*, and all five ran out of the building. I waited for several minutes, long enough for them to have reached the candy store, and to have seen the difficult shape of reality. I went out into the street. Vicente was crouched under one of the machines, leaning against the front of the store. Stanley and Willard were examining the chains and locks. José and Julio were lookouts, which is to say that Julio was crouched on the curb playing with some scraps of wood, while José, his hands in his pockets, spat assiduously into the street, apparently trying for distance. I yelled at them and they came straggling back.

Stanley is a typical gang leader, extremely talented at proposing exciting feats and needling the others into proving themselves. Because he is so young, his deeper motives are quite evident. It is not the adults he can't get along with, but his peers. All this leadership is a way of freezing the boys' relations with each other and sabotaging their relations with adults. He feels threatened on all sides. Now he is "testing the limits." The other boys, who have already tested them, and who anyway are not as desperate as he, are simply wasting their time.

Yet their sense of belonging to each other—however shaky it may be—is important. And they *should*, at least some of the time (how much of the time, God only knows), want to shake off the adults, get out from under that dreadful load and seize upon the excitement of a boy's world. Their problem is the city itself. Seen through the eyes of an adventurous boy, the environment is incredibly hostile. The only loopholes seem almost to *demand* acts of petty crime.

The boys ran through the building, invading the other classrooms. José refused a lesson. José, Willard, Vicente, Julio—all are quite accessible at this point. Stanley is not, and his effect on them is dreadful.

We're in for a bad time. We have little to offer them. Nor could we possibly offer them much in respect of their need for adventure and independent exploits. They need some independent contact with the large world, but that world is closed and hostile, and this little piece of it, the school, is where they'll explode.

2/18/65

José brought some boxing gloves to school, and there was such excitement that it was impossible to have lessons. Stanley and José began boxing in the room, Stanley, as usual, throwing furious punches and charging blindly with all his might, sometimes actually closing his eyes. I took them down to the gym. We got out the mats and made a boxing ring. Stanley and José put on the gloves. I told them that we had to agree on the rounds, and Vicente, in his glassy-eyed, frenetic way, shouted, "Twenty!" José echoed him, not knowing that he'd be dropping of exhaustion long before the twentieth round. I suggested three rounds, but both Stanley and José shouted contemptuously that that was not a fight at all. We settled on eight two-minute rounds, with two minutes in-between. From that point on I made one mistake after another, and still don't know what I should have done.

Stanley charged in like a torando, but his one punch was a roundhouse, and José managed to duck. We put chairs in opposite corners. Willard was Stanley's second. He fanned him with a handkerchief and massaged his shoulders, grinning all the while. Julio and Vicente worked over José, and he seemed to wish they would not, for all they did was shout advice to him in Spanish and argue with each other. Soon José was drawn into the arguments, and every rest period sounded like a Saturday night domestic quarrel in the tenements. As the fight progressed, the noncombatants became terribly excited, threw punches at imaginary opponents and dashed across the ring, sometimes interfering with the fighters. José was getting the worst of it and was far more tired than Stanley. By the seventh round he was losing badly. I had been giving them three and four minutes between rounds, and neither had noticed. José began to fantasize aloud. "You want one in the face? Huh, man? You want one?"— whereupon Stanley charged and smashed him in the face. José shook his head, assumed his fighter's pose again, and said, "How you like that? Huh?" Stanley mocked him: "I like that, man," and charged again. José took to this tactic himself, charging desperately. He succeeded several times in pushing Stanley off balance, and in landing punches that brought a surprised, infantile look to Stanley's face. But José hardly knew what he was doing. On one of his charges he drove Stanley out of the ring and collided with Willard, who all along had been throwing jabs and uppercuts in the air. Willard yelled at him to watch out, and José turned and struck him in the face. Willard threw several punches, all strong and accurate, and had José down in a moment, kneeling on top of him and punching his face. I pulled him off.

The boys were all shouting. Julio and Vicente cried to José, "Take off your gloves!"—meaning a bareknuckle fight. I didn't know what to do. I was convinced that if I were simply to end the whole thing, the animosity would remain and would end in even greater violence and perhaps enduring enmity. Yet José was exhausted and could hardly fight. Even so, he was screaming and was beside himself with rage. Willard, too, was keyed to a pitch, cursing savagely and trying to get at him. I thought it would be less damaging if Willard were to put on gloves, but while I tried to put the gloves on his hands, Julio and Vicente pulled José's off, and José charged. Willard struck him twice, so powerfully that the fight came to an end right there. José's nose was bleeding profusely. He was panting and screaming: "Look what you do to me! I'm gonna kill you, man!" He tried to stop the bleeding with one hand, and extended his other hand toward Julio. *"Dame la cuchillo! La cuchillo!"* I shouted to Julio to keep the knife in his pocket, but he eluded me and passed the knife to Vicente, who passed it to José. When Willard saw the knife, he became enraged and picked up a metal folding chair. José kept shouting, "I'm gonna kill you, man!" while Willard yelled back, "Come on and kill me! I'll break your ass!" "You think I'll kill you with all these people looking? I'll get you alone. You'll turn your back sometime, man, and I'm gonna kill you!" "Here's my back, man. Come on, kill me! I'll break your fuckin' ass!" "You better leave this school, because I'm gonna kill you!"

I had no difficulty staying between them. Neither one tried to get past me. The fight was over. I sent Willard and Stanley upstairs, and stayed in the gym a long time with José, Julio, and Vicente. José's nose stopped bleeding. After a long while he grew calmer. The whole fight, the very bringing of the boxing gloves to school, belonged so much to Jose's fantasy of himself that it was simply pathetic. There is so much courage in this fantasy—and such a distressing need, in this neighborhood, for raw courage and endurance—that I hardly knew what to say to him. I thought he would feel less like a loser if I spoke to him a little angrily. Also, he needed to know how the fight had started. I told him he had caused it himself by hitting Willard in the face. He denied that he had done this, and in fact was unaware that he had. Julio and Vicente bore me out, and it made an obvious difference to José. I asked him once again to give me the knife, and he did. Julio asked for it, but I put it in my pocket and said I'd give it to him after school, adding that anyone who brought a knife to school in the future would be sent home. And I have always returned these knives. It would be stupid to confiscate them. They'd be replaced immediately, and a gulf would grow between us. Too, they are personal property, just like that.

Kenzo walked into the gym, and his face blanched at the sight of José's swollen eye and nose. Julio called him a faggot and Kenzo pounced on him and put a judo hold on his neck. Julio screamed and surrendered.

Vicente: I don't have no judo class, man. I gotta find another one.

Kenzo: How come?

Vicente: We ain't got no teacher, man. Our teacher's in jail.

(He was referring to one of the men arrested the previous day in what the newspapers described as a plot to dynamite the Statue of Liberty. His picture had been in the papers, and his place of employment: judo instructor, Henry Street Settlement.)

Vicente: They said he was a communist spy, or sump'n. That's what I heard on television, man.

José was calm now, and I took them all upstairs to the front room. Willard stayed in the other room. Stanley came in for a moment to look at José. He said nothing, but as on other occasions seized José's hand and left a piece of candy in it. José made a face of disgust and started to throw it on the floor, but Vicente caught his hand, unwrapped the candy, and popped it into his own mouth, flashing José a big grin.

I decided to take them on a trip, and I asked for suggestions. Vicente's fantasies of a good time immediately poured out, some of them quite idiotic, he screaming at the top of his lungs and dancing from foot to foot. Julio began screaming, too, arguing with Vicente, and all the yelling brought Stanley and Willard running into the room. They wanted to go, too. Julio said, "If they go, we ain't goin'!" But as the squabbling continued, it became obvious that we couldn't forbid them. We decided to rent bikes farther downtown, near the project Willard lives in. As we left the room (I didn't notice it), Stanley stole the lunch cookies. When we were out on the street, I saw that he had them, which I didn't mind, for they could be replaced, but I told him to pass some out to the other boys. He refused and began dancing away up the street. By this time I was thoroughly disgusted with all of them, their incessant screaming, their violence, their fearfulness, their shallow, wretched personalities, their superstitions, their worship of Cadillacs and crooks, their stupid fantasies, their infantile anxieties, their impatience, their emptiness. I turned around without a word and walked away, fully intending to abandon them and go home. On the one hand, I felt at fault in doing this; it was simply dumping the whole problem in Mabel's lap, and she could not go home. On the other hand, I was goddamned if I would play that wretched game with them. I would not take an institutional responsibility in any sense. And I wanted them to know that they had to meet minimal obligations or I would not waste my time with them. I was not working to draw a pay check. Nor was I programmatically on the side of the children, or on the side of the oppressed. There are no such *sides*. Oppression is an evil. The stupidity it produces is also an evil. I was damned if I would accept a relationship with behavior that simply thwarted me. Better reject it out of hand.

Such were my thoughts, my furious thoughts. How long they would have lasted, or what form they would finally have taken, I don't know. The boys had been shouting to me, and I hadn't responded. Now I heard running footsteps behind me. Vicente, José, and Julio blocked my path, and the others came running up behind. They insisted that I come with them. I told them that they were a pain in the ass, that I would give them the money for their bikes, and that I was going home. But they insisted, and they were actually impressed with themselves to see what an effect they had had on me. Stanley passed out the cookies, dividing them evenly and making a great show of it. And I was touched to see that they were touched; at which point I realized that in some sense I was one of the boys, that I would never, probably at any age, be very much of a father, but would remain a temperamental yet perhaps not wholly unduti- ful older brother.

A half hour later we were all gliding along on bikes in Jackson Park, beside the East River. For the first time that day I felt good, pleased to see them speeding along in a gang, and pleased to be out in the open myself. Vicente's bike broke down, and I gave him mine and sat on a bench and smoked and watched a couple of tug- boats, and enjoyed the damp air blowing in across the water. We gathered in the bike shop when our time was up. The proprietor (half out of his mind, as all in this business are, driven into a quite accurate, quite pragmatic paranoia by the behavior of their clientele) no sooner turned his back than Julio and Vicente began stealing candy. I stopped them and chased them out, and later spoke harshly to Julio, saying that I would not allow the stealing. Damned, compulsive monkeys! (And I myself had been a petty thief at the insane age of eleven, and had struck a teacher who had hit me, and one night—with a cruel and delicious glee I would not mind tasting once again in my life—had driven the scoutmaster into a tear- ful rage by tooting on a little horn called a kazoo and then skipping away when he tried to catch me. I told Mabel of all this, and she said, "Then why do you get so upset about the stealing?" The chief reason, no doubt, is that I won't allow the boys to compromise me. But there is another reason, and an important one. My own boyhood gang was a middle-class gang. We were punished when we stole, but we were also excused on the grounds of our youth. Julio and the others are not excused. Their youth is taken away from them. All that is noticed is that they are Puerto Rican or Negro. They are punished *and* ostracized. It is hard for them to get back in. I don't want Julio to close every door we are trying to open. I want him to be able to go *back* to the bike shop, *back* to the candy store, *back* to the grocery store where we buy our supplies for lunch. I don't like Julio, and he doesn't like me, yet he knows I'll always include him and will stand up for him in the same terms I apply to the others. I feel it is correct—on the basis of all this—to make my demands of him. Which is not to say that in the long run there is much hope, or that these demands are especially realistic. They make sense, and there is no alternative.)

Julio, perhaps more than anyone else in the school, is destined for a life of crime. Like Stanley, he has great native intelligence, but while Stanley is disturbed and may possibly straighten out (or possibly be dead at the age of twenty, like another gang leader I knew), Julio's character already resembles that of an adult psychopath. Where the superego should be—where we see rebelliousness in the other kids, and contrariwise, the sense of a code—there is policy, shrewdness, and dissembling in Julio. He bullies the younger children more than any other of the boys. Once, when he thought he was unobserved, he stomped again and again on a rubber doll that was lying on the floor. He was not destroying it—it kept bouncing back into shape; his action was expressive and compulsive, and it was one of the few times I have seen Julio act with spontaneous feeling. He is malevolent and treacherous, is a master of deception, and detests everyone. He is good-looking (they all are, and this is certainly a noteworthy fact about these rejected boys), but Julio's handsomeness, unlike the others', is at times almost sinister. While Stanley is white, Julio is dark and Puerto Rican. The world of opportunity is closed to him, and given his intelligence, he must sense it in a painful way. His home life is dreadful. He has come to school with scratches on his face inflicted by his mother, and she herself, as we know, has been driven half out of her mind by poverty, children, overwork, and a husband who alternately beats and abandons her. Yet though everything I have said about Julio is true, it is by no means the whole story. There is still a child of hope alive in him, a wealth of small impulses which, if only they could attach themselves in the proper ground, might grow and flourish. It is one of the remarkable traits of the young, this tenacious survival of spirit and largeness of possibility. When I remind myself that all five boys came to us as *rejects,* I think less of their faults and more of the fact that the rejected can still be so alive with possibility. This is not to say that in some deep-down, Nietzschean way they were rejected because they are superior. Compared to peers in more fortunate circumstances, they are in a large sense terribly weak and undeveloped. I mean only that each one could grow, perhaps immeasurably.

2/23/65

Willard's older brother came back from Youth House a few days ago, and Willard has been upset and in an ugly mood. His mother tells us the brother is a bad influence. Stanley looks up to him and seeks his company.

A good bull session with all the boys; and then Mabel got them to reading while I worked alone with José. Julio and Stanley read well. They are nowhere near their age level. (Their presence in the sixth grade at the public school, like José's presence in the fourth, meant absolutely nothing but a lot of chicken scratches in the filing cabinets.) By "well" I mean that they read with obvious intelligence, the kind of intelligence which indicates that they could go far, and go far fast, if only they could be relieved of the dreadful conflicts within themselves and of the ravages of their lives. Stanley has a good head for mathematics. Willard is slow in everything, but as regards the material itself, is not uninterested. All are way ahead of José.

José spoke today of his lack of knowledge. It was his first direct admission of the shame he has always felt. He told me—looking away and almost hanging his head —that he had gone to school in Puerto Rico and was learning to read. When they first moved to this country, it had been he who had read his father's post cards, since his mother cannot read. But he said he had forgotten. I told him that when he could read English well, he would be able to read Spanish, too.

The dodge-ball game was ugly today—endless lying, arguments, and the possibility of fights. The boys asked me to referee. I have always refused in the past. I consented this time, and it made matters worse. It occurred to me that if I left the room, they would become more rational in order to play at all. I left and listened from the hall, and it worked.

On the way upstairs they burst into the auditorium, plugged in the jukebox, danced on the piano, rattled chairs, all screaming hysterically and trying to bait me into chasing them. I am really at a loss in such situations.

The building is not ours. We are not entitled to the auditorium except one day a week. If it *were* ours, then of course they could play there and break things if necessary, for the things would be their own. There is no solution to this mess—except time. We are all beginning to suspect that we cannot cope with Stanley.

2/24/65

Something must be working very powerfully on Stanley and Willard away from school. They are harsher and more bullying than at any time since their first days here. Willard's brother is obviously a factor, and certainly so, too, is the assassination of Malcolm X, whom the brother had learned to revere in reform school, where the Muslim movement is important.

They bullied the others harshly during the dodge-ball game, even objecting to their speaking in Spanish. Willard thought they were making anti-Negro remarks, which they were not. He threatened each one. Little Vicente, with Willard towering over him, shuts his lips in a straight line, averts his eyes, folds his arms across his chest . . . and holds his ground. Angry as he is, Willard cannot keep from smiling.

In the afternoon, after I had gone home, Stanley broke a window, turned on the fire alarm, and disrupted a class. He's been suspended for two days. We'll discuss keeping him.

2/25/65

Stanley out. Willard stayed out, too, to keep him company. All the others were positively happy. Kenzo, Vicente, José, and Julio played in the gym together, and for the first time in weeks I heard the sound of merriment in their voices.

José, at my request, has come to my apartment three times in the past week for lessons. He continues to improve, though very slowly. It is beginning to dawn on him that learning is an event, an experience; that it belongs to him and not the school; and that the initial confusion is not the permanent state of affairs.

7

I don't think the five boys learned anything at all during the period just covered by the journal. As I write these words, I experience something of the same defeat I felt at the time. Yes, it would have been a mistake to force classroom instruction upon them. That had been done in the past, and their appalling ignorance was one result of it. Nor would the smallness of our group have justified rigid discipline. The boys were far too unstable for that, too liable to collapse, too ready to rebel. Perhaps a more imaginative teacher than I would have hit upon some way of engaging them. Perhaps a more experienced one would have realized at once that the disorder was inevitable, and in the long run even desirable. Yet the sense of defeat lingers on. I mention it because it seems to belong intrinsically to the experience of teaching. There are many occasions when the best one can do is insufficient, and may even be, from the point of view of the child—and in a deep and legitimate sense—quite superfluous. One even realizes that this very sense of defeat—given the magnitude of the problems faced by such children—conceals sizable quantities of vanity and impa-

tience. Yet there it is. In libertarian schools it will be
occasioned, as it was at First Street, by a break in relations and routines. In conventional schools it will be
caused by the sullen resistance accompanying all the activities pursued under compulsion, in which case the
teachers' sense of defeat may endure for months or even
years.

Our original structuring had been of the "vertical," or
"family," kind. Regardless of age or ability, all the children had had access to one another. They had had places
and occasions, too, for separating according to age and
ability. The younger ones had provided rest and ease, and
even learning episodes, for some of the older ones. There
had been mutual teaching, encouragement, and very constructive (if noisy) play. All these benefits were turned
into liabilities by the arrival of Willard and Stanley. Their
routine brutality concealed a truly abject fear of experience, and it had the effect of curtailing the experience
of everyone else. José, Julio, and Vicente no longer played
with the younger children, or with the girls, or ventured
to expose themselves in the "soft" activities of singing
and dancing. All devoted themselves to acting tough . . .
and we found it necessary, simply in order to protect the
little ones, to devise routines that would isolate the older
boys. Our school became that much less of a school. If
Gloria or Susan were writing this account, they might still
speak of a wide variety of activities, of projects in science
and art, singing and dancing and music, and of the various
ways in which they used some of the conventional materials of an enriched environment. One of Gloria's pupils
at this time was the youngest of a large family of nonreaders. He had been sent to school "to learn to read," and
she saw immediately that he was about to ensnare himself in confusion and mere verbalization. He kept clamor-

ing to read, and she eased him instead into a great many games. He was unaware that the blocks and puzzles and cutout forms he enjoyed so much were all of a visual-motor, problem-solving kind. The reading materials which had been withheld were now gradually introduced, and the boy learned rapidly and well. His curriculum, his entire program, was radically different from that of other children of the same age working beside him in the same room. Susan, too—several months having passed—had a roomful of children working on different materials and going at different speeds. Because Eléna and Maxine were among them, Susan experienced something of the same wildness that Mabel and I were accustomed to with the boys. But Maxine and Eléna were changing spec-tacularly. Maxine no longer baited the roughnecks, and in fact was no longer so hugely hypnotized by sex. She had transferred her affections to a gentle, bashful boy named William Mueller (and could sometimes be seen chasing him, crying, "Come here, Bill Miller!"). Whereas during her years at public school her mother had found it almost impossible to awaken her in the morning, she was now "up and waiting"—and her friendship with William was certainly one of the reasons. She had already gone beyond her age level in reading and had caught up in math. Eléna, too—because she was bright, like Maxine, and because Susan had slowly weaned her away from the conviction that she was stupid—was moving at a spec-tacular pace. She had come to us at the age of ten, doing first-grade work in reading, and beginning second in math. Now (to quote Susan), "She would go on learning jags and would chase me around the school—in the art room, or during music—waving her workbook at me, de-manding that I check her answers or give her a 'test.' When Eléna wanted to learn something, she grasped it

almost always on the first explanation." Eléna had stopped
stealing, too, and could be trusted with large sums of
money. She often went shopping for our lunch supplies
and art materials—as did others of the girls—and she
could be relied upon now to return the exact change.
During this period, which among the older boys was one
of violence and rebelliousness, Susan's group constructed
a telegraph and sent messages from room to room, and
began a series of investigations with a microscope. When
this instrument first arrived, the whole school was fascinated. The children scurried about in search of materials to place under the lens. The older boys thought to
contribute and examine only blood and spit, which having done, they withdrew.

I instituted a sort of seminar with the boys, early-
morning sessions based upon the obviously compelling
events in their lives: violence, cops, crime. All these had
important ramifications, and the fantasies of the boys
seemed like logical starting places. The violence they
were so familiar with was not, after all, without cause,
but belonged to the political, economic, and class structure of our society. The cops—whom they detested, and
quite rightly—were adjuncts of a rule of law of which the
boys had no conception, partly because the police themselves routinely violated the law. (One night later in the
year, six policemen crashed through the door of José's
apartment, though they could have knocked and would
have been admitted. Without warrants of any kind, they
took the older brother to the station house. He was not
placed under arrest, but was questioned and later re-
leased. The boy was a known friend of a heroin addict and
thief—hence the raid—though he himself was neither an
addict nor a thief.)

I had no intention, in these sessions, of moralizing, or even of trying to impart more useful attitudes. I wanted only to penetrate the fantasy world in which they were so severely isolated. But I underestimated the desperation with which they clung to their conceits. Their vulnerability, and the real insecurity of their lives, was such that even small doses of reality tended to flood them with anxiety. When I mentioned events in the civil rights campaign, their faces darkened and they squirmed in their chairs, or jumped up and acted out episodes from television. Willard was only partly Negro. It was too painful. The other part was Batman. José was only partly Puerto Rican; the other part was Hercules. Robert Jay Lifton, in *Death in Life,* mentions a term coined by the Japanese for the survivors of Hiroshima and Nagasaki: *hibakusha,* "explosion-affected persons." These boys, in addition to their other problems, were *hibakusha,* though none of them could have recounted the events at Hiroshima. Like other revelations of their condition, this one, too, took me by surprise.

I had wanted to talk to them about police and courts and jails, and to make clear somehow that law was not simply an array of force, and the cop on the corner, and a vast saying of "thou shalt not," but was also, or should be, the protector of persons, including themselves, and of rights, including their own. I had no difficulty in arousing their interest, and we began to speak of a hypothetical crime; and from that we passed to a brief mention of court and jail. When I came to the link that joined these two—the police—an astonishing thing happened. They had been sitting or sprawling in chairs. Now all five jumped up and began shouting excitedly. They ran around the room, leaping and gesticulating and making all kinds of noises in imitation of mechanical sounds. They

were acting out fantasies of escape. *These escapes, however, were not from the police, but from an explosion,*
some vague catastrophe of war which, however vague it
may have been in their minds, was nevertheless quite obviously "the bomb." I was astonished at this development, for I had not mentioned war in any way, nor had
any of the boys. No doubt the fantasies of one ignited
those of another, yet the fact remained that this leap
from the police to war lay close to the surface in them all,
and was so highly charged that each one possessed an
idiosyncratic fantasy of escape. All of these fantasies
combined a scene of desolation with the danger of pursuit. One after another the boys shouted, "Boom! Boom!"
and threw their arms into the air. None of them identified
his pursuers, except that the pursuers were a kind of
army. José sped away in a car and stood in the hills in a
defiant stance, spraying bullets from a machine gun.
Julio piloted a jet plane and fled directly "to the jungle."
Vicente had a private plane and changed it to a jet on
hearing Julio's scenario; but he equipped it with guns
and shot down several planes on his way "to the woods."
Stanley had TNT and dynamite, and blew up whole hill-
sides of enemy troops. Only Willard imagined hand-to-
hand combat; he clenched his teeth and slit the throats
and bellies of his pursuers as he fled through what again
seemed to be a jungle.

I cannot remember which of them referred to the atom
bomb, but one of them did, and I inferred from the
imagery of several that New York had been blown up. By
"New York," however, they meant only the small part of
the city with which they were familiar. This became clear
as I questioned them. And it was strangely pathetic to
discover that this fearfulness, which rushed so easily to
the surface, and which possessed its own quite logical

associations of violence and violent fate, had nevertheless
construed only the palest version of the real threat we
all endure. The reality toward which I had hoped to
orient them was far more disordered than their disordered
young minds. I debated with myself about what to do.
Should I describe to them the real effects of the hydrogen
bomb? Would this increase their anxiety? And did they
have to know? I decided that it would not increase their
anxiety, but diminish it, for each one, according to his
lights, had already imagined the holocaust. If it was true
that the real threat of destruction could not be removed
from their world, it was true, too, that the effects of this
threat had been compounded in the nightmare or fantasy
transformation it had undergone in their minds. Catastrophe, as they sensed it, was ubiquitous, had no cause
or source, and tended to undermine the reality of everything else. And so I proceeded to place their "bomb" in
the real world. I said that it was far more powerful than
they had imagined. I sketched a map of Manhattan on
the blackboard. They took their seats again. I said that
the bomb came in several sizes, and I added three *x*'s to
the sketch, indicating direct hits on Manhattan of me-
dium-sized bombs. Again they leaped to their feet with
defiant shouts. "Shit, man, I get my jet plane . . . Zoom!"
But as I described the successive effects of the bomb—
the blast itself, the outer ring of flames and hurricane
winds, the horizontal fallout, the vertical fallout, the wind-
borne fallout—their fantasies ceased and they listened
with the sullen, resentful unease that is almost the birth-
right of their own and somewhat older generations, whose
legitimate hopes of life have been blasted by their elders.
I tried to make them understand that our problem with
the bomb was not what to do after it had fallen, but how
to prevent its falling, how to do away with it entirely. I

do not think that this was meaningful to them. Nor do I think that the session itself was of much importance. Perhaps it made their anxiety more real, a little less pervasive and destructive. Yet their flights into fantasy were, after all, mere symptoms, and there was not much point in attacking them directly. Only true ego growth would diminish their subjection to the unreal—skills, interests, and knowledge, the usual attributes of personal resources. We were supporting this growth—trying to, at least—in other ways. And so the value of this session, and of the others like it, was extremely limited. Some few of the real events they had converted into images were converted back again into events. Some little quantity of information passed from me to them. During the session I have just described, I asked Vicente if he knew how fast a bullets travels. "It travels fast, man! I bet it goes thirty miles an hour!" They learned that sound travels at a given speed, and light at a given speed, but bullets at various speeds, all of which exceed the speed of sound. The formulation that drove this home was that a soldier killed in battle never hears the shot that kills him. This was greeted by a solemn silence, except for Stanley, who nodded gravely and said, "Yeah."

On another occasion I spoke to them about the circulation of blood in the human body. I had in mind their fearfulness of injury, and the fantasy knife fights in which they all indulged while they carried real knives in their pockets. I plotted the session in my mind: I would draw a picture of a man with a knife, and show the veins and arteries and the heart, and show how the blood circulates, and the kind of damage caused by a gash, and how to apply first aid, making use of pressure points and the tourniquet. I would ask José to take off his shirt, and then with a piece of chalk I would mark "cuts" on his arms and chest, and ask the others to rescue him. The actual session was a total flop, and in fact had been stupidly conceived. I had not taken into account that the knives in their pockets were partly magical, were a species of talisman, meant to ward off evil not by use but by possession. In speaking so realistically of wounds and veins and pressure points, I was taking away their magic. Too, their fear of injury was vertiginous. It is not accidental that certain toughs faint at the sight of blood. The toughness, after all, is a line of defense, and beyond this defense there is nothing, so to speak, but an image: the inviolable self, vulnerable to almost everything—to ridicule, to affection, to compassion . . . to experience itself in almost any form. I drew the outline of a man on the blackboard, and drew the heart and veins and arteries; and they began to squirm and talk to each other in a hectic way. When I placed cuts here and there, and indicated the spurting of arterial blood and the oozing of venous, the talking became shouting. Their faces were sour and fretful. They punched each other and shouted threats and accusations. Stanley left the room and took Willard with him. Vicente began clamoring to go to the gym. I saw what a mistake I had made, how far I had wandered from the specific needs of these boys.

One of our sessions, however, was a distinct success. Only José and Vicente were present. They were entertaining each other with episodes from television. I listened more attentively than usual to this staple of their conversation. And I realized that they were suffering a confusion that is characteristic of very young children: they thought that the events were real. José had been speaking of Hercules, Vicente of Superman. José knew that Steve Reeves, who portrays Hercules, was a real man, but he actually thought, or almost thought, that this real man was Hercules. Vicente believed that Superman could fly. Did he also believe that Superman existed? When I asked him, he said, "Yeah, man! Don't you know?"

"Right here in New York?" I asked. "Could he fly by this window?"

"Sure he could, man!"—but then he saw that I wasn't referring to Superman's powers, but was asking if we could see him flying through the same air that we breathed. He was grinning, and his face expressed a strange mixture of conviction and doubt.

The thing that was missing from their experience was the understanding that the adventures they watched on television had been created by other persons. José had mentioned a Western in which there was a lot of shooting. I asked him if those were real bullets.

"Sure, man!" he cried. "What you think?"

"How do you know they're real?"

"Man, you can hear them! You can see the dirt fly up!"

"And the men who get shot—they're really dead?"

"Yeah, man!"

Both boys knew that the programs on television were made with cameras. "Knew" is not quite the right word, for though most of the relevant information existed in their minds, it had not been connected into meaningful wholes. But we had shown films at school and had taken many snapshots, and they understood what a camera was, and that a man had to hold it and that it recorded whatever he aimed it at. I asked José if a man just stood there with a camera and watched all those men die. He thought about this a moment, and then said that that was probably the way it was.

"And how did he know there'd be a gunfight? How did he know where to go?"

The issue suddenly became more real to him, and he looked quite puzzled.

And so I proceeded to tell them how films were made: that little charges were planted in the ground, which when they exploded threw up the dirt like bullets; and that the sound of guns was added later by means of a tape recorder, like the one they had played with several times at school.

Far from destroying their pleasure in films, these explanations increased it. They were fascinated. I told them how special effects were contrived in the studio, and how filmed backgrounds were used. Vicente—to my surprise —shouted, "Yeah, and when Superman flies, he must be layin' on a board, 'cause his chest gets flat right here." He put his hand on his chest. He was quite pleased with himself and repeated it to José. "It's true, man, every time he flies, he gets real flat right here." Persons who believe that the excitement of dramatic art depends on the inviolability of the illusion are quite mistaken. These filmed adventures had not collapsed into mere assortments of devices; the heroes were still intact, and all their attributes and exploits. But they had suddenly become social artifacts. And perhaps it even meant something to the boys that grown men and women put their own time into contriving these tales and acting in them. José was willing to grant now that Steve Reeves was an actor and lived in Hollywood, whereas Hercules was a figure of myth and lived in men's minds. To some small extent the scales had been reversed. The boys lived somewhat less in the make-believe world of their heroes, and their heroes lived somewhat more in the society that was common to all. They had known all along, in some unstructured way, that devices and illusions were passing before their eyes. It needed only a touch to bring this subliminal knowledge to the surface and give it a meaningful form. The interesting thing was this: That they *had* had a psychic investment in the fantasies of television. It lay not so much in their heroes as in the protective isolation of the dream world they were able to inhabit by insisting that their heroes were real. They abandoned that protection immediately in favor of a superior position: the understanding of how it was done.

During this entire period, which lasted several weeks, I kept making the same mistake, and it was a serious one: I kept wanting to teach. I wanted our school to be more relevant to the needs of the boys. And they, of course, kept throwing me off. What they needed, and obviously craved, was a dose of the big world. If they had been healthier, they might have ventured out; but they were incapable of organizing the independent activities they desired. All had been truants at the public schools. They had spent a lot of time in the streets, but rather in the style of stray dogs than adventurous young boys. First Street, in their eyes, was a haven, and they refused to leave it. But I had become anxious about the break in communication and kept trying to mend it, and this prevented me from thinking of their problems imaginatively, and from venturing beyond the school myself in my attempt to give substance to their experience.

8

José, as I have mentioned, had been able to read Spanish at the age of seven. By the age of thirteen he could read neither English nor Spanish. It was obvious that his problem was not a question of the mechanics of reading. Something primitive in the process had been destroyed. What was it? And why is it that precisely reading, which children can teach one another (Tolstoy mentions this repeatedly), should so often prove to be problematical? Why is it that a child who has performed the really huge task of learning to speak should then fail at the lesser task of learning to read?

Printed words must be understood as a variety of speech. In most written matter there is a voice. (There is little voice, of course, in government forms, tax schedules, and the like, which is precisely why they cannot be read, but must be decoded.) When we wonder about a student's comprehension of written words, our instinctive test is listening, not cross-questioning. If he can read the passage aloud with appropriate animation, we know that as far as the reading goes, his understanding is adequate. He has made the inflections of his own voice coincide with the changes and shades of meaning which form the voice of the writing.

Reading draws upon the riches of speech, running much the same gamut of dream and emotion, fact and analysis and conventions of logic. For this reason it is a task for which a strong motivation almost always exists. For the same reason, however, the exposure of self is critical and renders the whole process extremely susceptible to disturbance. The young learner is placed in an unusual dependency. One might say that he is *invaded* by the task, for unlike any other intellectual task, it uses as material the child's own chief way of coping with his world, that is, his speech. A young child is not aware of speech as something distinct from himself. Speech is the voices he can understand and the things he can say. It is wholly instrumental and expressive. And now suddenly he is confronted by a peculiar extension of talking that is not immediately instrumental. There is no inherent difficulty. A child can learn the "code" quite easily and can soon use it. But there is an inherent danger. The prime matter of the code already exists in the child in a highly individual form. Ideally, we want to add to this form—add the conventions of written language and the relevant skills. What we do instead, most often, is confuse the child and set up conflicts by insisting that the prime matter of reading is also standardized. We invade the child, displacing his own speech as the original stuff, and leaving in its stead mere *printed words*. Even under these conditions children can learn to read, but the organic bond between reading and talking is reduced to almost nothing, and many "competent" readers sound like machines or parrots. We might put it this way: the five-year-old child, learning to read, is thrown back, as it were, into certain of the dependencies of infancy. He will attempt inevitably, as he did in infancy, to make some sort of match between the demands of the environment and his own needs. When we treat reading as a process wholly separate from him, we are creating an environment which tells him that his own needs cannot be trusted as a guide, though they are in fact, and always have been (prior to school), the very best guide he possesses. Too, we are destroying—precisely —the instrumentality of the instrument he has already acquired: his ability to talk. This is why children can often learn to read better if they are not taught at all, for no child will voluntarily do such things to himself. The results of these errors are familiar. The odd thing is that the way around them is so easy—and isn't taken. It is odd, too, that while any good teacher can tell you—or any child show you by his actions—that learning to read involves forming parts and wholes in a number of different ways, we have only two distinct *methods* of teaching reading: the phonic and the Look-Say. *Neither of these methods, as a method, can be derived from an analysis of successful learning.* Such an analysis reveals at once that both ways of grappling with written language belong to each other and are properly used idiosyncratically. To elevate them to the status of *methods*—though it may serve to codify and standardize the teaching of teaching—destroys the usefulness they possess when they are left at the disposal of the learner. In short, there is no way to standardize and mechanize the teaching of reading. It is inherently a spirited, highly individual process.

This was one of the first insights of Sylvia Ashton-Warner in her marvelous work with the young Maoris. She discovered that learning to read was so very personal that it touched immediately on dreams and other highly charged experiences in the lives of the children. There was a kind of personal magic in it. To gain a word was to gain some measure of control or mastery over the fears and desires associated with the word. Thus her beginners' vocabularies were not "look," "see," "run," "Spot," "run," but "ghost," "kiss," "kill," "love," "darling," "alligator," "beer," "knife," "thunder," "together."

> Whereas he had spent four months on "come," "look," "and," he spent four minutes on these . . . they were one-look words. So from these I made him reading cards, and at last Rangi was a reader.

In proceeding thus with her gut-words, Ashton-Warner preserved the organic unity of feeling, speaking, and reading. One might say that she created an environment which gave to the learning of reading some of the same highly individualized support we give routinely to the learning of speech. Just the opposite had been done with José, and his problems were compounded by the change from Spanish to English. Reading, for him, had few of the attributes of speech, and none at all—except in negative ways—of the attributes of feeling. He could not imagine his own identity waiting to meet him in books, as it met him on the streets and in his play with other boys. In fact, he still stumbled over the word "I." It is worth mentioning here that this collapse was not the merely negative phenomenon it is taken for by so many educators. There was something self-protective concealed within it, for the identity which did in fact lie in wait for him in the books that do exist—which is to say, in the society which does exist—was precisely that of a second-class citizen, shunned where others are welcomed, needy where others are comfortable, denigrated where others are praised. A white middle-class boy might say, with regard to printed words, "This is talk, like all talk. The words are yours and mine. To understand them is to possess them. To possess them is to use them. To use them is to belong ever more deeply to the life of our country and the world." José, staring at the printed page, his forehead lumpy, his lip thrust out resentfully—anger, neurotic stupidity, and shame written all over him—seemed to be saying, "This belongs to the schoolteachers, not to me. It is not speech, but a task. I am not meant to possess it, but to perform it and be graded. And anyway it belongs to the Americans, who kick me around and don't want me getting deeper in their lives. Why should I let them see me fail? I'll quit at the very beginning."

At the same time that such thoughts tormented him, he esteemed the powers of those who could read, and he could remember quite clearly reading the post cards from his father. He was determined, at First Street, to learn to read. Or so he thought. The truth is, he wanted to cease failing; he wanted to *have already* learned to read. He did not know what it meant to learn, and he did not know what it meant to read. His own grim determination was another of the obstacles that stood in his way. As Gloria had done with the young child from the family of nonreaders, I banished books from our lessons. But José was thirteen; I could not put visual-motor games in their place. For a long time our only equipment was a notebook and some pencils—and a great deal of conversation. I wanted to get back, in some way, to the stage of reading at which written words still possessed the power of speech. And so our base of operations was our own relationship; and since José early came to trust me, I was able to do something which, simple as it may sound, was of the utmost importance: I made the real, the deeper base of our relationship a matter of physical contact. I could put my arm around his shoulders, or hold his arm, or sit close to him so that our bodies touched, or lean over the page so that our heads almost touched. Adults, and especially adult Americans, are not used to this kind of touching, except of course as it expresses affection. Children, however, and adults of other cultures, touch and hold and lean and press quite as a matter of course. The importance of this contact to a child experiencing problems with reading can hardly be overestimated. José was frequently at some sort of border line in his sense of himself: struggling to comprehend, or to cope with his shame and frustration, or to cope with the excitement of flashes of understanding. Little eddies of anxiety moved around and around him—yet he was not thrown back, in his need for support, upon attitudes or emotions; our physical contact gave him security. Nor was it my body beside his that meant so much, but the fact that the presence of my body vivified his awareness of his. He knew where he was: he was in his skin; and when the little bursts of panic made his head swim or his eyes turn glassy, he did not have to run away or reject the task *in toto*. He could gather himself together, because his real base—his body —was still there. I know that in the course of our lessons I committed errors and God knows how many omissions, yet this physical base was so important and so reliable that it provided all kinds of leeway. It took the sting (though not the seriousness) out of my rebukes, it expressed a concern I could not have put into words, it gave a reality and continuity to sessions which were sometimes of the most ephemeral content. If one single formula were capable of curing the ills of our present methods of education, it would be this physical formula: bring the bodies back. This statement, I know, is incomprehensible to many persons, especially to those who, reading the word "body," think not of the bodies of persons, but of various ideologies of The Body. This is not the place to amplify this thought. Let me point out, however, that among children all important feelings, desires, and interests take physical forms. The one great physical phenomenon of the public schools consists precisely of squirming in the chairs. If the coercive discipline were relaxed, what a wealth of motion there would be! And how rational and productive would be the procedures which might arise from taking these physical manifestations quite seriously!

(I am reminded here of one especially noisy day when the boys rushed from the classroom to get to the gym. Vicente was in such a state that his excitement bordered on frenzy. I caught his arm in the hallway and knelt in front of him. I put my hand flat against his diaphragm and said, "Vicente, breathe so it pushes out here." He did not think my request a strange one, or ask for an explanation. He simply looked at me the way children do, still tugging to get free yet accepting my action. He took one deep breath, right under my hand. "Now let it all the way out." He pursed his lips and expelled the breath, responding spontaneously to the pressure of my hand. The frenzy melted from his face. The tight little shoulders, which had been drawn upward toward his ears, relaxed and dropped down to a normal position. His voice, which had been hurtling through the chambers somewhere near his scalp, took up residence in his throat again. He chased away after his gang, still shouting, still excited, but he was in his body now, and his actions would make sense. It was for a similar reason that in moments of extreme conflict I occasionally shook, never struck, the children. Just three, actually, and just once apiece: Maxine, Vicente, and Stanley. All three occasionally went berserk, were sometimes dangerous, many times intolerable. Shaking them by the shoulders made their heads spin; it was a big, total-body sensation; and simply in order to orient themselves, they had to get back into their skins, had to come to their senses. Which is, of course, the meaning of that phrase, for "senses" does not mean agreement, judgment, and rationality, but the sensory ground on which, alone, agreement, judgment, and rationality can be given form.)

I had known from the beginning that José had learned very little in school, yet I was surprised by his ignorance. It was the ignorance of a boy who again and again had drawn back from experience in fright and resentment. He did not orient himself in space and time as do middle-class boys of thirteen. He did not know in what month he was born, or the months of the year, or the meaning of hours, days, weeks, years, centuries. And this is not to say that he lived with the sensory immediacy of a child. His sensual experience was similarly impoverished. Eléna, José's sister, assimilated information and skills with sometimes dazzling rapidity. So did Maxine. Both, compared to José, were sensually much more alive.

One day we were looking at a picturebook of the Pilgrims. José understood that they had crossed the Atlantic, but something in the way he said it made me doubt his understanding. I asked him where the Atlantic was. I thought he might point out the window, since it lay not very far away. But his face took on an abject look, and he asked me weakly, "Where?" I asked him if he had ever gone swimming at Coney Island. He said, "Sure, man!" I told him that he had been swimming in the Atlantic, the same ocean the Pilgrims had crossed. His face lit up with pleasure and he threw back his head and laughed. There was a note of release in his laughter. It was clear that he had gained something more than information. He had discovered something. He and the Atlantic belonged to the same world! The Pilgrims were a fact of life.

One of the pictures in the book showed the Pilgrims at prayer. José said, "God was born in the year *one*, right?" I said, "Right," and again I wondered what this meant to him. I asked him what year it was. He said, "Nineteen sixty-four." But when I asked him how many years ago Christ was born, he said, "Way, way, way, way, *way* back." This was the answer of a far younger child, not a boy of thirteen. I said, "Yes, way back. How many years exactly?" He responded with his customary guessing and bluffing, correcting himself according to the expressions on my face. "Three hundred! No? Two hundred! No?"

On another occasion he spoke of cities and states with a peculiar confusion. I asked him which was bigger, a city or a state. He said, "A city!" I told him that the states were bigger, that every state had several cities in it. And then I asked him if he knew where New York City was. I thought he would say, "In New York state." But he wrinkled his forehead and looked away, trying to dope it out. He turned back to me and said, "Uptown." I need not point out in what special sense this answer was quite correct.

It would have been pointless simply to undo the errors in José's view of the world and supply him with information. It was essential to stand beside him on whatever solid ground he might possess. Nor could I proceed as if he were a five-year-old just learning to read. This is not to say that we could make no use of Ashton-Warner's excellent methods, or of Tolstoy's brilliant descriptions of the reading problems of the peasant children. These needed only to be adapted to José, whose "reading problem" had grown so extremely complex that I found it necessary to remind myself that I, too, was a part of it.

We talked a great deal, getting to know each other. One of the first incidents he described to me was violent and tragic, like others I was to hear later. It was a fight, fatal on both sides, between his mother's brother and another man. It had happened in Puerto Rico. José became excited as he told the story, and jumped up and acted it out. ". . . and then he shoved the knife in him right here (pointing to his own chest). But my uncle pulled up his heart, you know. You know? Like this, man . . . when you breathe, your heart goes up and down like this . . . right? So when the knife came in him, he pulled up his heart. Oh man, it jus' missed his heart like this. An' then my uncle pick up a big rock an' smash him with it."

José's uncle died three days later in the hospital. His opponent died shortly after the fight.

He had told me this story to help explain his mother's current visits to the eye clinic. She had been deeply disturbed by her brother's death. José said nothing about her feelings, but described how one night, not long after the fight, she had come into the kitchen for a glass of water. When she turned from the sink, she saw her brother as if he were alive. He was sitting at the table smoking a cigarette. She tried to scream, but her voice caught in her throat and she fainted. José was quoting her when he said that her eye trouble dated from that night.

Often, while we talked, José doodled in his notebook, drawing little pictures of things that interested him. I asked him to draw the scene in the kitchen when his mother had fainted. He crouched over his notebook eagerly, and it was obvious that he recalled the images of their home in Puerto Rico with great relish. The kitchen resembled some I had seen in Mexico; there was no glass in the windows, and the floor was apparently of dirt, but there was electricity, a gas stove, a refrigerator, and a sink, though no running water. He drew a cupboard, put a picture on the wall, and a calendar. Here was a table and a chair, and now he drew a man with a cigarette sitting in the chair, sending curlicues of smoke toward the ceiling. His mother lay on the floor between the table and the sink. The glass had fallen from her hand, and a puddle of water spread out around her.

José knew the alphabet and could write words if someone spelled them for him. We chose some sentences from his story. I spelled the words and he wrote them beneath the picture.

Soon other events appeared in picture form in his notebook. One was a family moving day in the Lower East Side. Relatives had gathered from all branches of the family and from various parts of the city. They had borrowed a pickup truck, which in José's picture was piled high with beds and chairs. Two men carried a bureau. A girl carried a lamp. José drew himself marching along beside the truck, with a mop over his shoulder. Again the story was written beneath the picture, but tags were added to the drawing, identifying the various members of the family. Still another picture dealt with the juvenile violence so common in those streets. Three boys armed with sticks and knives faced two others, armed only with sticks; but the two (José was one of them) had seized the lids from some garbage cans and were holding them up as shields.

Sometimes we reviewed these stories together, though usually we never returned to them. I didn't want them to become chores or lessons. I did take words, however, from José's narrations and printed them on vocabulary cards and in little lists in his notebook: "brother," "mother," "sister," "dream," "knife," "fight," "cigarette."

For brief periods of every day—five or ten minutes—we studied these in a relatively formal way, together with neutral words such as "look," "see," "book," etc. My reason for holding these separate little lessons was not to teach him, but to put enough pressure on him to precipitate the anxieties and subterfuges which had characterized his entire experience of school. These were the real contents of the lessons. I do not mean that I psychologized. That would have destroyed everything. I simply made room for the emotions and responses he had always felt but had never acted upon. Sometimes he would become angry—at himself, at me, at the task; it was hard to tell, because he would clamp his jaw and glower, convinced that he had no right whatsoever to be angry. Once I said, "You're pissed off, aren't you?" He scowled still deeper and said, "Yeah." "So why don't you yell, or something?" When he saw that I meant it, he opened up his mouth and roared, "Shit!" Then he giggled. Then he became angry again and said, "I hate those fuckin' words!"—smacking the word list with his hand. I suggested that he smack it good and hard, and he doubled up his fist and pounded the words. Then he picked up his pencil and obliterated the words with fierce black lines, and gouged the paper with the pencil. His face was flushed, but his anger had changed into an excitement that was not unpleasurable. He did not tear out the page or throw the notebook on the floor. He seemed to have reached the end of that impulse. He looked at me with a very animated face. I said, "I'll write one new word for you, and then we'll go to gym," and I wrote "pissed off" in his notebook. He laughed exuberantly and jumped up and shouted, "Pissed off!" and then, "Let's go to gym!"

There was much else about himself that he could not accept: his confusion, his self-doubt, and above all, his ignorance. He could not bring himself to speak the words, "I don't know," which meant, too, that he could not ask for help. But gradually, as he came to understand that he was not being tested and graded and did not have to *perform,* he dropped his pathetic bluffing and ventured to say, "I don't know." Having found that it was safe to say this, he began almost to wail it, and from this point moved on, very slowly, to an entirely new understanding, namely, that learning was a process, an experience: you began in darkness and ended in light. During all this time, our reading lessons consisted of our own voices, our own handwriting, and events from his life. The physicality of our relationship provided security and a simple datum of reality. He could terminate the lessons whenever he chose, or could refuse them entirely, or could extend them. Which is not to say that I was passive in this regard. I always expressed my own opinion, and sometimes very firmly. Even at such times, however, the final decision was José's. If I was especially insistent, he was forced to consult with himself and find out if he really meant what he proposed. Sometimes the answer was "no," and he would consent to another ten minutes of lessons; sometimes it was "yes," and the lesson would be quite brief, or would take the new direction proposed by himself, or would not begin at all.

Occasionally I read to him, sometimes alone and sometimes with two or three others—Vicente, Julio, Kenzo. These sessions, in their group form, were not successful. The only story that really engaged them was Tolstoy's *Prisoner of the Caucasus.* We spent three days finishing it, and they retained everything from one day to the next. *Tom Sawyer* fell flat, as did *Huckleberry Finn,* and I had to abandon both. Where the Tolstoy story was full of action and mortal danger—and above all, was exotic—

the others referred continually to middle-class norms and touched the boys' feelings of alienation. Too, they were attuned to television, the movies, the nervous pace of the streets; it was hard to find tales that would hold them. The proper stories, as Tolstoy points out in his educational writings, are not those written *about* their experience, but those arising from it. In some sense, the boys should write for each other, at least to provide a material for the crucial first step of finding a recognizable and relevant experience in books. More work like Herbert Kohl's may be the answer here. (It has been tried successfully in England, as Joseph Featherstone tells us in his *Report.*) Kohl discovered, in his public-school classes, that the children did not understand that the language in books was the very same language they spoke to one another. He got them to write of their own lives, not worrying about punctuation and grammar (for these can be derived later, according to meanings), and suddenly children who had been unable to write compositions were producing poignant stories of their lives at home and in the streets. Too, they were interested in one another's work, and this provided a subject matter for reading. Now learning was possible, for as Dewey tells us, learning is not a process distinct in itself, but is a by-product of engagement with subjects.

> Under normal conditions, learning is the product and reward of occupation with subject matter. Children do not set out, consciously, to learn walking and talking. One sets out to give his impulses for communication and for fuller intercourse with others a show. He learns in consequence of his direct activities. The better methods of teaching a child, say, to read, follow the same road. They do not fix his attention upon the fact that he has to learn something and so make his attitude self-conscious and constrained. They en-

gage his activities, and in the process of engagement he learns. . . .

—*Democracy and Education*

(José and I never did reach this stage of engagement with a compelling subject. His difficulties were too extreme. He was trapped too desperately in awareness of himself. My strategy was to take him *through* this awareness by giving him the means to turn it to account. Thus I often—toward the end of the year—insisted that he cope with learning precisely *as* a process, for this brought his conflicts to the surface, and they could then be dealt with. With a more normally developed child, a strategy like this would be superfluous, and even damaging.)

But there is another consideration, too, with regard to reading stories aloud, and it deserves attention: the daytime—especially when we are dealing with restless and active boys—is simply not the right time for stories. Tolstoy mentions this several times in describing the peasant children of his own school.

In the evenings in general . . . the hubbub is not so great, and the docility and confidence in the teacher are greater. The pupils seem to evince an abhorrence for mathematics and analysis, and a liking for singing, reading, and especially for stories.

Perhaps if our own system of primary education were not modeled so harshly on the methods of factories, and were not so blatantly designed to facilitate the labors of administrators and teachers, we might find that the evenings would be uniquely suited to particular studies. Certainly nothing would be lost by bringing school into some kind of harmony with the daily cycles experienced by everyone. (Parents would do well to consider it. The evening is not a bad time to get the kids out of the house.)

It was not until the end of the year that ordinary books finally took their place in our reading lessons. This happened in a natural and desirable way. Vicente, who had done most of his reading with Gloria, took to visiting our room at the end of José's lesson, bringing with him the book he was currently engaged in. He would sit down beside me and read aloud until he had satisfied himself. He never asked for help or allowed me to interfere in any way, but would simply read for a while and then stop. José lingered and listened while Vicente read. One day he went to the book closet and rummaged about for a long time, and came back with a book. He had chosen it, I think, by noticing the relative proportions of pictures and words, knowing that few words, big pictures, and large type meant infallibly that the book had been designed for beginners. In the next three days José read three first-grade readers with ease and understanding. On the one hand, this was not much of an accomplishment for a thirteen-year-old boy. On the other hand, he had reversed a habit of failure that stretched back for six years, and had made a definite and not unpromising beginning. Most important, his attitude had brightened enormously.

I am sure that other teachers, reading of these sessions with José, will have recognized many opportunities I missed, and will have thought of materials which might very profitably have been introduced. One line of approach was suggested two years later by a lecture of O. K. Moore's, the inventor of the "talking typewriter," which has worked such wonders with autistic children and with late learners. The "typewriter" is enclosed within a booth so that the child is assured complete privacy. The keyboard "responds" with a voice ("*a*," if that letter has been struck; "boy," if that word has been written), and with pictures, and with infinite patience. The booth, and all its contents, is a tiny environment, and the environment is controlled completely by the child. It is meant to be used only for short periods of time, and can be programed for various ages. Moore told of two teen-age Harlem toughs, both nonreaders and school-haters, who once they were assured of the privacy of the booth, played endlessly with the responses programed for six-year-olds. *They were filling in for themselves a developmental stage they had missed.* Soon the boys were able to read, and they began carrying books home after school, books disguised very heavily in wrapping paper and odd-shaped parcels, for they would have died of embarrassment if *A Child's Book of Fairy Tales* or *The Boxcar Children* had been discovered tucked away beside their switch-blade knives. Hearing Moore tell of this, I realized that I could have done something similar with José, for I could easily have allayed his embarrassment, and I know that he would have responded to the childish literature he had never experienced—*Mother Goose,* fairy tales, and the like. I believe, too, that a Puerto Rican teacher, at home in both English and Spanish, and familiar with both cultures, could have helped José far more than I. This is so obvious, and there are so many mixed-up Puerto Rican children in the city schools—whose average of intelligence, according to my own impressions, is remarkably high—that one can only wonder why the large-scale training and recruitment of Spanish-speaking teachers has never taken place.

* 9 *

I have mentioned how important we found the writings of A. S. Neill and the example of his Summerhill School in England. There was another school, too, whose history meant much to us, and of whose existence not many persons have been aware. This was the free school that Leo Tolstoy set up for the peasant children of his own estate, Yásnaya Polyána. He himself taught in the school for three years, and wrote brilliantly of it in a short-lived magazine published at his own expense. These writings—out of print for decades—have been reissued recently by the University of Chicago Press (*Tolstoy on Education*).

In moral and religious matters, Tolstoy at that time was quite conventional (though one can hardly call the earnestness of his beliefs conventional); otherwise he was iconoclastic, a good century ahead of his time, and very often expressed thoughts and described practices identical with those of A. S. Neill. He developed themes, too, that we find again in the pages of John Dewey, stressing the experimental nature of education, its tendency toward social equality, the persisting need to reexamine the past so as to escape the dead hand of authority, and the importance of bringing the school into active relations with the life of the times. The choicest things in these essays, however, are Tolstoy's descriptions of the children responding to the freedom, or "the free order" (as he calls it), of their school. These descriptions are so vivid and alive, and are so instructive, that I would, if I could, quote the entire book, though I know that by now many persons must have obtained the new edition. What these pictures from life bring home to us is the actual anatomy of inborn human faculties, and how they flower under conditions that support their growth. And how different this is from the writings of our own educational researchers, who though they stress the importance of intrinsic motives and patterned growth, write as if they had no faith whatsoever in the existence of these things, placing their reliance, as ever, on the opinions and orders of a handful of administrators!

Since the descriptions I have just mentioned are too lengthy to quote, and are too delicious to summarize, let me give a few extracts from other sections that will indicate the nature of the school and its bearing on present-day libertarian practice.

In spite of the preponderating influence of the teacher, the pupil has always had the right not to come to school, or, having come, not to listen to the teacher. The teacher has had the right not to admit a pupil, and has had the possibility of bringing to bear all the force of his influence on the majority of pupils. . . . The farther the pupils proceed, the more the instruction branches out and the more necessary does order become. For this reason, in the normal non-compulsory development of the school, the more the pupils become educated, the fitter they become for order, and the more strongly they themselves feel the need for order. . . . Now we have pupils in the first class, who themselves demand that the programme be adhered to, who are dissatisfied when they are disturbed in their lessons, and who constantly drive out the little ones who run in to them. In my opinion this external disorder is useful and not to be replaced by anything else, however strange and inconvenient it may be for the teacher. I shall often have occasion to speak of the advantages of this system, and now I will say only this much about the reputed inconveniences: First, this disorder, or free order, is terrible to us only because we are accustomed to something quite different, in which we have been educated. Secondly, in this case, as in many similar cases, force is used only through haste and through insufficient respect for human nature. We think that the disorder is growing greater and greater, and that there are no limits to it,—we think that there is no other means of stopping it but by the use of force,—whereas we only need to wait a little, and the disorder (or animation) calms down naturally by itself, growing into a much better and more permanent order than what we have created.

How often have I seen children fighting, when the teacher would rush up to take them apart, which would only make the separated enemies look awry at each other, and would not keep them, even in the presence of a stern teacher, from rushing later against each other in order to inflict a more painful kick! How often do I see every day some Kiryúshka, with set teeth, fly at Taráska, pull his hair, knock him down, and, if it costs him his life, try to maim his enemy,—and not a minute passes before Taráska laughs underneath Kiryúshka,—it is so much easier personally to square up accounts; in less than five minutes both become friends and sit down near each other.

The parents' dissatisfaction with the absence of corporal punishment and order at the school has now almost entirely disappeared. I have often had occasion to observe the perplexity of a father, when, coming to the school for his boy, he saw the pupils running about, making a hubbub, and tussling with each other. He is convinced that naughtiness is detrimental, and yet he believes that we teach well, and he is at a loss to combine the two.

The two lower classes meet in one room, while the advanced class goes to the next. The teacher comes, and, in the lowest class, all surround him at the board, or on the benches, or sit or lie on the table about the teacher or one of the reading boys. If it is a writing lesson, they seat themselves in a more orderly way, but they keep getting up, in order to look at the copy-books of the others, and to show theirs to the teacher.

According to the program, there are to be four lessons before noon, but there sometimes are only three or two, and sometimes there are entirely different subjects. The teacher may begin with arithmetic and pass over to geometry, or he may start on sacred history, and end up with grammar. At times the teacher and pupils are so carried away, that, instead of one hour, the class lasts three hours. Sometimes the pupils themselves cry: "More, more!" and scold those who are tired of the subject: "If you are tired, go to the babies !"

All the evening lessons, especially the first, have a peculiar character of calm, dreaminess, and poetry, differing in this from the morning classes. You come to the school at fall of day: no lights are seen in the windows; it is almost quiet, and only tracks of snow on the staircase, freshly carried in, a weak din and rustling behind the door, and some urchin clattering on the staircase, taking two steps at a time and holding on to the balustrade, prove that the pupils are at school.

Walk into the room! It is almost dark behind the frozen windows; the best pupils are jammed toward the teacher by the rest of the children, and, turning up their little heads, are looking straight into the teacher's mouth. The independent manorial girl is always sitting with a careworn face on the high table, and, it seems, is swallowing every word; the poorer pupils, the small fry, sit farther away: they listen attentively, even austerely; they behave just like the big boys, but, in spite of their attention, we know that they will not tell a thing, even though they may remember some.

Some press down on other people's shoulders, and others

stand up on the table. Occasionally one pushes his way into the crowd, where he busies himself drawing some figures with his nail on somebody's back. It is not often that one will look back at you. When a new story is being told, all listen in dead silence; when there is a repetition, ambitious voices are heard now and then, being unable to keep from helping the teacher out. Still, if there is an old story which they like, they ask the teacher to repeat it in his own words, and then they do not allow any one to interrupt him.

"What is the matter with you? Can't you hold in? Keep quiet!" they will call out to a forward boy.

It pains them to hear the character and the artistic quality of the teacher's story interrupted. Of late it has been the story of Christ's life. They every time asked to have it all told to them. If the whole story is not told to them, they themselves supply their favourite ending,—the history of Peter's denying Christ, and of the Saviour's passion.

You would think all are dead: there is no stir,—can they be asleep? You walk up to them in the semi-darkness and look into the face of some little fellow,—he is sitting, his eyes staring at the teacher, frowning from close attention, and for the tenth time brushing away the arm of his companion, which is pressing down on his shoulder. You tickle his neck,—he does not even smile; he only bends his head, as though to drive away a fly, and again abandons himself to the mysterious and poetical story, how the veil of the church was rent and it grew dark upon earth,—and he has a mingled sensation of dread and joy.

Now the teacher is through with his story, and all rise from their seats, and, crowding around their teacher, try to outcry each other in their attempt to tell what they have retained. There is a terrible hubbub,—the teacher barely can follow them all. Those who are forbidden to tell anything, the teacher being sure that they know it all, are not satisfied: they approach the other teacher; and if he is not there, they importune a companion, a stranger, even the keeper of the fires, or walk from corner to corner by twos and by threes, begging everybody to listen to them. It is rare for one to tell at a time. They themselves divide up in groups, those of equal strength keeping together, and begin to tell, encouraging and correcting each other, and waiting for their turns. "Come, let us take it together," says one to another, but the one who is addressed knows that he can't keep up with him, and so sends him to another. As soon as they have had their say and have quieted down, lights are brought, and a different mood comes over the boys.

At times, when the classes are uninteresting, and there have been many of them (we often have seven long hours a day), and the children are tired, or before the holidays, when the ovens at home are prepared for a hot bath, two or three boys will suddenly rush into the room during the second or third afternoon class-hour, and will hurriedly pick out their caps.

"What's up?"

"Going home."

"And the studies? There is to be singing yet!"

"The boys say they are going home," says one, slipping away with his cap.

"Who says so?"

"The boys are gone!"

"How is that?" asks the perplexed teacher who has prepared his lesson. "Stay!"

But another boy runs into the room, with an excited and perplexed face.

"What are you staying here for?" he angrily attacks the one held back, who, in indecision, pushes the cotton batting back into his cap. "The boys are way down there,—I guess as far as the smithy."

"Have they gone?"

"They have."

And both run away, calling from behind the door: "Good-bye, Iván Ivánovich!"

Who are the boys that decided to go home, and how did they decide it? God knows. You will never find out who decided it. They did not take counsel, did not conspire, but simply, some boys wanted to go home, "The boys are going!" —and their feet rattle down-stairs, and one rolls down the steps in catlike form, and, leaping and tumbling in the snow, running a race with each other along the narrow path, the children bolt for home.

Such occurrences take place once or twice a week. It is aggravating and disagreeable for the teacher,—who will not admit that? But who will not admit, at the same time, that, on account of one such an occurrence, the five, six, and even seven lessons a day for each class, which are, of their own accord and with pleasure, attended by the pupils, receive a so much greater significance? . . . Their continued willingness to come to school, in spite of the liberty granted them, does not, I think, by any means prove the especial qualities of the Yásnaya Polyána school,—I believe that the same would be repeated in the majority of schools, and that the desire to study is so strong in children that, in order to satisfy their desire, they will submit to many hard conditions and will forgive many defects.

Many times, reading the pages of Tolstoy, I have been struck by the differences between the peasant children and some of ours. What would those sturdy lads have thought of Julio, Vicente, and Stanley, who could not speak to adults at all—let alone figures of authority—without cringing or blustering? The young peasants were children of oppression. We find phrases of Tolstoy's—"a fine musician," "a remarkable mathematician," "the correctness of his poetical conceptions"—and realize that these richly endowed children are destined for the fields and pantries, and we sense the revolution in the not-too-distant future. Yet it seems to me that some of the children at First Street suffered an even greater deprivation, a disorder and impoverishment that struck at the very roots of life. In the place of fields and growing things, animals, trees, weather, the sky, they knew only the nerve-shattering noises of the streets, the dingy buildings, the crowded sidewalks, the starless gray pall that hangs over our heads where the sky used to be. Where the peasant children acquired the skills of farming and carpentry and dozens of other necessary occupations, and therefore knew that they were indeed necessary persons, ours had acquired nothing and could do nothing, and did not at all feel necessary to the inner life of labor that sustains a country. They were, and felt, superfluous. At the same time, they were battered and invaded from all sides. Store windows, billboards, posters—all tempted them to want things and urged them to buy. Television took the place of family voices at night. Their parents were distraught. There was nowhere to go. The streets were hostile and confining. The hallways smelled of piss and wine. It was little wonder that our older pupils were mistrustful and violent, impatient, resentful, undeveloped. It *was* a wonder—an unending one—that they had preserved so much of the vitality of youth, and that they responded so quickly to radical changes in their environment.

Before opening his school at Yásnaya Polyána, Tolstoy had toured schools in France, Germany, and England, and had familiarized himself with the growing literature on education. His critique of prevailing customs appeared in the earlier issues of the magazine, together with his own closely reasoned theories of education, of which not the least important feature was that they were based as much upon considerations of morality as upon the nature of the process of learning. The relation between his own practice and this earlier critique can be seen in such observations as these:

> School is established, not in order that it should be convenient for the children to study, but that the teachers should be able to teach in comfort. The children's conver-

sation, motion, and merriment, which are their necessary conditions of study, are not convenient for the teacher, and so in the schools—which are built on the plan of prisons— questions, conversation, and motion are prohibited. . . . Schools which are established from above and by force are not a shepherd for the flock, but a flock for the shepherd.

Instead of convincing themselves that in order to act successfully on a certain object, it is necessary to study it (in education this object is the free child), they want to teach just as they know how, as they think best, and in case of failure they want to change, not the manner of their teaching, but the nature of the child itself. From this attitude have sprung and even now spring (Pestalozzi) such systems as would allow to *mécaniser l'instruction,*—that eternal tendency of pedagogy to arrange matters in such a way that, no matter who the teacher and who the pupil may be, the method should remain one and the same.

I have quoted chiefly the remarks that bear upon the relations of teachers and pupils. Tolstoy experimented considerably with curriculum and methods of teaching. If these experiments seem less relevant to our situation today, it is because we have already invested immense labors of research in these matters. We are not at a loss for structured curriculum, and there is no lack of variety and refinement in materials and methods. We lack only the essentials: a working relationship between pupils and teachers, a living bond between school and community.

One last observation of Tolstoy's is worth stressing here —since America is uniquely cursed with a reading problem—and this is that learning to read is not difficult, but easy. What is needed is to remove the obstacles that prevent reading from assuming its inherent relationship with speech, and cease the practices that destroy the motivation which for this subject is ordinarily strong and deep.

In November of 1967, in an address to the Manhattan Borough President's hearing on decentralization, Paul Goodman presented the case for mini-schools and based much of his argument upon a brilliant summation of the conditions that are necessary if a child is to learn to read. The public schools, he pointed out, systematically destroy these requisites.

> According to some neurophysiologists, given the exposure to written code in modern urban and suburban conditions, any emotionally normal child in middle-class surroundings will spontaneously learn to read by age nine, just as he learned to speak by age three. It is impossible for him not to pick up the code unless he is systematically interrupted and discouraged. . . .

Goodman's speech first appeared in the *Chelsea Clinton News*. It attracted letters of approbation, but also —from teachers and principals—expressions of disapproval. They could not believe that a child, without instruction, could do so much. Nor could they believe that learning to read is a far easier task than learning to speak. Tolstoy, not once but many times, records conversations such as these:

> I asked him [a fourteen-year-old peasant boy] syllabication and he knew it; I made him read, and he read without spelling out, although he did not believe he could do it.
> "Where did you study?"
> "In the summer I was with a fellow shepherd; he knew, and he taught me to read."
> "Have you an ABC book?"
> "Yes."
> "Where did you get it?"
> "I bought it."
> "How long have you been studying?"

"During the summer: I studied whenever he showed me in the field."

Again:

. . . a boy ten years of age once brought his brother to me. This boy, seven years old, read well, and had learned to do so from his brother during the evenings of one winter. I know many such examples, and whoever wants to look for them among the masses will find very many such cases.

At his own school Tolstoy made use of the mutual teaching that works such wonders among children. (As Joseph Featherstone tells us of the liberalized public schools of England: "At first it is hard to say just how they do learn reading, since there are no separate subjects. A part of the answer slowly becomes clear, and it surprises American visitors used to thinking of the teacher as the generating force of education: children learn from each other.") Other methods used were group reading, memorizing of poems and prayers, and individual, undirected work. Both the phonic and the Look-Say techniques played their part. Everything was based, however, on the first of the four methods Tolstoy describes:

The *first*, in use by the mothers of the whole world, is not a scholastic, but a domestic method. It consists in the pupil's coming and asking to read with the teacher, whereupon the teacher reads, guiding his every syllable and the combination of syllables,—the very first rational and immutable method, which the pupil is the first to demand, and upon which the teacher involuntarily hits. In spite of all the means which are supposed to mechanize instruction and presumably facilitate the work of the teacher with a large number of pupils, this method will always remain the best and the only one for teaching people to read, and to read fluently.

* 10 *

I have said that children are capable of positively curative effects on one another when their relationships are allowed to evolve naturally. Obviously there are limits and exceptions; and I am not speaking here of children thrashing about in a vacuum of neglect, but working out relationships against the background they are entitled to expect of adult protection and concern. By "natural" I mean such situations as we ordinarily observe when children are at play—without adults—in parks and vacant lots, on picnic outings (their parents nearby, but not involved in their games), on hikes, and sometimes—though it is difficult—on the city streets. We may be surprised at such times by the children's energy and spirit, but when we pay attention to the small details of their relationships, we see something that is quite familiar: the sense of decency and fair play that is taught in the home during the earliest years. We adults, of course, are the original source of this ethical sense, but by the time a child is three years old, another source has been firmly established and is far more fertile, demanding, and attractive than anything we can offer. This larger source

is the experience of the child himself, his world of playmates and excitement, of games and projects and discoveries. A moment's reflection tells us why this is so: the
first rules of behavior that we teach our children, far from
being mere maxims, are immediately and profoundly functional. The child sees quite clearly that he must share his
toys and candies, or the activity he enjoys will cease; that
he must honor his agreements, or the game will end; that
he must show consideration of others, or he cannot have
friends. The social necessity proves itself at all times and
in thousands of ways, and as our children grow older, our
original teachings are consolidated and made specific not
by any effort of ours, but by the sheer weight of necessity.
This is not to say that our own words and deeds become
valueless (for they never do), but that the scales have
been reversed: we now have little to offer, and the child's
own world has much. Most of what he craves is in that
world; it must come to him from his peers, and from
those who are slightly older, and from his own activity.
Nor do the children hesitate. They are quite willing to
deal with the demands of others and with the necessities
of many different kinds of situations. They are far better
at this sort of thing than we adults. We refer to it lightly:
"They make friends easily," or, "Oh, children always find
a way of playing together." We forget, or do not notice,
that the way they find is neither haphazard nor irrational,
but is a matter of observation, discernment, generosity,
intelligence, patience. Further, it is based squarely upon
the social concessions that govern the life of the home.
We are usually wise enough not to interfere with all this
when it's taking place in the backyard or the living room,
but as soon as the children are placed in schools, or in
other situations deliberately organized for their benefit,
we suddenly act as if they had no capacity at all for the

practical sociability we have already seen them to be masters of. We place all decisions in the hands of adults, and proceed to prescribe everything for the children: what they shall play, and for how long, and how they shall relate to one another. The rich and complex process we may have been observing in the yard comes to an end. The ethical necessity ceases to arise from the child's own experience, and now lands on his head from above, often in such grossly simplified forms that it can no longer be called ethical.

I would like to give some examples from First Street of how the children helped one another and mutually favored the process of growth. It was almost always in forms that teachers could not duplicate. It was in forms, too, that could not have existed except with a great deal of freedom. First, however, I would like to contrast the richness of children's natural play with the stultifying rigidity of play that is organized by adults. No better example can be found than that of the Little League, for what boys, left to their own devices, would ever invent such a thing? How could they make such a boneheaded error as to equate competition with play? Think of the ordinary games of boys—in sandlots, fields, parks, even stickball in the street. They are expansive and diverse, alternately intense and gay, and are filled with events of all kinds. The boys make much of one another's personalities, one another's strengths and weaknesses, and their witticisms fly back and forth with unflagging vivacity. They do not stop their game to argue a fine point, but rather the arguments are great features of the game; they are vociferous and long-drawn and run the gamut from sheer emotionalism to the most legalistic pedantry. What may seem to be a shouting match is in fact filled with close distinctions. (I heard a boy win such a match by introducing the word "immaterial." "Whatta ya mean immaterial!!" "It's immaterial, that's all!" "Yeah?" "Yeah!" "Whatta ya mean it's immaterial!!" "It just doesn't matter, that's what!" "Oh . . ." If the other had lost his momentum before the mighty word, it was clear, too, that he was gaining the word.) Between innings the boys throw themselves on the grass. They wrestle, do handstands, turn somersaults. They hurl twigs and stones at nearby trees, and yell at the birds that sail by. A confident player will make up dance steps as he stops a slow grounder. If an outfielder is bored, he does not stand there pulling up his pants and thumping his glove, but plays with the bugs in the grass, looks at the clouds, makes up a droll saying to shout at the duffer at bat—who immediately answers in kind. There is almost always a dog on the field, and no part of the competition is gayer or more intense than that between the boys and the dog, who when he succeeds in snapping up their ball, leads them off in a serpentine line that is all laughter and shouts, the dog looking back over his shoulder and trotting with stiff legs, until finally he is captured and flattens his ears as they take back their ball. No one has forgotten the score or who was at bat. The game goes on. Often birds and squirrels share the field, and sometimes a noisy crew of younger kids, who must scamper out of the way from time to time, and who shout childish versions of belligerent wit at their young elders. Everything is noticed, everything is used. The game goes on until darkness ends it, and the winners can hardly be distinguished from the losers, for by then everyone is fumbling the ball and giggling and flopping on the grass.

I have put all this in a generalized way, but the game I have been describing is actually one I witnessed recently in a New Jersey park. At the other end of the same park a Little League game was in progress. The coaches and officials were off-duty cops, doing their bit, yelling insults at the players, and the most vulgar kind of mockery. Everything was forbidden. "Keep yer eye on the ball, ya moron!"

But a game with cops is in a class by itself. The standard Little League game, no matter how gentle its officials may be, is an affair of uniforms and scoreboards, umpires and coaches, record books and publicity. And there in the stands, all around the boys, is an audience of adults (who should be doing something themselves), just waiting to be proud of them. How put-upon those boys are! They are strained and silent. They try to act manly and serious, and one sees at a glance that they are anxious and uncomfortable, and deeply resent having to prove themselves. The winners exult. The losers weep. What strange occurrences in the play of children! And who invented it? Not boys themselves, but nervous adults seeking to allay their own anxieties.

I am not exaggerating when I say that the play of children can be positively curative. Powerful factors are at work, and they combine into a dynamic that resembles that of the psychotherapeutic methods based on ego growth (though actually it is the other way around).

Children at play are intent upon pleasure and excitement, and in order to enjoy themselves they must relate to one another in terms of existing capabilities. They arrive at a sense of these capacities in the most pragmatic way, making adjustments of all kinds, until finally they achieve what they desire, which is the greatest possible élan of play. This does not mean that they ignore one another's defects. On the contrary, they often seem harsh in their indifference to hurt feelings. If a crippled boy is playing in the game, no one pretends that he is not crippled, no one chooses him as a teammate, not until the very end, and then someone is sure to shout, "He can't run at all! If we gotta take him, you gotta give us Harry, too!" Yet if we look closer at this sort of thing, we see that the boys are not so much harsh as literal. The boy *is* crippled. He *can't* run. And in his own heart he knows that his feelings are not important to the boys, whereas the game *is* important. It is important to him, too, more important than his feelings. Furthermore, he can play only as a cripple . . . and if we wait to see what happens, it will be clear that this literalness, or harshness, is the only real acceptance the crippled boy can know. He joins in, and goes as fast as he can. The situation will change as the boys grow older. The expansiveness of play will give way to the rigors of competition, and the crippled boy will no longer have a chance.

But physical defects are not the only kinds of liabilities the children take note of and adjust to. They are acutely aware of temperament and traits of character. Vicente, as I have mentioned, was very babyish during his early weeks at First Street. He had to have his way, and threw tantrum fits when he could not get it. These traits were quite apparent during the dodge-ball games, and the other boys were annoyed. But they did not call off their game, or forbid Vicente to take part. Nor did they *only* criticize him. Nor did they play as if he were a "regular boy." They complained to him directly—"Quit stalling!" (when he spited them by freezing the ball)—and at the same time they slightly lowered the demands of the game, granting him many concessions. They did not, however, lower the game to *his* level, but only so close to it as to make him reach and exert himself. This combination of concession, pressure, criticism, and acceptance worked a powerful effect, as one might well imagine. Yet it was the ordinary dynamic of children at play—*at play without adults.* For if I had intervened, if it had been I who had yelled at Vicente instead of the other boys, there would have been no good effect, for I had not granted him concessions. Nor was I his rival. Nor would my criticism represent to him the same loss of pleasure, or the same hope of praise, as did that of the boys. Nor could Vicente's particular abilities mean much to me, as they came to mean much to his teammates. He was as agile as a squirrel, and though his teammates groaned when he threw badly (and he would turn and yell at them), they laughed with glee and approval when he put his hands in his pockets and dodged the hardest throws of their opponents. His face would light up when he heard their voices, and he would turn to them with a wide grin and an exultant shout. I watched this so often that I came to realize that what the boys were doing, quite instinctively, and out of necessity and self-interest, resembled, in its dynamics, the things I had done myself as a teacher and therapist (I was then in training) with the severely disturbed children at another school. For I had tried to relate to their strengths so as to add to them, and had dealt with symptoms only as actions, and had created precisely the demands that they could meet, given my own support and assistance. I had noticed, too, that even the disturbed children could help one another, though less frequently and in a far more limited way than normal children can.

When Stanley arrived at First Street, the boys' good effects on one another were much diminished. Yet even Stanley, from time to time, responded to the inducements and pressures of unsupervised play. One such occasion stands out in my mind and is worth describing, for it not only reveals the dynamics of play in a clear-cut way, but indicates that the nonintervention of the teacher is not a passive or nothing-at-all sort of thing, but exerts a particular kind of influence on the children.

The boys were playing dodge ball in the gym, Vicente, José, and Julio against Stanley and Willard. Stanley kept stepping over the center line when he threw the ball. The boys complained bitterly that he was cheating, but he threatened them and told them to shut up. All were afraid of him, but his cheating was really intolerable, and finally Julio yelled across the gym to where I was sitting on the floor, watching their game, as usual, from a distance.

"He keeps steppin' over the line!"

I reply only with a nod.

"Well, it's against the rules, man!"

Again I nod, indicating clearly that I know he is right.

Now José shouts, too, for they are all upset. "Well, tell him to quit it, man!"

I shake my head "no" and shrug. They understand that I'm saying, "It's your affair, not mine." They don't like this a bit. It increases their annoyance. Julio, who is the best player on the floor, and who is by far the angriest, makes a violent gesture with his arm and yells, "Shit, man, I quit!" and walks off the court. But now Stanley runs up to him with a cocked fist.

"You gonna quit, huh? Well, I'm gonna break your ass."

Julio cringes, but stands his ground and mutters, "I don't care, man."

Stanley is glaring at him, and Julio, somewhat mopingly, returns his stare. One can almost see the desires and apprehensions cross their faces. Both boys want to keep playing. The game was exciting; otherwise the argument would not have arisen. The rivalry was intense; otherwise the cheating would not have been so blatant, so much a deliberate insult. Stanley knows that he cannot force Julio to play. Even if his threats succeed, Julio will play half-heartedly, and Stanley, who is a good thrower, is especially dependent on Julio, who is a good dodger. Stanley sees his own pleasure in the game evaporating. He knows, too, that if he attacks Julio in earnest, the whole game will be destroyed, for the excitement of competition really does depend on prior agreements, and a fight would wipe these out. Too, Julio's teammates, though they are not fond of him, will certainly express their solidarity with a fellow Puerto Rican. All of these deliberations are more or less visible on Stanley's quite intelligent face. He had been sticking out his chin and looking at Julio through narrowed eyes. Now he grunts and punches Julio lightly on the arm. Julio mutters, "Fuck you," and walks off the court. He hesitates a moment, and then leaves the gym. Vicente and José call to him, "Julio! Come on!" *"Maricón!* Come back!" But he has disappeared, and so they curse him and then yell, "Throw the ball, man! We can beat you anyway!"—though they had been losing from the beginning. Stanley throws, and the game goes on, but it's woefully lacking in excitement. Willard has said nothing all this while. His silence, however, and his sullen face make clear that his pleasure has been spoiled. Stanley notices this at once and tries to talk the game into life, raising a great hoopla and throwing as hard as he can. His own face, however, is wooden. Vicente and José are put out too quickly. The next round commences. Julio appears in the doorway and watches. Vicente yells to him, "Shit, man, come *on!*" but Julio shakes his head and mumbles, "No man." Now Willard suddenly lifts his voice. "Come on, Julio, he won't cheat no more." And Stanley, who is holding the ball, yells, "That's right, chicken! Come on, chicken!" and hurls the ball at Julio, who catches it and hurls it back. Stanley catches it, and screaming, "Come on, chicken! Come on, chicken!" charges up to the line—not an inch over—and throws the ball at Julio again. This time Julio dodges the ball, but he dodges onto the field of play, and José immediately cups his hands at his mouth and yells at Stanley, "Come on, chicken, *quawk, quawk, quawk!*" and in a moment the game is in full swing. The three Puerto Ricans, who are masters of derision, flaunt themselves as targets, sticking out their asses and waving their arms. They cup their hands at their mouths and yell in unison, "*Quawk, quawk, quawk, quawk!*" Stanley is grinning. He charges up to the line—not stepping over—and shouts, "Buncha fuckin' chicken over there!" and hurls the ball. Julio dodges the ball, puts his hand at his groin and shouts, "Yeah, man, you want a worm!" Once again the game is merry, obscene, and intense, though I should not say "once again," for the boys are in much better spirits than before. Most important, they leave the gym as one gang when the game is over, talking animatedly back and forth.

The effects of this game on Stanley and Julio hardly need comment. But what of my own refusal to intervene? What did it mean to the boys that their teacher wouldn't enforce the rules? Did it mean that he didn't care? Hardly, for they had come to know me through hundreds of other situations. They knew that I did care, and they knew very accurately (probably better than I) just where my caring ended. My refusal meant the most obvious thing. It meant not only that the game was theirs, but the rules of the game as well. And so I was not withholding myself, but was in fact putting myself in relation with something much larger than the game, something which the boys had again experienced in other contexts. This larger thing was their independent life in the world. My proper role vis-à-vis their independence was that of an observer and protector, and this was precisely the role I had taken. The effect of this was to locate all questions of ethics and conduct in the experience itself, that is, in the boys themselves, and not in some figure of authority. The further effect of this important shift in responsibility was that each boy was able to experience the *necessary* relationship between his own excitement and the code of conduct which joined him to others in a social group. Which is to say that their play—*because it was unsupervised*—acquired the moral pressures which are inherent in games, for at bottom this is precisely what morality is: the sense of the necessary relation between self and others, group conduct and individual fulfillment.

It is worth mentioning here that most of the games children play are not invented by themselves, though certainly they are embellished a great deal and often give way to less highly structured, purely creative play. The games are a form of lore, a tradition which in certain aspects reaches back into tribal origins. We tend to notice chiefly the physical aspects of games—the movements and skills, the excitement—and these are so important that we have no doubt of their great value to children. But the internal dynamics of the games—the strong and simple structures which bring rules, skills, individuals, groups, losses, rewards, energy output and rest into coherent wholes—these we often ignore, though it is just these that deserve to be called social artifacts. They have been arrived at in the most pragmatic way, often over the span of centuries, and the fact that they still exist is proof that we prize them highly. I point this out because we adults—teachers especially—watching children at their games, tend to think that because the children are new, we ourselves have a great deal to offer. We neglect to observe that we are competing with a durable and compelling tradition.

Of the boys, it was Vicente who benefited most in his contacts with other children; of the girls, Maxine. This is not to say that the other children received little benefit from one another, for they received a great deal, but the changes in Vicente and Maxine were spectacular.

Maxine's career in the public schools had been disastrous. She had gone from bad to worse, and her move to First Street was in the nature of a last chance.

I have been stressing the fact that the idea of freedom, to be intelligible, must be stated in terms of actions and individuals; and I have just mentioned that children at play support one another's ego growth. Let me describe Maxine's experience—both at the public school and at First Street—in terms of the behavior that most deserves to be called symptomatic; and let us see how the different environments affected her, and what role was played by the children themselves.

Maxine was a great "tester of limits." Like most neurotic behavior, this testing was self-defeating. She would scream and quarrel over some object which in fact meant little to her; or she would antagonize the teachers when in fact she wanted their friendship. This behavior was clouded and obscure; it was not functional in the immediate situation. Yet it concealed a tendency that *was* functional—or that might be, if only it could be clarified. This is worth spelling out, for the behavior that is described loosely by the phrase "testing the limits" is often misinterpreted by writers on education. Children who engage in it are not interested in license. Nor are they wasting their time, though certainly they are in a dilemma. The chief source of misunderstanding is this: that the idea is often applied exclusively to the child, as if it described a characteristic, or character trait, whereas it is meant to be applied to the child *in* his particular environment. It describes the dynamics of a situation, not the behavior of an individual.

Maxine was somewhat frightened by her own impulses. She needed to know in what way she could rely upon others—children and teachers both—to handle the impulses she could not handle herself. But she was also frightened of the other children, not physically, but as competitors and rivals, for in her eyes her age-mates were far more mature than she was. And so she needed to know what special privileges she might obtain, and where she might establish her own security. Hence she needed to know exactly where the power lay. It was as if she were asking herself on what terms she could be part of a group, on what terms have her personal wishes gratified. What good thing might be offered her in return for giving up her infantile desires? She wanted to know, too, which aspects of her teachers' behavior constituted the true authority of adult life. Which aspects could be trusted, and which persons, for she was far too necessitous to allow herself to relate to merely capricious behavior. All this was the meaning of her testing the limits; and it is worth mentioning here that such testing is quite normal at an earlier age (and therefore looks vastly different) and occurs routinely in the family circle. The goal of all this activity, though Maxine herself might have sensed it only in the most disorganized way, was precisely what any adult would agree was necessary to her growth: the organization of self and world—a self that might be more than impulse, social activity that might be more than constraint. Her needs were so extreme that she tried to make every occasion answer them. And here we see why such behavior is especially disturbing, for the needs that Maxine experienced in extreme forms are in fact basic in every child's life, to say nothing of the lives of adults, who experience them in moments of severe temptation. Her antics touched deep chords in her classmates and teachers. She was irresistible. If one were to draw back and take a comic view of the situations she created, the figure that would emerge would be precisely that of Harpo Marx.

The word "limits," then, does not mean rules and regulations and figures of authority. It refers to the border line at which individual and social necessities meet and merge, the true edge of necessity. This is as much as to say that the question, Who am I? belongs to the question, Who are you? They are not two questions at all, but one single, indissoluble fact.

How did Maxine ask this dualistic question? She asked it by stealing Dodie's soda pop, and by shouting some loud irrelevancy when Rudella was trying to question her teacher, and by taking all the magnets from the other children and kicking her teacher in the shins, and by grabbing Eléna's cookies at lunchtime. And what answers did she receive? But let me describe the public-school answers first, for she had done the very same things in the public school. She had stolen someone's cookies, but it was the teacher who responded, not the victim; and so Maxine could not find out the meaning of her action among her peers. Nor could that long and subtle chain of childrens' reactions—with all their surprising turns of patience and generosity—even begin to take shape. And when Maxine confronted the teacher directly, shouting in class and drowning her out, she was punished in some routine way and was again deprived of the individual, relational response which would have meant much to her. Yet she kept pressing on, creating crisis after crisis, always insisting upon relation.

Now the other half of testing the limits becomes clear. For what *were* the limits? The teacher herself was constrained by orders from above and by the inexorable demands of the schedule. She had to earn a living, had to secure herself with superiors and observe many regulations which violated her own better judgment. She could not express her feelings or act upon them, and was forced to cultivate a patience that often resembled mere inhibition. One would say that she herself was in a quandary of limits. Where did the edge of necessity lie? Was she sacrificing herself to an unworthy notion of social demands? Who held the power? The UFT? The supervisors? The parents?

The quandary of the teacher affected Maxine. It deepened her confusion and deprived her of relation. And it frustrated—precisely—her need for limits.

The forms of necessity are the same for children as for adults. Necessity cannot be argued with; it is overwhelming in one way or another, which is to say that it possesses a superior rationality, a persuasive function, an unanswerable force, the power of numbers. Let us imagine Maxine searching for the edge of necessity. She understands that her teacher is compromised, for she sees that her judgment has no scope and that she rarely acts upon either insight or feeling. The teacher is an instrument in other persons' hands. But who are those other persons? And what power does the teacher have? For Maxine wants security, and she must know. What, too, are the demands of the group? But then what is *the group*? There seems to be none, for the children are not allowed to establish real relations among themselves. We know that Maxine feels herself to be a little odd and guesses that her needs are special. How shall she bring this to anyone's attention? Whose attention? And what can they do?

The testing goes on and on . . . and the reason does not lie in Maxine, but in the fact that under such conditions as prevail in the public schools—or in any highly institutionalized way of life—there is simply no such thing as *limits* in the true social and psychic sense. Everything is arbitrary.

At First Street Maxine tested the limits and arrived—lo and behold!—at limits. She snatched up Dodie's soda pop and proceeded to drink it: one swallow, two . . . Dodie gapes at her wide-eyed . . . three swallows . . . "Hey!" Dodie lunges for the bottle. Maxine skips away, but Dodie catches her, and though she does not strike her, she makes drinking soda pop quite impossible. Maxine has much to think about. Apparently the crime is not so enormous. Dodie allowed her two swallows, but was obviously offended. More than that Dodie will not allow. An hour later they are playing together. Dodie did not reject her. You can play with Dodie, but you can't drink up all her soda pop. She runs fast, too, and I bet she'll hit me some day. (Dodie did finally hit Maxine one day . . . and they still remained playmates . . . and the days of stealing soda pop were long gone.)

Maxine takes Eléna's cookies. That's over in a minute. Eléna throws her to the floor and kicks her in the rear, cursing at her in Spanish. The kicks don't hurt, but they're kicks all the same. This is no source of cookies! But Eléna is impressive in her ardor, and perhaps she's a source of security, a really *valuable* friend. An hour later they are playing in their "castle." Eléna is the queen, and Maxine, for several reasons, chooses to be her baby.

Maxine shouts while Rudella is speaking to Susan, her teacher. Rudella is disgusted. "Why don't you shut up, Maxine! You're always makin' so much *noise!*" Other voices second her. "Yeah, Maxine!" "Shut up, Maxine!" No one punishes her. Susan says, "What is it, Maxine? If you're in such a hurry, go ahead and tell us." Or Susan, too, gets angry and yells at her. In any event, Maxine again has much to think about. Susan's anger is immediate and personal; nothing lies beyond it. Susan takes herself seriously, and Maxine must take her seriously, too. As for the kids, when they are all yelling at her together, they are too much even for her own formidable powers of resistance. While she can absorb endless numbers of demerits, endless hours of detention, endless homilies and rebukes, she must pay attention to this massed voice of her own group. She needs them. They are her playmates. But her need of them is balanced by their need of her. There is a basis here for give and take. Too, Maxine's own peculiar needs have been accepted, not that they will be answered necessarily, but they have been accepted as her very own attributes. Her anxieties are out in the open. So, too, are the many impulses she has such difficulty in mastering; and wonder upon wonders!—the others can handle them, can actually handle them in the exact form in which they arise! Maxine heaves a sigh of relief. She can do her worst and she'll still have a social group around her, because people really *can* take care of themselves. And she knows now where the power lies. It's right there under her nose. The kids have some of it and the teachers have the rest. And they really have it, because there's no principal, no schedule, no boss. Why even the teachers blow their lids! George spanked her the other day when she took all the magnets and kicked him in the shins. Just like Eléna, only worse because the spanking hurt. Yet they played together half an hour later and he wasn't mad any more.

Given the radical environmental change at First Street, the inherent rationality of Maxine's testing gradually came to the surface and achieved its purpose. For the limits were there to be discovered, the true border line, in all its particularity, at which Maxine's unorganized self met the more organized demands of the people who made up her group. Her need for relation was answered, and with it her need for security. Nor was she obliged to feel so very special in the oddities of her needs, for *all* the kids were special, all spoke up in distinctive ways and had immediate access to the teachers and to each other. No one had to wonder what mysterious hierarchical necessities lay beyond the teachers' words and actions. There was no ulterior power. Good sense arose in the occasion, as did everything else: feeling, judgment . . . even the day-to-day conception of the appropriate tasks of learning.

Yet though the teachers were free to be as good as they might, as flexible, forbearing, and patient as they might, the consideration they showed the children was nothing compared to what the children showed one another. We had a lot of roughnecks. There were many aggressions and insults. The children's patience and forgiveness outran them all. Even the older boys, with their well-founded dislike of Willard and Stanley, found ways of forgiving and forgetting. They were able to maintain the contact that is essential to the growth of relationships, which in themselves are the media of all change. It is obvious that children are obliged to do this. The decisive contexts of their lives are always determined by adults. No child chooses his city, his neighborhood, or his block. No child chooses the moment when his family will pack up and go somewhere else. No matter where they are, the children need one another. The violent rejections of adult life are luxuries they cannot afford. The important thing is that they do have the ability to take one another into account.

They do find ways of resolving their differences. In any other context, these ways would be proverbial. Writing on education, one must point them out: patience, forgiveness, acceptance.

Consider, too, these other differences between the lives of children and the lives of adults, for though we know that our world is a disastrous one, we are not fond of observing that precisely the weight of its disasters distinguishes our own lives from the lives of our children:

Children relate to one another by means of enterprise—play, games, projects. Which is to say that they are never bogged down in what are called "interpersonal relations." For interpersonal relations are precisely those words, deflected acts, and emotions which occur when shared activity ceases or becomes impossible: our long conversations, our opinions, our attitudes. We "relate" *to one another,* that is, we jockey around in the sticky ambience of personality traits, neuroses, insecurities, trivial aggressions, practiced egotism, regret, bitterness, self-love, complacency, arrogance, vengefulness, etc. Children do not and cannot. They penetrate this ambience quickly—it is always rudimentary anyway—and they get on with some shared activity that is exciting.

Nor do children have false pride.

Nor have they conceived of the ambitions which often lead adults to treat other persons as objects.

Nor are they interested in the formalized power of office, class, etc.

Nor do any of them develop the specialized repertory based on the weaknesses of others—as adult society abounds in special services, and those who specialize find themselves relating to, and ultimately depending upon, the insufficiencies of others. Children relate to one another's strengths and abilities, since only these make enterprise possible.

Nor do children speak jargon to one another, or abstractions, but a vivid and living speech.

Nor do they sacrifice activity to comfort.

Nor is their hopefulness, like the hopefulness of many adults, compromised by aborted judgment, a barrier against disillusionment; but takes an almost animal form of unconscious faith, so that we see it as energy, appetite— almost as creative will.

I have drawn adult life much too bleakly, but I think the point is clear. If we were to imagine a neurotic or unhappy child, and were to begin to name the qualities of the environment we might wish for him, we would list the things I have been describing. We would say, let it be an environment that is accepting and forgiving; and let it be one that takes him out of himself and involves him in group activities; and let the inducements to sociability be attractive and vivid, yet let them be measured accurately to his own capacities; and let there be real pressure in the environment, let it make definite and clear-cut demands, yet let the demands be flexible; and let there be no formal punishment or long-lasting ostracism; and let there be a hope of friendship and hope of praise; and let there be abundant physical contact and physical exertion; and let the environment offer him a sense of the skills and the varieties of behavior that lead to greater pleasure, greater security . . . and let the rewards for this kind of growth be immediate and intrinsic in the activities themselves.

These attributes of a healing environment are almost

self-evident. Surely it is evident, too, that this environment is precisely the ordinary one of children at play among themselves.

It would be wise to refer to the play of children, too, for a statement of the minimal obligations of any school. Here again the most ordinary attributes will serve us: the brightness of the childrens' faces when they are hard at their games, the vivacity of their voices, the swiftness of their invention, the accuracy and drollery of their observations. One might speak—without any sentimentality at all—of the *gay intelligence* of childhood. This is not to discount the passions and gravity of childhood, or its incidental violence, or the fitful opacity which sometimes makes children, like animals, seem mysterious; it is only to observe that once children are in motion among themselves, the quality of gay intelligence becomes apparent immediately and characterizes their games. No one needs to be reminded that this is one of the loveliest of human traits. It has been a theme of praise in literature and philosophy, to say nothing of daily life. We do need to remind ourselves, however, that the gay intelligence of childhood is not the product of schools, but of family life and nature and certain of the accumulated experiences of our culture. It is what we *give* to the schools when we give them our children. If we were completely at a loss to state the positive goals of education, we might still insist upon a minimal responsibility: do not destroy what already exists. *If you cannot add to the intelligence of childhood, at least do not destroy it!*

This would be our charge to the schools if we were to put words to our instinctive hope of life. In my own experience, *all of the parents I know* of school-age children reveal this hope in a negative form, that is, they express the fear that the schools will brutalize their children. Nor am I speaking only of middle-class whites. Negro and Puerto Rican parents experience this fear in an especially poignant way, for it is confirmed in short order. Their children, who like all children attend their first classes eagerly, with naive pride in their new notebooks and long pencils, soon come home with puzzled and anxious faces, faces which harden in two or three years into the sullen resentment which reflects the progressive loss of intelligence several studies have shown to be a feature of school life in the slums.

No school at all is better than a bad school. Nothing else in the child's environment is capable of such systematic destruction. Yet no school at all amounts to neglect, for no other provisions have been made.

The more one pursues this thought, the more it becomes apparent that the deeper problems of primary education cannot be solved in the schools. They are the problems of communities. Yet the idea of planning schools around the lives of parents as well as children—and I do not mean involving parents in their children's activities, or in adult education—is so rarely mentioned that one would suppose it were anathema.

* 11 *

Birthday party for Dodie. It was in Susan's room, just after lunch. The favors and candies, the colored-paper decorations (a surprise), and the sense of a special occasion excited the limitless cravings of certain of the kids. Their voices grew louder and louder. It was as if we had pulled a switch and tons of coal were hurtling down a chute, together with some kind of musical accompaniment. It was as if a Texas Twister had swept through a playground, scooping up dozens of children, and cats and dogs as well, and parakeets and bells . . . and then the vortex opened (as it always does!). Little groups drifted off to the sides. Dodie and Rudella stepped into the hallway. The little ones clustered together and went upstairs with Gloria. The older boys were rummaging in the closet, and Kenzo, rather gingerly, looked over their shoulders to see what they were doing.

I went to the front room and sat down to catch my breath, i.e., a lungful of Gauloises. Little Michael Hasty, the very light-skinned Negro, not yet eight, walked through the doorway with careful steps. He had made himself a birthday cake, an inverted dixie cup with a candle rising from its peak. His shoulders were curved protectively and he was shielding the flame of the candle with one hand.

Michael is probably the loneliest kid in school. His face is sorrowing, and there is something chilled and wan in his gestures. But there is great rage in him, too, and a panic fear that lies close to the surface. He can tease sadistically, and when he is frightened, he lashes out with blind savagery.

He said, "Look what I have, George."

Stanley came into the room just then. "Hey!" he yelled. "Gimme a candle!"

Michael drew back and said, "No . . ."

Stanley narrowed his eyes. "If I tell you to gimme a candle, you better gimme a candle."

Michael ran behind the desk, but Stanley leaned across and blew out the candle, then with a swift blow knocked it off the dixie cup. Michael's face looked as if he were screaming, though he made no sound. He hurled the paper cup at Stanley, catching him square on the nose. Now it was Stanley's panic that came pouring out. The cup was almost weightless, but he blinked and turned white, and then screamed with rage and leaped over the desk. Before I could reach him, he had struck Michael twice.

I stood between them. Both were shouting now. Michael was terrified. He cried, "I'll get a knife, you mother-fucker! I'll kill you!" (This from a boy not eight.) Again the blood drained from Stanley's face. I was surprised at how frightened he was. He stopped struggling with me and ran to the closet at the back of the room, where he threw aside a pile of fabrics and old hats. When he came back, he held a long butcher knife in his hand.

"Here's a knife, you mother-fucker! Let's see you kill me!"

Michael caught his breath and said in a small voice, "He got a knife, George."

I took the knife from Stanley. Michael ran from the room. I was holding Stanley by the arm. I was angry and was yelling, "No knives in school!" He struggled and cursed. "I'll get all the knives I want, you mother-fucker! Take your fuckin' hands off me!"

I gripped him firmly by both shoulders and began to shake him, not a brief shaking, but a long, long, long shaking that made even his arms go floppy. His face changed moment by moment, as if masks were falling away. The scowling thug-face vanished, revealing the face of a boy almost twelve whose head was spinning and who was simply trying to get his bearings. Then that face, too, vanished, and there was the face of a young child who had a plea to make and wanted to cry. Baby tears formed in his eyes and trickled down his cheeks on both sides of his nose. I stopped shaking him and sat him in a chair beside me. While he tried to catch his breath, I told him that I would never let anyone attack him with a knife. Nor would I let *him* attack anyone with a knife. Nor would we allow any knives at all in school. He started to say something, but I repeated the whole statement word for word, and he listened to me with a slightly bowed head.

3/17/65

The most thoroughly middle-class child in school is little Bertrand Kleist, whose parents are radical activists. He's a sturdy, bright, brash six-year-old, well cared for and optimistic. Both Willard and Stanley have taken a shine to him and treat him like a mascot when we go on trips.

The three of them sat together on the uptown bus, and Stanley threw his arm around Bertrand's shoulders. In such moments Stanley is genuinely affectionate. One would hardly know him, as several days ago he sat for ten minutes beside Laura, very gently brushing her hair.

We had divided into three contingents to take the buses, and now we gathered again and made our way into Central Park, thinking to watch the St. Patrick's Day parade from the little bluff in the sixties behind the temporary grandstands. Several police were stationed there, however, for the express purpose of chasing people away. I asked one of the cops why we could not use this very logical, completely adequate site. He didn't know, and in fact was embarrassed by his own behavior. He cracked a sad smile and said, "You have to ask the man downtown. I'm just a soldier."

A couple of our kids ran down the hill and sneaked into the reserved bleachers. In a moment our entire school followed suit, clambering over the stone wall and hoisting one another up into the stands. A typical First Street operation. We were not made for this world.

But the people in the stands, a mixed lot of children and adults, were amused by our invasion and stretched helping hands to us and made room for us to sit. And so we settled down in the best of seats.

The air was brisk and there was a lively spirit in the stands. I bought a dozen bags of peanuts and passed them around to our kids and our helpful neighbors. It seemed there might be a little gaiety after all.

National Guard and ROTC platoons marched at the head of the parade, and marched by in a pall of silence. So much for public enthusiasm for the military.

But now here came a bevy of jodhpured debutantes on

frisky brown horses, and a lively cheer went up. The cheer was followed by a lone voice: "Hey, Beautiful! Hey, Beautiful! Not you, ugly, the horse!"

It was Stanley. His hands were cupped at his mouth. Beside him sat Michael Hasty, observing his every motion. As Stanley's voice died out, Michael's rose up. "Hey, Beautiful! Hey, Beautiful! Not you, ugly, the horse!" His hands were cupped at his mouth. When some more soldiers marched by (again in silence), Stanley yelled, "Give 'em a medal!" and Michael repeated it, word and tone. Now came a squadron of dignitaries dressed in tails, with bright red ribbons across their chests. They doffed their hats as they passed the stands, and Stanley yelled, "Throw 'em a dog biscuit!" and his echo repeated, "Throw 'em a dog biscuit!" I was on the topmost plank of the bleachers. They were three rows away. I had been leaning forward calling to them, and now I shouted again, but a host of bright red uniforms had come in view—the Cardinal Spellman High School Band—and both Michael and Stanley were shouting full blast, "Here come the faggots!"

By this time we were no longer in good standing with our helpful friends. To make matters worse, Michael and Stanley began to argue. Stanley glared at him and cocked his fist. Michael became panicky and lashed out. His blow caught Stanley flush on the nose, first with an effect of fear, far out of proportion to the pain and the size of the seven-year-old who had caused it; then with vindictive rage. He began to pummel Michael.

The people in the stands drew away from them. I picked up Stanley and lowered him to the ground by his wrists. He stood there cursing and screaming, trying to climb back into the stands and hit Michael some more.

"I'm gonna kill that mother-fucker! You fuckin' faggot, I'm gonna kill you!"

Stanley is white, Michael a light-skinned Negro. Soon all the Negroes and Puerto Ricans in the stands were taking Michael's side against Stanley. A big Puerto Rican boy began to climb down from the bleachers, intent on settling Stanley's hash, and I had to prevent it.

In the meantime Mabel, who like thousands of others had noticed Stanley's location, had made her way down the bleachers. She appeared beside him, and after a few minutes took him away to sit with her contingent.

The parade grew duller and duller. The people in the stands were bored and restless. Susan and I, taking advantage of Stanley's absence, gathered up our kids and left. Michael stayed close to me. We stopped at our local luncheonette and drank sodas before going back to school, and just as the chorus of the straws rose up, that rattling, slurping, amplified sound in the bottom of the glass, Mabel walked in with the rest of the boys, probably to buy them sodas. Stanley yelled and rushed at Michael. I stopped him and spoke to him firmly. It was clear in my own mind that we could not keep him if he persisted like this. I told him that if he hurt Michael, he would have to leave the school.

"I'm not gonna hurt 'im, I'm gonna kill 'im!"

I repeated my words.

"I don't care! I'm gonna kill 'im!"

By this time the manager of the luncheonette was urging us to get the hell out. The squabbling continued on the sidewalk, Michael cowering behind me.

Stanley repeated his threat. I told him the decision was his own. And then suddenly, wholly unexpectedly, he said, "Okay—just one punch."

Michael promptly stepped out from behind me and said, "Okay, one punch," and braced himself. Stanley hit him hard on the arm and walked away.

Michael had asked me earlier to walk him home, and so I went down the street with him. But after a couple of blocks he said, "I'm okay now, George. I can go by myself."

He had been especially frightened because he had seen the enormous switchblade knife I had taken from Stanley that very morning. Stanley had brandished the knife so as to be sure that I would see it. It was clear that he wanted to know if I would keep my word and take it.

3/18/65

Since I had gone straight home after walking Michael part way, I still had Stanley's knife in my pocket. Stanley greeted me in the morning by yelling for his knife. I told him I would give it to him after school, and he mustn't ever bring it again.

"Gimme my knife!"

"No knives in school."

"I want that knife!"

"Anyone who brings a knife to school gets kicked out for the day."

"I don't give a shit! Gimme my knife."

I went into the front room to hang up my coat. José, Julio, and Vicente were tinkering with an electric hot plate. Willard was looking at a picture book of Vermont. We had been talking about the sugar maple trees, and how the sap was collected and boiled down to make syrup, and how the syrup was boiled again to make sugar. I had brought a jar of syrup with me and we planned to convert it to sugar. The boys wanted a taste of it. Stanley appeared in the doorway. "Gimme that fuckin' knife!" I told him no one could have a knife and stay in school, and I said it angrily, for I was fed up with him. He began shouting still louder, in a rhythmic, determined way: "Gimme that fuckin' knife! Gimme that goddamn knife! Gimme that goddamn mother-fuckin' knife!"

I took the knife out of my pocket and slammed it into his hand. Then I took him by the neck and the seat of the pants and ran him down the two flights of stairs and pushed him out the front door, saying come back tomorrow without the knife. And then I went upstairs, huffing and puffing. And there was Stanley. He had come in the other entrance and up the other staircase. I grabbed him again, and hustled him out again, and invited him back again without the knife, and went huffing up the stairs again. This time he waited about five minutes, then burst into the room, shouting and cursing and threatening everyone. Not only was I too tired—and defeated any-way—but he so obviously wanted to stay in school (this confirmed truant) that I knew I couldn't make a third attempt. I took him to another room and closed the door (for I didn't want him to be humiliated), and shook him by the shoulders until his face began to clear, and then (not easily, but successfully, thank God) turned him over my knee and paddled his ass as hard as I could. The tears had started coming out during the shaking, and now they came out more freely—child tears. I sat him beside me and held him firmly, not to console him, but to make him listen. I told him he could not have his knife in school; I would give it back to him after school (I had taken it again).

"Yeah? You said that yesterday and you didn't give it back to me."

"Why didn't I give it to you?"

"I don't know."

"Because I didn't come back to school, that's why. Where did I go?"

"I don't know."

"Who was walking beside me?"

"Michael."

"Why was he walking beside me?"

A little smile came to his lips. "I don't know."

"Yes, you do know. Because you scared him, that's why."

When I let him go, his face was clearer and calmer than I had ever seen it. He looked so different that José, passing him in the hall, turned around in a double take . . . but said nothing.

Spanking Stanley made me realize that I couldn't handle him. Not that the spanking was wrong. It was exactly right (and could not be repeated). He is terribly alienated from the child in himself, and is consequently driven by the child's fears. I treated him as a child by spanking him. I had set up relations with the part of himself he had rejected. And I had let him know that I could cope with the behavior he is unable to handle himself. But just that is the rub, for though in principle I *can* cope with it, in fact I cannot. I've been over this road before, and I know that I can't take it again.

Years ago, at the school for juvenile schizophrenics, there had been an eight-year-old boy who seemed the personification of evil. He was a strikingly beautiful child, dark-haired, with enormous soft eyes, long lashes, and red, red lips, richly curved. The sound of another child crying sent him into paroxysms of glee. His body would begin to tremble, he would arch his back and jump up and down stiff-legged, striking the tips of his fingers together. He would sneak up behind the younger children and pinch or hit them. He collected bugs and tore off their legs and stored the squirming corpses in a jar. One day, during play period, he found a piece of broken glass on the grounds and stabbed two of the children. Neither wound, fortunately, was serious, though one required several stitches. And so—as we were debating now about Stanley—we debated among ourselves about this child. Only about half of the children were capable of progress. Ivan was among the most intelligent, and was one of the few for whom we felt hope. But the chief consideration was this: that if we rejected him, his life was as good as over, for the only facilities in the state were tantamount to dungeons. We decided to give him one last chance. I had never worked with him. Another teacher took my children, and for three weeks, five hours a day, I devoted myself to Ivan. Later, he became a member of my group, but for those weeks we belonged exclusively to each other. It seemed that he was trying to outwit me, to discover a weakness, an escape hatch for himself. Just the opposite was true, for though he hurled himself against me with open desperation, and with what at times seemed like demonic energy and cleverness, what he really wanted was to discover that I could contain him, which in his eyes meant protect him from himself. Maxine, Vicente, and Stanley are "impulsive." One would hardly describe Ivan that way. A vibration would seize him—quivering, apparently, along his spine—and then, in effect, would hurl him at someone else. My task was chiefly one of anticipation: to be there before the impulse seized him, and then, often by the use of gentle force, to help him cope with it, as I often put my arm around him and walked beside him, teaching him different ways of breathing. After three weeks it was as if he had heaved a great sigh of relief. He felt safe. He settled down among the other children of my group. I was his right-hand man, and he had even become proud of the fact that I would not let him hurt people.

I've thought of Ivan again and again while watching Stanley, especially in this regard: that where one would have thought cruelty was the delight of Ivan's soul, it fell by the wayside once he had experienced a superior kind of functioning. Part of his problem was that the aggressions that are normal to human life had not developed properly. He did not—to use Frederick Perl's word—"destructure" his food with his teeth, either by biting or grinding, but tore it to bits with his fingers and sucked up the bits and swallowed them. Nor did he use his hands with the normal aggressiveness we take for granted when we make our routine changes in the environment. He used his hands like the claws of birds: only the nails. Even when he struck another child, it was not like the blow of a hand, but of a flap of wood attached to his arm by a string. His breathing, similarly, was out of phase with the requirements of his body when he was in motion. Such things as these—there were many others—were what we worked with, trying to restructure them. As the months went by, Ivan experienced brief moments of adequate functioning. These were so important to him that he could be seen, at other times, trying to imitate himself as he had been at his best.

Stanley, compared to Ivan, is a normal boy, though obviously he's disturbed. He is like Ivan in that he cannot tolerate his peers, but terrorizes them and sabotages their relationships. I know that if I were to take him under my wing, protect him from himself, and assume the responsibility for the impulses he cannot handle, we could bring him around. But the truth is that I cannot do this. I haven't the patience anymore, or the commitment, or—most important—the love. This became clear to me when I spanked him, for I saw how correct it was —not correct in itself, and definitely not correct as punishment (which it wasn't; it was force and anger), but correct as the first step in a long chain of close responsibility, amounting in the end to a functional parallel of love. I could not sustain that chain. Nor was First Street a school for disturbed children. And so the spanking was wrong, which is tantamount to saying that we must get rid of Stanley.

Willard has grown weary of Stanley's dominance. He understands that he is a kind of cat's paw; but he is unable to cope with Stanley's cleverness.

Willard and I are never close. He never confides in me. Yet he has come to see that I like him, rather that I like certain things within him . . . and he must esteem these same things himself, for today, as he began to snarl at Kenzo and raise his fist, he threw me a sidelong glance, and an almost shy smile sped across his face. He lowered his hand and walked away.

Willard and José are gradually becoming friends. They speak to each other more often now, and smile. The similarity of their characters is the reason for this. Both are self-respecting in essentially healthy ways. Both are rational. Both are brave. They want to win praise more than anything else.

I gave Stanley's knife to Mabel, and she gave it to him at the end of the day.

3/21/65

Today, for the first time, the boys changed sides in their almost endless dodge-ball series. Willard came stepping across the line, grinning broadly, insisting that Julio and Vicente go play with Stanley, and he and José would stand them.

But just because of this sudden change, the game lacked the intensity it has always had, for it used to soak up a great deal of animosity.

I had noticed a plastic lid in the locker room, the top to some kind of cannister, shaped like the frisbees, or "flying saucers," the kids sail to one another in the parks. I sailed it into their midst and said nothing. They picked it up immediately and began to throw it at one another, substituting it for the soccer ball. And now, for the first time since the arrival of Willard and Stanley, they began to play, truly play, with a quality of gaiety and imagination.

They had all seen the James Bond film *Goldfinger*, in which the great menace is a hulking Oriental who wears a derby with a rim of razor-sharp steel. He murders several people by sailing this lethal derby through the air and slitting their throats. The plastic lid became the *Goldfinger* derby. And a special rule was immediately invented: you couldn't touch it until it came absolutely to rest. So much for its magical powers! There was a great deal of shouting and playacting. One after another came forward to the line, wearing the lid like a derby and making terrifying faces which sent the others scampering away in mock horror. Above all, there was a great deal of laughter.

Willard's brother, who had been home from Youth House for several weeks (during which time Willard was in a foul temper), got in trouble again and is back at Youth House. Mabel spent the morning helping Willard and Stanley write him a letter. In the afternoon the boys worked at their first group project: a pool table. They all went to the lumberyard with Mabel, and then to the hardware store to buy tools: a coping saw, nails and screws, glue.

3/25/65

Three officials from the public schools came today to inspect us. They were like a race apart as they moved among us with their poker faces, their stiff gestures, dark suits and ties. At a cursory glance they were grotesque or comical. When one looked into their faces, however, one saw that it was their function that was grotesque, their role in the vast clockwork of the machine. The men themselves were paying the price. They were variously embarrassed, ashamed, angry, bored beyond feeling. The face of one—the most pleasant and intelligent—had the sensitive flush of a heavy drinker.

All were considerate and did not want to disturb our routines. Partly this was because they themselves were so crashingly exposed to view, for all our groups are small, and when an observer walks into a room, everyone turns and observes him.

The authorities have never given us much trouble, and today we understood why, for the officials kept recognizing Problems from the past. They wanted to keep them in the past.

"Hello, Stanley. Ah! I see Willard is here, too!"

And another: "There's Vicente. I see you have your hands full. Is that José Portillo?"

One of them stepped into Susan's room, and seeing Maxine bent over a book, busily drawing something on a piece of paper, muttered under his breath, "My God! Is that Maxine?" She looked up and saw him and said, "Hi! You wanna see something?"

We conferred with the officials later. We had expected to be put on the defensive, but they spoke like appreciative visitors. "I think it's a wonderful thing you're doing with these kids." We could not find any common ground. The conference was brief. In their eyes we were one of the Safety Valves of the district, and they didn't want to clog us in any way.

One of them had come into my room while I was working with José. He said, "Would it ruin things if I sit here a while?" I nodded and said, "Yes, it would." I felt sure that he understood what I meant—that José would collapse. He sort of winked at me and went out again. Later I explained to him, and he said, "I know, I know. We had José four years down at PS—."

Stanley, after a few days of calm, has gone back to his terrorism. His effect on everyone is simply disastrous. We called a meeting of the whole school to decide what punishment should be meted out for bullying. The bullies were present and tried to caucus in their own behalf, but the younger kids were firm, and everyone was fed up. It was decided that anyone hitting a younger child should be suspended for one day. But this is a hard rule to enforce. The meeting itself will have more effect than the rule.

During shop Stanley kept threatening Julio, not always directly, but playing on his nerves, pounding extra hard with his hammer and muttering, "I'm gettin' pissed off. I'm gettin' pissed off." The other boys, because of their fear of Stanley, threaten whomever they can, and give vent to their anger by punching the ones who can't punch back.

I was trembling with anger when I left today. And with disgust and contempt.

3/30/65

Two teacher conferences this week: what to do about Stanley? No one doubts his bad effect on the others, yet if we throw him out, it means Youth House in short order. Too, this is the only school he has ever *attended,* and he's obviously getting something out of it. We called his psychiatric social worker, who has seen him once a week for a year. He agreed to join us for supper at Rappaport's. Gloria and Susan decided not to come, and said that they would go along with whatever we decided.

The supper crowd was slowly gathering at the restaurant. There are still some faint traces (here and at Ratner's) of Second Avenue's heyday of Yiddish Theater, though they are faint indeed and have been washed over by several waves of the New. I recognized some theater people at a long table near ours. Their off-Broadway play had folded under a barrage of bad notices, and they had spent the afternoon taking it apart. They were silent and avoided one another's eyes with that peculiarly childlike chagrin of actors. They had wanted to be loved.

Stanley's psychiatric social worker came in at last, and we all recognized one another, though none of us had met. He was in his late twenties, blond and sincere, with the traces of a Southern accent. We ordered and began talking about Stanley.

The young psychologist had only recently taken his doctorate, and now was cultivating the mannerisms of the trade, all crashingly evident against the still-boyish good nature of his face. Here was the Penetrating Glance, the Long Pause, the Double Nod. (The latter consists of a nod, a pause, and another nod. The first nod indicates that he has heard you; the pause indicates that you have not put it in a form that he can accept; the second nod says, "Go ahead, anyway. I'll clarify it later.") Here was the Answer-That-Corrects-The-Question, and here, too, was a maneuver that is hard to name, though I have seen it many times. Its effect is at once paternal and arrogant, undermining and supportive. The practitioner lifts his brow while you talk, with an effect of casting doubt on your every word, word by word; and then when you have finished, he lowers his eyes modestly, abstaining rather elaborately from speaking a single word of criticism. None of these mannerisms seemed to have the slightest thing to do with what was being said. It made me think of a friend of mine the day he graduated medical school. We were helping a third friend fix his car, and I said, "Hunh. I scratched myself." The new doctor held my scratched finger in his hand and gazed at it gravely, tugging at his new mustache. In years gone by, playing ball and in the woods, we had suffered together innumerable cuts, gashes, scratches, bumps, bruises, etc., and had paid them scant attention. This was the most pored-upon, most gravely studied scratch I had ever sustained. At last he said solemnly—with a truly striking note of patience for the follies of mortal men—"You'd better put some Merthiolate on that." In a similar way the young psychologist told us that Stanley needed "firm limits."

"I know you believe in freedom, but don't go overboard. He needs limits. Don't be afraid to spank him."

Also: "He can relate quite well to adults on a one-to-one basis."

In short, we all agreed about Stanley—which had no effect whatever on the Penetrating Glances, Double Nods, and Long Pauses. Yet the psychologist had been touched by Stanley, and his own concern for him was touching.

"You know," he said, "there's simply no place for him to go. If you close the door on him, he's really out."

It was this aspect of the problem we had hoped to hear something about—the alternatives. He mentioned the many signs of Stanley's high potential. And it was true that when you thought of Stanley in isolation—apart from his disastrous effect on the other kids—you became aware of his intelligence, his imagination, his needs, his unhappy life at home. The thought of kicking him out was painful.

We asked him if he thought Stanley was getting much out of the First Street School.

"Definitely. It's the only time in his life he's *wanted* to attend school. He talks about it a great deal."

This was exactly what we hadn't wanted to hear.

Mabel and I went to her apartment later and sat down with a piece of paper and a pencil, and began mapping out a strategy to minimize Stanley's effect on the other kids. Mabel decided to sacrifice her morning period with the little ones. I rescheduled José, and said, yes, I would work with Stanley alone for an hour every day. And then it seemed ridiculous to make such plans. I could *not* work with Stanley, for it would mean psychotherapy, and I could not work as a therapist except by giving myself, really and truly, to the patient's needs. I had broken off that career for just this reason; it had torn me apart, and after four years of it I had realized that I was no longer willing.

I said, "We have to get rid of him," and picked up the phone and began dialing the psychologist to tell him the bad news. Mabel looked glum. I had that awful feeling that goes with really injuring another person. I said, "Shit," and hung up the phone.

We began figuring again, trying to rearrange our activities. Again I said, "We *can't* do it," and picked up the phone. This time I dialed the whole number, then dropped the phone abruptly, as if it were hot. Now that I describe it, I realize that a very particular kind of self-indulgence is hidden here.

"Maybe we can hire a teaching assistant, a high-school kid, or a college kid, maybe somebody from SNCC, and have him help us with lunch and take the older boys out every day."

We went back to our figuring.

At least we had admitted that neither one of us had what Stanley needed.

4/13/65

We've tried two teaching assistants. The first was too inhibited and genteel, the second too intellectual and wordy. The boys thought him an oddball and mocked him, and he was unhappy. Now we have a seventeen-year-old Puerto Rican boy who lives on Second Street (where he was robbed at knife point just a few days ago). He's a good athlete and is lively and outgoing, but his only models are the public-school authorities and the waddling cops of the PAL, who can't even pick their noses except with aggressive and threatening gestures. In short, he's too much a product of the streets, too prone to push the boys around and to be censorious in a narrow and terribly authoritarian way. But we must give him a chance to get the hang of our style.

The days are getting warm, and there have been unsettling flashes of blue sky. Gloria's kids, and Susan's, are doing marvelously. The older boys are at a loss, restless because of spring (as I am) and driven by Stanley. They want to go out by themselves, and at the same time are afraid to leave their haven. They are overwhelmed by the city and their own sense of insufficiency, and so they hang around and talk tough and reject almost everything we offer.

Mabel had an idea that at first I didn't like, but turned out to be excellent. This was to form the boys into work crews and pay them well for their work. The idea of earning money galvanized them, and they flew here and there with buckets and mops. Unfortunately, there is not enough work to make a really big difference, though no doubt we can find some little bit every week. If the place were our own, there *would* be a lot, and it would matter a great deal to the boys to have a source of income at school compatible with their efforts. This, after all, is precisely the situation of the teachers, and it has not corrupted us, but has given a necessary life dimension to our presence here.

Today, for the first time in weeks, José asked me for a lesson. We had a good one. He is still so far behind that I don't very often feel optimistic, but when I reread my earlier descriptions of him (as I have just now done), I see what a long way he has come. He doesn't collapse at all anymore, and has learned enough from his own little notebook to be able to branch out into printed matter. I bought him a set of flash cards, and he's interested in them, not as *drill* or *review*, but as objects: cards, words. Sometimes Vicente comes in after we've finished and sits beside me and reads. José, instead of leaving the room (as he would have formerly), hangs around and listens.

We held a big spelling bee today, with cash prizes for the winners (and consolation prizes for the losers, who were crestfallen and glum). Money is a magic word. I've never seen them throw themselves into an organized activity with such eagerness. Unfortunately, we can't repeat it. The school is too small. The winners won by a great margin, and predictably would win again and again— Eléna and Kenzo.

4/16/65

Someone donated a bike to our school. Stanley and José stayed in the gym together and rode it, after the other boys had left with Ramon, our seventeen-year-old assistant (who is not working out very well).

José was wearing a red shirt, and he took it off. I picked it up and said, "Did you ever see a bullfighter?" It was all they needed. The bike rider became the bull and the other waved the "cape" at him.

Stanley leaped off the bike laughing. "*Toro* gets away! *Toro* jumps on him! *Toro* gets him down! *Toro* tickles him!"

They played imaginatively and without fighting, and I was pleased to see it. Stanley can do this when he is alone with someone. Later, at lunch, he was Al Capone again, disturbing everyone and creating a foul atmosphere.

I took the boys aside for a while after lunch and told them about the bullfights I had seen in Mexico. They were interested, as they are interested in all things brave, violent, and dangerous.

4/26/65

I suggested a lesson to José. The other boys were sitting around us. He stuck out his chin and said, "Fuck you."

His lips were curved in a little smile, and there was a curious appeal in his eyes. It was obvious that he wanted a lesson but was afraid to say so in front of the boys. In a joking spirit, I said I'd lug him into the classroom, and that was that. "Yeah? I'll break your ass, man," he said, still smiling. So I ducked down and scooped him up on my shoulders and carried him into the other room and set him down on the desk like a sack of grain. I called to Mabel and asked her to lock us in, José was grinning now, very pleased at having been rescued from his dilemma.

I opened the new word cards. José lay full length on the desk, and I sat beside him. He objected to the great number of cards—there were about a hundred—but I said, "These are new words. Don't try to read them. Let's just see what we have." I flipped the cards one by one. He recognized many—to his own surprise—and these we put in a separate pile. I made a second pile of words I thought he might like to learn in the near future. The third pile was for hard words. Now each card became the occasion of a little conference. I turned up the word "pretty." "Yeah," he said brightly, "put it there," meaning the second pile. And so with several others. And in the process of saying that he wanted to learn them soon, he learned them on the spot and was unaware of it. It was odd. The cards themselves were physical objects, and the words began to seem like objects, too, as if we were sorting out possessions. Soon I asked him to make up sentences for each word, even the ones he couldn't read, and we kept turning cards and talking about words for a long time, a very peaceful, easygoing kind of game.

The rest of the day was a mess, our typical mess with Stanley, too boring to describe.

5/5/65

José and Willard play the insult game, their own version of The Dozens. Each one tries to heighten his opponent's insults and turn them against him. It is a traditional Negro game, so I have read, though we find something very like it in Shakespeare, too. Often the insults are as foul as can be, and this appeals very much to boys the age of José and Willard.

Willard makes a circle with the outstretched fingers of both hands. "This is your mother's hole, man."

José is losing badly because of his limited English. He says, "Fuck you."

Willard grins and says, "Takes two to fuck me." He calls his own prick a hot dog, and says he'll put mustard on it and use José's ass for a bun.

José says, "Man, your mother's hole was so dirty you came out black."

If José had said this two months ago, Willard would have bloodied his face. Now he only blushes, gives his "topping" grin, and says, "I like my color, man"—and goes right on with the insults.

We've been showing films in school, and our rewind spool was broken. I took José and Vicente to the store with me to get another, José on his bike, Vicente and I on foot.

José on a bike is like José at everything else: he has to believe that he is much better than he is. He comes into blind corners without braking, goes past trucks without wondering what may be emerging on the other side. And rather than cope with all this, he takes his hands off the handlebars to show how good he is.

"Man, he's gonna have a lot o' wrecks." Vicente shook his head. We could just see José in the distance.

A moment later José swerved to avoid a pedestrian, hit a parking meter, and went sprawling.

Willard has been operating the projector at all our showings. He goes about this in an interested and intelligent way, and is the only one who can thread the film correctly. He's improved a great deal in temperament and in his ability to make friends.

We have expelled Stanley at long last. The children know ruthlessly what they want. All are glad that he's gone—no one more so than Willard.

5/7/65

Mabel and I took a gang of the kids up to Bear Mountain. Stanley being out, the spirit of the school has improved remarkably. Of the boys, we took Willard, José, Julio, Vicente, and Donald, a new boy. Of the girls, Rudella, Eléna, Dodie, Dolores, and Hannah.

The country, as usual, was exciting to them, and then calming.

We had only a dim idea of where we were going, and trusted to serendipity, which delivered us to the entrance of a large summer camp in the woods, closed still for the winter and barred by a long iron pipe. We could see the calm level of water from the road.

It was closed, but was it closed *and* locked? No, it was not. We took out the bar, drove in, replaced the bar . . . and held our picnic on the shore of the lake.

The boys ran around to a little cove and took off their clothes and jumped in the water. José and Willard did not want to be seen and covered themselves with their hands, but Vicente climbed a rock and stood there as if he meant to piss across the world, shouting, "Hey girls, you wanna see my prick?"—his voice ringing like a bell over the water.

The girls turned away, some giggling, some making faces of disgust. Rudella said, "Those stupid boys!"

But a few minutes later, seeing the arcs and splashes of their naked bodies in the lake, that woebegone female look crossed their faces. Boys have all the fun. They found a creek to wade in, however, and soon were calling out to one another merrily.

We ate our lunch by the lake, cleaned up the grounds, then drove to the old Bradley iron mine and explored it.

A good day. All returned tired. The girls struck up songs in the bus.

5/12/65

With Stanley out, there's no need for Ramon, our assistant, and we've let him go.

Other bikes have been donated. We're out a good bit of the time now, which is good. Lessons are brief, even those with José. The boys have responded with some interest to simple geography and maps. Maybe the wanderlust of spring brings it alive for them—or for us. José locates everything by its relation to Puerto Rico. He had drawn a rocket ship nearing the moon, and way down below was the outline of our Eastern coast. To my surprise, it was more or less correctly drawn—except for Puerto Rico, which was very large, but in proper shape. I discovered that he had drawn that first and then had pieced in the rest.

5/18/65

To the Bronx Zoo with José and Vicente and little Michael Hasty. The other boys, and some of the younger ones, went to Staten Island with Mabel.

All that idiotic gang defiance of adults is ended. Both José and Vicente are fond of me, and they obviously prefer being able to show it. Nor are they afraid, any longer, to express their desire for attention. In short, the kids make better use of us now that Stanley is gone, and better use of their own freedom.

It was a good day. José was interested in many things and stood for a long while before certain of the cages, asking questions and making comments. He pointed, laughing, to a large eagle with a white ruff around its neck, and glossy black feathers on chest and wings. "Look," he said, "he's rich"—gesturing, stroking the fur collar on a rich man's coat. Vicente still cannot stand long in one place. He rushed from exhibit to exhibit, crying out in his piercing voice, "Hey, look at this! Look at this!" He was carrying cigarettes, and I wouldn't let him smoke them. He ran away, grinning back at me over his shoulder, and lit a cigarette and flourished it, swaggering down the pathway between the cages. Soon he was frowning and coughing, and a moment later was trotting at my side like a five-year-old, holding my hand. Little Michael has not yet made friends with them, and he drifted along, in front of us, behind us, rarely coming close or speaking, except when José and Vicente went off by themselves, and then he would talk to me.

We gathered at the honey-bear cage just at feeding time. There were five of the bears, furry and brown, about the size of housecats. They paced nervously and clambered on their tilted log . . . and then the food tray appeared. Three of the bears began eating, but the others retreated to corners, crouching abjectly. The boys noticed this and wondered what it meant. I could only theorize: those were females (I could see that the others, in any event, were males). The females became impatient and inched forward, and one of the males turned aside and threatened them. The females assumed postures of submission. There were three distinct positions: head turned aside; head turned aside and laid flat; complete curling up, as in sleep. The boys were interested to learn that these postures were signals (I had been reading Lorenz), and that the animals understood each other by means of them.

We didn't leave the zoo until three. The boys were exhausted. As soon as we took our seats on the subway, Vicente fell asleep, first with his head against my shoulder, then dropping it into my lap. José leaned against my other shoulder, and soon he too was fast asleep, collapsing backward against the seat. Only Michael didn't sleep. He stood between the cars for a long while, watching the tracks, then finally came and sat down beside us. I had to shake Vicente and José to wake them up at Fourteenth Street.

"Wha . . . ? Wha . . . ? Oh!"

They opened their eyes bewilderedly, then leaped for the door with embarrassed grins, shouting good-bye over their shoulders.

5/20/65

The subculture of poverty. In this world the kids assume that *whatever* is said will be to their disadvantage. We were standing in front of the school, arguing about where to go. Many opted for the beach, including José but José had no bathing suit and was complaining loudly. Mabel said, "Maybe we can rent bathing suits when we get there."

"Bullshit!" cried José. "I wanna go to the beach!"

I said to him, "I'll give you five dollars right now if you can repeat what she said."

"What?"

"I'll give you five dollars if you can repeat what she said."

By now everybody was listening.

José yelled, "Sure, man!" So I said, "Go ahead."

His jaw was stuck out pugnaciously and he was looking at me with narrowed eyes. Slowly his eyes rotated to one side. His brow grew wrinkled. His jaw dropped. A slow flush spread across his face, and he smiled sheepishly.

"What did she say?" he said.

6/18/65

Last day of school. We went to Alpine Park again, on the New Jersey side of the Hudson, a good place for us, small, almost always empty except for a few fishermen. It runs in a narrow strip right close to the river, with picnic tables, fireplaces, a winding path that leads off into the trees along the bank. Behind us were the wooded cliffs of the Palisades, in front the water and the awesome immensity of the city, beautiful at this distance.

We had piled the whole school into the microbus, kids holding kids on their laps, kids and teachers sitting on the floor. A cop looked in the window just as we left the school, and his jaw dropped. "Christ," he muttered, "drive careful, buddy."

Boys and girls—what primitive differences become apparent as soon as you leave the city! Within five minutes of our arrival the girls were setting up house under the branches of a tree, and the boys were running in all directions. José talked with a fisherman. Willard and Julio examined the fireplaces, then ran and hurled stones into the water. Vicente plunged headfirst into a trash basket, looking for God knows what.

Maxine, Eléna, and Dolores had gone shopping that morning, and we were well supplied with frankfurters and hamburgers, marshmallows and pickles, buns and potato chips. I asked the boys to round up firewood. No one refused. No one responded. I might just as well have asked the sea gulls. I got some myself, and laid a bed of paper and sticks in two of the grills, then piled on charcoal. I doused the little piles with lighting fluid . . . and the sudden blaze and burst of smoke brought the boys at full speed. Fire! I can't remember what they were saying, but they jumped around excitedly, constantly shouting. Nor —now that the fires were going—could they resist the compulsion to feed the flames. They scurried about in search of firewood, and each added his stick to the blaze. In the meantime the girls and teachers had laid out food on a nearby table. I explained to the boys that the fires must burn a good while, and that when the flames and smoke had subsided and the charcoal was glowing, we would cook our food. Their answer to this, having already provided themselves with long sticks, was to run pell-mell to the table. They came back with skewered franks and thrust them into the smoke and flames. Susan, who had heard my fire lecture and had seen its results, was sitting at the table laughing and laughing. Soon all of the kids were crowded around the fires roasting franks. Gloria and Mabel laid out a row of hamburgers. We had brought a plastic squeeze-jar of mustard, and Maxine seized it and sped about among the cooks and eaters, yelling, "Mustard! Mustard! Who wants mustard?"—dispensing it in such quantities that we kept hearing, "Hey, Maxine! That's *too much!*" Marshmallows followed the franks, and soon there was that glassy-eyed lull of repletion that goes with fire watching and overeating. The lull was broken in the most predictable way, and predictably, it took us by surprise, for the boys had circled the fires, and now, as if at a signal, unleashed their snub-nosed, eager little pricks, like puppies bounding into the light, and gave the flames a good ammoniac sousing. It was so vulgar, so inevitable, so humorous, so historical and universal, that we teachers—who always refrained from pissing out our suburbanite friends' backyard grills—rocked back and forth with laughter and let the ritual run its course.

Now again the primitive differences, for the girls, even Maxine, helped the teachers clean house, stowing paper plates and bun ends in the baskets nearby. Some tied a long rope to a tree, and twirling the other end, started a jumping game. Others threw a beach ball back and forth. All, in effect, were playing close to home. The boys, however, had scattered again. After a while I gathered them. I had brought a length of stout rope, and I held it up and shouted, "Let's make a swing!" and they came running, for there are few rope swings in a city boy's life.

We took the path that meandered through the trees along the bank. At the head of the path was a wooden sign: FOR EXPERIENCED CLIMBERS ONLY. José studied it grimly. He said, "For . . . ," and could say no more. Julio read it out: "It says, 'for experienced climbers only.' " José said, "Bullshit," and all went ahead of me up the path. The best sight of the day occurred just then, for Willard and José were going side by side and had thrown their arms around each other's shoulders. We found an overhanging tree, and soon the boys were leaping from a rock, rope in hand, swinging out over the water and back again. Several planks had washed ashore, and one of those platform skids you see on the docks. José took off his clothes, and seizing the skid, launched into the river. The others followed suit. The river was polluted, but I thought they would survive, and so I cautioned them only to stay close to shore.

Songs in the bus again as we rode back home. Eléna and Maxine led the singing, song after song, and it was the teachers who learned from the kids, for though we had been present at all of those sessions with Barney, we had not learned one-fifth of what the children had. They were still singing when we arrived in the East Side—so many words! so many verses! I would never have thought it could be so pleasant, or that the angel of peace would settle so long in our chaotic midst.

I drove kid after kid to his home or block, and teachers, too, until only Willard and José were left in the bus. They were sitting side by side in the back, where they had sat the whole ride through. They had not participated in the singing, but they had listened. For several weeks now Willard has been at peace, his face calm hours on end, and even happy. I could see him in the mirror, and I realized that he had been smiling all day long, for their conversation had ebbed down to nothing and his face had become a mask. He jumped out at his corner and turned with a tense grin to José. "See you on the block, man." I said good-bye to him, but he avoided me and didn't answer. José said, "Yeah, man, see you on the block." I caught sight of José's face as I maneuvered the bus back into traffic. He had begun to weep. His shoulders were drawn up and he covered his face with one hand, trying to stop the tears. Then he gave way to it, and sat with his arms at his sides and his head erect, tears streaming down his face.

I said nothing to him, but ten minutes later stopped the bus in front of my apartment and asked him to wait. I brought down a pelt I had bought years ago in Guatemala, a civet cat, I think, tawny with black spots. He was wiping away the tears with his sleeve. He wanted to know if I had shot it, which I hadn't, but had bought it in the Indian market after an unsuccessful hunting trip. I showed him the bullet hole that had killed it. When I let him off at his block, he threw it over his shoulder, and I could see him adjusting it, flattening it out, as he went down the street.

Some friends of ours have invited José and Eléna to spend a week at their farm in New Hampshire. Mabel and I will deliver them, and then go on to Maine and try to rent a house. Other friends—in Vermont—are taking Rudella for a while, and her younger brother, who'll come to First Street next year. Then later in the summer Gloria and Mabel will take a whole crowd up to Maine. They want me to go along, but I don't think I will. I've had my fill of children for a while, and I'd like to get away.

* 12 *

The crisis in public education, like the hastening dissolution of other of our social institutions, creates anxiety and doubt, and we respond as anxious people do: we try to impose order by force, imagining that if we can obliterate the symptoms, we will have cured the disease. We speak increasingly of control, as if we feared that everything would collapse into nothing if we let loose our (illusory) hold on things. And so I have been urging one simple truth through all these pages: that the educational function does not rest upon our ability to control, or our will to instruct, but upon our human nature and the nature of experience. I have been trying to describe their attributes as they appear in action, for— in kind—they are the bases of all teaching and all learning. Dewey calls them the *starting point* of education. If these deeper attributes of our lives are often obscured by anxiety, they also survive it. They are the source of talents far stronger than our gift for bureaucratic planning. I have been urging that we trust them, that we show some little faith in the life principles which have in fact structured all the well-structured elements of our existence, such principles as our inherent sociability, our inherent rationality, our inherent freedom of thought, our inherent curiosity, and our inherent (while vigor lasts) appetite for more. What this means concretely is that we must rescue the individuals from their present obscurity in the bureaucratic heap: the students, because they are what this activity is all about; the teachers, because they are the ones who must act. I have been describing our attempts to accomplish just this with Maxine and Vicente, José and Eléna, and all the rest. I know that we failed in a great many ways, yet the task we set ourselves is the relevant educational task in our country today.

I have spoken in detail of the schools of A. S. Neill and Leo Tolstoy. I have said little about the philosophy of John Dewey, though it is just his thought that remains the deepest expression of the methods and ideals I have described. This is worth commenting on, for there are many people who still assume, more or less routinely, that the "progressive education" of the Deweyan schools was a fair testing of Dewey's thought. This was not the case, as Dewey himself gently observed in 1936, in *Experience and Education,* when he pointed out the lapses and excesses of the new schools and stressed the extreme difficulty of acting educationally upon a philosophy of experience. The same people—educators, teachers, and writers on education—will doubt that such an informal and shaggy milieu as that of the First Street School could possibly represent the application of Dewey's ideas in the present. They forget that Dewey was not describing method but technique, and that technique must vary according to the needs of the times and the needs of individuals. They might imagine, too, that because Dewey proposed experimental science as the model for education, the heart of the school must be the laboratory, or possibly the shop, and that the entire operation must have the neatness and finality of a successful physical experiment. This was not what Dewey meant. He stressed again and again—and as early as 1902—that it was not the external procedures of empirical science that needed to be adopted, but the dynamics of the relationship between science and experience. Science organizes experience in a unique, and uniquely imitable, way. It cannot afford rigidity, or merely rhetorical reverence, yet it builds upon the past. It is instrumental, wholly alive in the life of the present, yet it is open to the future and is no enemy of change. Free thought is its essence, yet it is disciplined by its devotion to emergent meaning. It places the highest value upon ideas, cannot function without them, defines them scrupulously, yet never enshrines them into final truths. It is always collaborative. Egotism, vanity, the power lusts of the individual will—all these are chastened by the authority of truth and the demonstrable structure of the natural world. These were the attributes Dewey cited in proposing empirical science as a model for the social effort we call education. The model was especially vivid in that he held it over and against the authoritarian tradition, which had never bothered to provide itself with a philosophy, had never rationalized its methods, and rendered the act of learning—as Dewey insisted—a mere accident.

It might be well to contrast Dewey's thought, and the style of his thought, his habit of mind, with the prevailing style of our educationists, not only to observe the difference between a philosopher and an Expert, but to see how and why our educational establishment is hostile to Dewey's deepest meanings (as it is hostile to the related philosophies of Neill and Tolstoy). And I must confess that I am not capable of performing this analysis impartially. Nor would there be much point in performing it at all if it were not for the fact that organized mediocrity wields such power in our country at present. Where the influence of a philosopher rests upon the authority of his thought, the influence of our educationists rests upon professional connections with the centralized power of the educational establishment. Their thought, taken simply as thought, is often so feeble as to provoke astonishment. This is frequently true of the most influential of them all, Jerome S. Bruner, director of the Center for Cognitive Studies at Harvard. Bruner's books are not without their virtues, but I shall leave it to others to praise them. I would like to concentrate for a moment, in an admittedly biased, unfair, and perhaps ill-tempered way, upon an analysis of the characteristic failure that renders Bruner's contribution, in my opinion, pernicious. Nor am I speaking only of Bruner. His failings are characteristic of the field. The positive purpose of this negative critique will be evident in a moment.

Bruner's most recent book is *Toward a Theory of Instruction*. Its thought—compared to the actual practice of the public schools—seems to be enlightened and humane. It calls attention to inborn motives, natural curiosity, the give-and-take of all social affairs. It is based at every turn upon years of research. Yet there is a flaw in the grain. As such it is no great matter. But when it is transformed into the hard facts of the environment of the schools, it becomes—as I shall show—an important matter indeed.

Bruner describes the inborn motives of the will to learn, numbering among them "the deep-sensed commitment to the web of social reciprocity."

The conduct of our schools [he writes] has been curiously blind to this interdependent nature of knowledge. We have "teachers" and "pupils," "experts" and "laymen." But the community of learning is somehow overlooked. What can most certainly be encouraged—and what is now being developed in the better high schools—is something approximating the give and take of a seminar in which discussion is the vehicle of instruction. This is reciprocity. But it requires recognition of one critically important matter: you cannot have both reciprocity and the demand that everybody learn the same thing or be "completely" well rounded in the same way all the time. If reciprocally operative groups are to give support to learning by stimulating each person to join his efforts to a group, then we shall need tolerance for the specialized roles that develop—the critic, the innovator, the second helper, the cautionary. For it is from the cultivation of these interlocking roles that the participants get the sense of operating reciprocally in a group.

Bruner's criteria here are not drawn from life, nature, experience, but from the closed system of the schools. He has addressed himself to the question, How can we improve our schools? Perhaps it is obvious that his answers are administrator's answers. It may not be obvious, however, that his question is the question of the technocrat. For given the current crisis in education, the question, How can we improve our schools? would satisfy neither the scientist nor the philosopher. Both would ask instead, How can we educate our young?

I would like to anatomize these thoughts of Bruner's. And I would like to do it in such a way as to make clear their ultimate environmental effect upon the young. If there is any doubt that the identical voice percolates endlessly downward through the pyramid of control, here are two other examples:

> What we would propose . . . is that we should learn still more about how children learn, and how different children learn differently, before any solutions are proposed. When

we have enough data, we think it may be possible to con-
struct a better fit between the objectives of the curriculum
and the pupils' perceptions; and certainly a better fit between those objectives, the evaluative system, and the pupils'
evaluative map.
—Mary Alice White, *The Urban Review*, April, 1968.

(These words are such a quintessence of the self-absorp-
tion of bureaucratic research, that I feel obliged to under-
line them, as it were, in red. Who would suppose that this
educator was writing in 1968? Drop-outs, illiteracy, vandalism, savagery, loss of intelligence, loss of spirit, apathy
rising into nausea, nausea rising into rage—these are the
facts for many millions of pupils and families in their experience of the public schools. They are such facts as indicate the basic responsibility of educators. Yet how
responsible this one manages to sound while she holds
them at arm's length in deference to her trivial data, her
"better fits" and "evaluative maps," and her animistic
belief that the curriculum itself possesses "objectives"!)

There is no point in giving the other example.

And I would prefer not returning to Bruner, were it not
for the fact that our society, in empowering its technocrats,
has disenfranchised the scattered millions who might
otherwise cohere into rational communities—the only adequate base for the educational function. It is no news that
we have become a heartless technocracy. It may need to
be said, however, that we are far along toward becoming
a mindless one as well. This is the distinction I would like
finally to make, the distinction between true thought, true
mind, and mere intellection, for if ever a nation stood in
need of wisdom (as I believe we can find in the pages of
Dewey), our nation does, and needs it now.

How is thought reduced to mere intellection? Ultimately, as I shall try to show, by a failure of love. More

obviously by failure of imagination, sympathy, observation —failure of response. Nor is the absence of response a merely negative phenomenon. We do not find a gap where response should be. We find instead the attempt to control. This displacement corresponds exactly to the failure of thought that we refer to when we speak disdainfully of "abstractions"; for we do not mean that thought should use no abstractions, but that when abstractions are allowed to usurp the place that belongs to what can only be called the body of the world, they no longer appear as vital components of thought, but as *mere* abstractions.

Bruner tells us that every child experiences a "deep-sensed commitment to the web of social reciprocity." Now in a rough-and-ready way this seems to be a true statement about life. At the same time it is quite obvious that children do not experience webs and commitments, but rather experience other children, adults, games, objects, etc. Are we haggling about words? Far from it. We want to speak of motives, desires, needs. We want to know how experience transpires for the child himself, and for the adult himself. We want to know what the quick of it is, the life of it. It is fatal to our investigation to fall into the error of believing that our own abstract descriptions— "commitment to the web, etc."—actually transpire as facts in the immediate experience of those we are observing. To allow this to happen is to lose sight of the object of study. It is to begin to tabulate one's own abstractions under the impression that one is speaking, still, of the organic unfolding of life. Whether we are aware of it or not, we have begun to limit and control the phenomena. Let us look at the consequences of this failure. It is chronic, and its consequences are pervasive.

We see, first, that the essential philosophic and scientific question passes by. How shall we educate the young?

Bruner is not interested. He speaks, rather, of instruction, and is concerned to improve its efficiency within the existing framework of the schools.

Now that high-sounding phrase, "deep-sensed commitment to the web of social reciprocity," appears in its true colors as the "give and take of a seminar." "This," he tells us, "is reciprocity." Is it? Is it not rather the Administrator himself, the Social Engineer, the School Monk, leaning back in his chair with his hands behind his head, his necktie informally awry, uncorking the Horn of Plenty by chatting with his students instead of subjecting them, as he might, to the terrors of a test? Reciprocity, social reciprocity, the web of social reciprocity, deep-sensed commitment . . . and we end with the "give and take of a seminar"! One would have thought that reciprocity referred to the peerage of existence, to our own approaching death and the extending life of the world in the lives of the young. And to the student's uniqueness, and to our own. And to the fact that experience, as it emerges, is always some way new, and always evolves in situations—situations, moreover, in which we can only give *our* part, not the other person's part. The questions that belong to reciprocity are questions of volition and of needs, the needs of the individual and those of society: Shall we compel the student's presence? Shall we compel his attention? Shall we "evaluate" him without his consent and for purposes of our own which we keep hidden? Shall we predetermine the duration and content of our encounter? Shall we prescribe in advance the limits of our own response, as we do prescribe them when we know so blandly, so deeply that we mean to instruct?

I think it is clear that when Bruner talks of reciprocity, he is thinking really, perhaps unknown to himself, of control, social engineering, manipulation. For we now discover that it is not the present lives of the students, their present interests, enthusiasms, aversions, loyalties, ideals, passions, rivalries, etc., that must be allowed to animate them in the classroom; but rather certain "roles" are available—"the critic, the innovator, the second helper, the cautionary"—and the wise administrator will guide the students in their exploration of these roles so that they "get the sense of operating reciprocally in a group"; and God knows, get no sense whatever of being alive in the quick of other lives, the quick of exciting thoughts, earnest resolves, strokes of invention, wit, and perhaps (can it be said?) an ardent love of learning! If an educationist can say of a youth, "He assumed a role," the youth will have experienced everything *but* a role. He will have been fired by some idea, some response of understanding or conviction. His real desires will have leaped toward some real object or person. In "operating reciprocally," people do not "get the sense" of it at all, but are actually *engaged* with each other, for real.

How odd, really, our educationists are! They discover the autonomy of indwelling motives and patterned growth —and then insist on manipulating these autonomous things. They affirm the value of instinctual life—and propose systems which make it count for nothing. They proclaim a reverence for facts, and immure themselves for years in experimental labs, from which they emerge in a haze of abstractions, agreeing chiefly on one thing: that more research is needed. And when this research brings them to the truisms known to every mother, and they might at least rest, they haven't the modesty to admit it and hold still. (What vast researches Bruner cites in order to establish that babies poke around and look at things— "curiosity is the prototype of the intrinsic motive"; that the three-year-old girl wishes she could chop up her food as well as her five-year-old brother—"desire for competence and aspiration to emulate a model"; and that nine-year-old boys are quick to run errands, to suggest expedients, and love to be praised for their real as opposed to unreal contributions—"deep-sensed commitment to the web of social reciprocity.")

The environmental effect of this kind of thinking, this mere intellection, this failure of mind, is quite clear. The school itself becomes manipulative. And the manipulation is hard to resist, for it seems to rest upon such enlightened deference to "inborn motives" and "autonomous functions," though it violates and invades those functions at every turn, pinching the energies of life, rounding them off, arranging them, producing in the end a feeble image of growth, where what is wanted is growth itself.

If I have been ill-tempered in my complaint, let me relieve the monotone by giving the other example, after all.

> Now, while rules of deference may be asymmetrical and a superordinate person may have rights to certain familiarities or invasions of the metaphorical boundary around the self that the subordinate cannot reciprocate, yet the superordinate still must respect the subordinate and not press too far. Thus, while it may be expected that teachers have the right to touch pupils, particularly in a friendly manner, it would not be expected that the same right be freely exercised by pupils.

This choice lyric is from a book called *Realities of the Urban Classroom*. (G. Alexander Moore, Jr.) It was financed by government and foundation money (the title alone deserves a grant), and is perhaps an example of the "data" Miss White tells us we need so much more of "before any solutions are proposed."

How different philosophic thought is from the technocratic intellection of which I have just given examples!

Education, for Dewey, is a function of experience and a fact of life, not the activity of a closed system of schools. Nor do schools introduce something different in kind into the experience of the child, but work with processes and capacities already given, already considerably developed.

> The educator who receives the child . . . has to find ways for doing consciously and deliberately what "nature" accomplishes in the earlier years.

It follows, then, that we must not set up conditions which violate the very processes upon which the enterprise rests. As I have mentioned elsewhere, Dewey insists that the very first of these is the instrumental nature of the child's acquiring, and of all that he acquires, for he acquires, nothing in a vacuum, everything in what Dewey calls "the continuum of experience." And so the teacher cannot merely instruct, for in the whole of life there is no occasion within which mere information, divorced from use and the meanings of experience, appears as a motive sufficient in itself. The task of the educator is to provide experience. In order to do this, he must first *interact* with his students, not as a teacher, but as a person; for there is no other way to provide the second essential of experience, which is *continuity*. Dewey does not mean here merely the continuity of a curriculum, but the continuity of lives within which the school itself is but one of many functions. Now certain conditions are indispensable to interaction and continuity. If the teacher is to interact, he must know his students individually. But how can he know them unless they are free to reveal themselves, each one in his uniqueness? From considerations such as these,

follow the structure of the school, the freedoms, responsibilities, and relationships I have described in earlier chap-
ters.

There are many reasons why Dewey's ideas are hard to
realize. They are arduous and subtle even in the thinking
(whatever may be said of the plain-pine Yankee homeli-
ness of his style). They are especially arduous in the doing.
Like Tolstoy, he understands method not as mere formal
conception that antedates its own occasion, but as *what
happens.* The so-called "methods" of education taught in
our colleges cannot in fact be used. They are mere poten-
tialities, are often impediments, and are worth nothing
until they vanish and reappear again as technique. And
technique cannot be taught, though it can indeed be
learned. The reason is simple: each appearance of technique, each application, each solution, is unique. The work
of the teacher is like that of the artist; it is a shaping of
something that is given, and no serious artist will say in
advance that he knows what will be given. Dewey would
certainly approve the suggestions made by Paul Goodman
and Elliott Shapiro that group therapy be central to the
training of primary teachers. The teacher's instrument is
himself. Group therapy puts us in touch with ourselves.
It clarifies emotions and reduces the blind spots in behavior. We cannot pass from the mechanical conceptions
of method to the living reality of technique except by
passing through ourselves.

Let me describe three of the deeper reasons why
Dewey's thought is so hard to translate into action. It
requires, first, that the educator be modest toward experience, modest toward the endless opening-outward and
going-onward of life, for this going-onward is the experience of the young. Precisely this fact of life, however,
evokes anxiety, sorrow, regret, and envy in the hearts of

adults. It is not easy to give oneself wholeheartedly to the flow of life that leaves one, literally, in the dust. If we often scant the differences between the young and ourselves, and prefer the old way, the old prerogatives, the old necessities, it is because, at bottom, we are turning away at all times from the fact of death. Yet just this is what modesty toward experience means: a reconciled awareness of death. It is a difficult spiritual task; and it lies right at the heart of the educational function.

To be open to experience means, too, that we cannot repeat past successes with past techniques. We cannot organize the educational event in advance. Certainly we can plan and prepare, but we cannot organize it until we are in it and the students themselves have brought their unique contributions. And so there is a point beyond which our tendency to organize becomes inimical to experience, inimical to teaching. Much that belongs to teaching precisely *as* a profession is therefore inimical to teaching. Yet just this tendency to organize and to elevate the gratifications of the profession—the status of expertise, the pleasures of jargon, the pride of method—is composed largely of two things, both inescapably human and hard to transcend: anxiety and vanity. Here again, a difficult spiritual task.

Yet it may be that neither of these tasks amounts to quite the impediment to Dewey's thought that we find spread large in the social and economic structure of our country as a whole. In Dewey's conception, the vital breath of education flows to the schools directly from the community. The function of teaching arises in the community. The product of teaching returns to it. Writing in 1902, 1916, 1936, Dewey did not envision, and could not, the incredible consolidation of centralized power that has taken place in our country since World War II. Educa-

tion must be *lived*. It cannot be *administered*. And we
have become, as a nation, a wretched hog wallow of administrative functions. The hope that animates Dewey's
educational thought, and that he stated in greatest detail
in *Democracy and Education,* seems downright utopian
today.

> . . . character and mind are attitudes of participative re-
> sponse in social affairs . . . it means that we may produce
> in schools a projection in type of the society we should like
> to realize, and by forming minds in accord with it gradually
> modify the larger and more recalcitrant features of adult
> society.

What might Dewey today, with the degeneration of our
social institutions well in mind, propose as the first task of
education? It seems to me that he would be alarmed especially by the social effects that appear as individual
traits, in some sense traits of character. The illiteracy of
youths who were born intelligent, and who have been
schooled, is the kind of individual collapse which, on the
face of it, is a social effect. The distrust of adults now ram-
pant among the young is a social effect (for it is profoundly unnatural). The savagery and violence of so many
children in the slums; the passivity, the willingness to be
bossed of so many children in the suburbs; the poor health
(by world standards) of our young; the extraordinary increase in juvenile crime—all these are social effects. They
are the handiwork especially of our politicians and educators, though obviously they are the product of our society
as a whole. Dewey based much of his thought upon considerations of the fundamental human nature visible in the
young. One of the remarkable facts of life (it is perhaps
the only thing that saves us from ourselves) is that this
indwelling nature, prior to its exposure to school and to

the crushing effects of public life, reaches, in the vast majority of cases, a quite adequate development in the life of the home—reaches it in the most ordinary, routine, taken-for-granted way. (And this remarkable corollary needs to be stated: that after leaving the home, as a more or less total environment, the child will never again, in all his experience of professionals, experts, and trained personnel, encounter services as adequate to his own growth as were those of his mother and father, sisters and brothers, relatives and friends.) Dewey referred to this routine development of the child as the starting point of education. But it is a starting point that continues. It remains, through the whole of life, the only possible foundation for the educational function. Nothing can be added to it. Nothing should be subtracted. Growth and development are a shaping of powers that already exist. And so it seems to me that Dewey would tell us today that our first task is to recover this routine adequacy of the child, these ordinary human powers, from the neglect, abuse, and degeneration into which they have fallen. There is no other foundation upon which to build. In short, we cannot speak of teaching and learning at all unless we speak of ways and means of sustaining the powers that are visible in the child when first he comes to class. This, of course, is what I have been describing in telling of the First Street School. We were Summerhillian and Tolstoyan, but more deeply than either of these, we were Deweyan.

I hope it is clear that I have not been proposing First Street as the model for a system of education. I do certainly propose it as a model for the indispensable first step. And since the first step is in fact the continuing foundation, I do propose the kinds of relationships we established at First Street, the kinds of freedom enjoyed by teachers and children and parents, the respect for experience, the absence of compulsion, the faith in the inherent sociability of children; I do propose all these as the environmental model for an entire system, for they belong intrinsically to the educational experience, and not just to the rationale of a school. As a school we were far too limited to provide a pattern for other schools (which will have problems of their own), and this, I am sure, has been so obvious that I hardly need mention it. A pattern has been suggested by others, however, and there were many times—our good days, our best trips through the city— when this pattern drifted before my eyes: all through the city, but especially in the poorer neighborhoods, where the need is greatest, there are little one-, two-, and three-room schools for young children in storefronts and ground-floor apartments, several to a block. The teachers live in the neighborhood and the schools belong intimately to the life of the block. Adults, adolescents, and the young all have a role and a stake in the schools; all are joined in a natural continuum. The adolescents are part-time aides, tutors, leaders in games and expeditions. Some are salaried, others are volunteers. All know the young, for they are neighbors' children, and brothers and sisters. Parents come and go as they like. Some cook lunches, help on trips, supervise cleanup and special work details. Some are salaried, some are volunteers. They are not working with younger members of "the public," but with their own children's playmates. The children in the schools feel secure and cared for. They have formed dependable relationships with adults who are important to them, and whom they see in the streets. They have made friends and working alliances with other children on the block. They know whom they belong to, and who belongs to them. The gigantic public schools, in the meantime, have been transformed into centers of specialized activities. Some are devoted to the arts, others to physical sciences, others to social studies conducted as community action. The children gather at these centers at specified times to make use of laboratories and special equipment, and for games and athletic competition, and to produce plays and pageants, and to taste the excitement of the larger world that is spread out all around them. And it *is* excitement, for though they gather now in large numbers, they are not rendered anonymous, but still know whom they belong to, and who belongs to them. There is a lively rivalry between the block schools, and much opportunity for social exchange. Nor are these larger centers known any longer simply as schools. They have become community centers and belong absolutely to the people of the neighborhood. They are filled with adults at night, and with youths and children. There are social dancing and games, orchestras, films, jazz groups, facilities for crafts, open classes for adults, meeting rooms for political action. And there is no one present, not a soul, who believes that the buildings, or any of their functions, belong to the State. They belong to those who use them. The uses are so intimately a part of life that the idea of compulsion has come to seem grotesque. The educational bureaucracy has dwindled to almost nothing, and responsibility now rests where it should: on the shoulders of those who are closest to the children, and those who, for reasons of their own, care most.

The idea of block schools, storefront schools, minischools, has been put forward on a number of occasions by Paul Goodman and Elliott Shapiro. The existence of First Street itself owed a great deal to Goodman's influence. I would like to quote the words of both. They are available elsewhere, and perhaps need not be repeated here. But they are important, and will bear repeating.

Nat Hentoff gives us the words of Shapiro in *Our Chil-*

dren Are Dying (an unfortunate title, I think, for a positive and valuable book):

> Take this neighborhood. It's poor. Stores go out of business, leaving many vacant storefronts—some with back yards—that could be used as classrooms. From 110th to 145th Streets and between Seventh and Eighth Avenues, there are the equivalent of forty to fifty potential classrooms. Why not use them primarily for young children—with the back yards as school-yards, and with libraries interspersed here and there? The libraries could be for parents as well as children and could be open until eight or nine in the evening. We would be coming right into the heart of the community, creating the kind of reciprocal relationship between the community and the schools that you don't find anywhere in this city—or in the country. We'd be on constant display, and people would be welcome to come in and see what we're doing. And if they wanted to, they could help as parent aides. The plan would take care of classroom shortages and would represent *real* decentralization. It could be a stimulus toward the creation of a new society. I've proposed this idea to the Board, with the estimate that it would take $4,000 to transform each vacant store into a classroom. The Board's estimate was $10,000, but even $10,000 isn't that much when you consider that the average classroom in a regular school costs more than $60,000 to construct. . . . The storefront classrooms could increase the possibilities of integration. As you spread out along the avenues, you would break through district lines and move into neighborhoods that would allow for different racial balances. (Shapiro points out, too, that the way to attract middleclass whites to ghetto schools is to make precisely these schools the very best.)

At the Borough President's hearings on decentralization in November of 1967, Paul Goodman put the case like this:

> For ages six to eleven, I propose a system of tiny schools, radically decentralized. As one who for twenty years has

urged democratic decentralization, I am of course interested in the Bundy Report, but here I am thinking of decentralization to the level of actual operation. By tiny school I mean twenty-eight children with four teachers (one grown up to seven children), and each tiny school to be largely administered by its own staff and parents, with considerable say, also, for the children, as in Summerhill. The four teachers are:

A teacher regularly licensed and salaried. Since the present average class size is twenty-eight, these are available.

A graduate from the senior class of a New York college, perhaps just embarking on graduate study. Salary: $2,000. There is no lack of candidates to do something interesting and useful in a free setting.

A literate housewife and mother, who can also prepare lunch. Salary: $4,000. No lack of candidates.

A literate, willing, and intelligent high school graduate. Salary: $2,000. No lack of candidates.

Such a staff can easily be racially and ethnically mixed. And it is also the case, as demonstrated by the First Street School, that in such a small setting, with individual attention paid to the children, it is easy to get racially and ethnically mixed classes; there is less middle-class withdrawal when the parents do not fear that their children will be swamped and retarded. (We have failed to achieve integration by trying to impose it from above, but it can be achieved from below, in schools entirely locally controlled, if we can show parents it is for their children's best future.)

For setting, the tiny school would occupy two, three, or four rooms in existing school buildings, church basements, settlement houses otherwise empty during school hours, rooms set aside in housing projects, storefronts. The setting is especially indifferent since a major part of activity occurs outside the school place. The setting should be able to be transformed into a clubhouse, decorated and equipped according to the group's own decision. There might be one school on every street, but it is also advisable to locate many in racial and ethnic border areas, to increase intermixture. For purposes of assembly, health services, and some games, ten tiny schools could use the present public school facilities.

The cost saving in such a setup is the almost total elimination of top-down administration and the kind of special services that are required precisely because of excessive size and rigidity. The chief uses of central administration would be licensing, funding, choosing sites, and some inspection. There would be no principals and assistants, secretaries and assistants. Curriculum, texts, equipment would be determind as needed—and despite the present putative economies of scale, they would be cheaper; much less would be pointless or wasted. Record keeping would be at a minimum. There is no need for truant officers when the teacher-and-seven can call at the absentee's home and inquire. There is little need for remedial personnel since the staff and parents are always in close contact, and the whole enterprise can be regarded as remedial. Organizational studies of large, top-down directed enterprises show that the total cost is invariably at least 300 percent above the cost of the immediate functions, in this case the interaction of teachers and children. I would put this 300 percent into increasing the number of adults and diversifying the possibilities of instruction. Further, in the conditions of New York real estate, there is great advantage in ceasing to build $4,000,000 school buildings, and rather fitting tiny schools into available niches.

Goodman describes the pedagogical advantages of such a system, with special reference to the teaching of reading. He then goes on to make a point which tends to outrage teachers and educators. It is one that I agree with, and have seen borne out in my own teaching experience.

I am assuming that for the first five school years, there is no merit in the standard curriculum. For a small child everything in the environment is educative, if he attends to it with guidance. Normal children can learn the first eight years' curriculum in four months anyway, at age twelve.

I would like to quote the rest of Goodman's address, for it sums up a great many things succinctly, many of which we experienced as life issues at First Street.

I see little merit, for teaching this age, in the usual teacher-training. Any literate and well-intentioned grown-up knows enough to teach a small child a lot. Teaching small children is a difficult art, but we do not know how to train the improvisational genius it requires, and the untrained seem to have it equally: compare one mother with another, or one big sister or brother with another. Since at this age one teaches the child, not the subject, the relevant art is psychotherapy, and the most useful course for a normal school is probably group therapy. The chief criterion for selection is the one I have mentioned: liking to be attentive to children. Given this setting, many young people would be introduced to teaching and would continue with it as a profession; whereas in the New York system the annual turnover approaches twenty percent, after years of wasted training.

As I have said, however, there are fatal political and administrative objections to this proposal. First, the public school administration does not intend to go largely out of business. Given its mentality, it must see any radical decentralization as impossible to administer and dangerous, for everything cannot be controlled. Some child is bound to break a leg and the insurance companies will not cover; some teen-ager is bound to be indiscreet and the *Daily News* will explode in headlines.

The United Federation of Teachers will find the proposal anathema because it devalues professional perquisites and floods the schools with the unlicensed. Being mainly broken to the public school harness, most experienced teachers consider free and inventive teaching to be impossible.

Most fatally, poor parents, who aspire for their children, tend to regard unrigidly structured education as downgrading, not taking the children seriously, and also as vaguely immoral. In the present black power temper of Harlem, the possible easy intermixing is itself not desired. (Inciden-

tally, I am rather sympathetic to black separatism as a
means of consolidating the power of black communities.
But children, as Kant said, must be educated for the future
better society which cannot be separated.)

In spite of these fatal objections, I recommend that instead
of building the next new school building, we try out this
scheme with 1,200 children.

Shapiro, too, mentions the suspicion with which the poor
look upon free activities in school. Certain of the First
Street parents, similarly, objected to the noise, the lack of
punishment, and the apparent disorder of our classes.
They thought we were horsing around. But they were in
contact with other of the parents, who did not share their
views; and of course they noticed the changes in their own
children. Before the year was well out, they had reversed
their opinions. This seems a more likely pattern than settled opposition. Shapiro mentions some relevant events. He
had just become principal of Public School 119 in Harlem.
The parents, for many years, had been apathetic.

The parents didn't trust us, and they had good reason
not to. One of the problems with parents in this kind of
neighborhood is supposed to be that they're nonverbal. But
they often have good reasons for not saying much to school
administrators. They're thinking, "Why don't the children
have readers to take home, and why don't they have more
other things, too?" But often the parents don't ask, because
they sense the principal is loyal to the system and not to
the children, and they figure, "What's the use? He's not going
to do anything to change the system." So it's an act of intelligence on their part to refuse to enter into what would be
a phony dialogue.

Here the parents were slow to accept that we were talking
honestly about the deficiencies of the school. We told them
what we were doing was impaired because we didn't have
resources to do very much. That kind of admission was

something new in their experience. We admitted, for example, that we didn't have enough books, and finally we got the parents to write to the Board and ask for more. Between their efforts and ours we did get more, and then we discovered that many of the same parents who had seemed inarticulate were very verbal and quite sophisticated. We began with only ten parents coming to meetings, but eventually we were getting seven hundred and fifty at important meetings. The other day the room was so full that I, one of the speakers, had to stand in the hall.

Let me say a word here of the effect of First Street on the pupils' parents. It is one of the most important things, and I haven't said much about it.

There was a great deal of contact between parents and teachers. It was continuous and purposeful, and gradually became more social and diverse. There were chats after school with the mothers who came for their children. But all parents had all teachers' phone numbers, and they called frequently to ask questions, give information, make complaints and suggestions. The parents got to know one another. The social exchange itself was inspiriting, but soon there was much more, for they had many needs in common and found that they could help one another. They swapped clothing, took care of one another's children, chipped in and hired an older child to escort the young ones to school. Some banded together and devised strategies for confronting the Department of Welfare (they have continued—now in stronger and more political forms). Some became interested in civil rights, and are now involved in black power and community actions. Many invited the kids to their homes. Many helped at school during special activities and on trips. Several took turns cooking lunches (fried chicken was one's specialty), and the girls took turns transporting these lunches, wrapped in foil, from home to school. (Our fried-chicken days were notable.) One father, a restaurateur, held open house for us once a week. The improvement in the kids had a strong effect on family life, not only because hope was revived, but because the kids were no longer sources of trouble and criticism. As the kids became happier, so did the parents. Not all changes took communal forms. Some were romantic. One mother blossomed suddenly into an off-Broadway actress. Two found new husbands. Was this an effect of the school? Who knows? A woman looks prettier when she isn't frantic with worry and depressed by the feeling of isolation. I claim it for the school. All these parental changes had further effects on the children. To some small extent, these new relations among their parents turned the neighborhood in the direction of community.

And what was the fate of First Street?

In the lives of the children and their parents, enterprises like the First Street School are at best stopgap operations. Teachers have asked us what "long-range effects" we produced. People who have worked among the poor do not ask this question. To minority groups living in city slums, and especially to welfare families, the routine problems of life are like an avalanche: they accumulate and come faster. The long-range effects are simply the effects that continue, and there is no doubt about what they are: poverty, neglect, abuse, racism, barrenness of environment.

Our money was running out. Early in the second year we teachers sat down together and drew up an appeal for funds to present to the foundations and government agencies. The general crisis in education had come to rank high among the many crises of our country, and there were new organizations in the field, foundation-endowed and prestigious, calling themselves *urban* this and *urban* that, and speaking a great many words in behalf of the poor. It seemed to us that our school was exactly the sort of thing they would sponsor. And so we described our methods and the results we had achieved, and gave the histories of the children, quoting their parents and teachers to show how they had changed. We stressed the economy of our operation and the high morale of the parents, and suggested that many schools like ours, spread through a neighborhood, might become the focal centers of community relations. It was a simple and straightforward brochure, and was neatly printed. We addressed a copy to every foundation in the country and to every relevant government agency, and trundled them all to the post office in a baby carriage. There were so many copies that we had to make two trips, the carriage filled to the brim each time.

The results of this effort were zero. Three letters arrived, on expensive stationery, with resounding titles across the top, saying *urban* this and *urban* that, expressing the kind of sympathy that costs exactly a postage stamp and a sheet of paper. A few months later I received a word of explanation, and since it came from the horse's mouth, it might be worth describing.

I was introduced to a Foundation man at a party, a former fund-raiser and present lesser-responsible in the lower pastures of the educational establishment, those levels which, not because of their contact with the poor, but because they are not as elevated as the upper or Federal pastures, are looked upon as the living edge of Reality, and are charged with the duty of developing the vocabulary of change. They publish glossy magazines (*The Urban Review*) and fill them with artistic photographs of

Negro children. They launch "basic research" into the ills of the cities (the Urban Institute), when in fact a whole library of expert testimony already exists and has existed for ten years. My informant was a big, good-looking man, with long, bushy sideburns, horn-rimmed glasses, and a London-style suit. He had been drinking a lot, as we all had, and was very amiable. I went back to the enormous coatrack in the hall and took a copy of our brochure out of my briefcase. His mini-skirted girl friend hung on his shoulder while he looked at it. He had frowned at first glance, but now as he turned its pages, he began to smile and shake his head. With every "tsk, tsk" that came out of him, his girl friend threw me bright, sympathetic glances. His smile seemed to be permanent, but his face had grown kindly.

"This is not the way you do it," he said.

"What do you mean, not the way?" I said.

He shrugged, as if the errors were too numerous to cope with. "Your format is dead," he said at last. "And it should be on glossy paper." He looked up and saw my face and said, "I'm not kidding."

I know that my face had grown angry. He grew angry seeing it, and proceeded to bawl me out. "If you're serious about raising money, you'll listen to me, because I'm telling you how it works. I'm not saying it's great that it works that way. That's a different matter. Right? If you want a personal response, all right, I'm impressed by what you've got here. It's real grass-roots stuff, and that's what we need. I wish to hell I could have talked to you before you sent it around. I could have *got* you a grant."

"It's not a question of whether you deserved it or not," his girl friend said, "it's a question . . ."

Her interjection angered him. "You haven't got a project

here at all." He was leafing the pages again. "You're just slopping around with a lot of hunches. What controls do you have? What are your premises? Where are your research personnel? You don't list any . . ."

The party was noisy. There was a burst of music and he had to shout. A well-known jazz group was playing at the other end of the apartment. The apartment itself looked like an uptown art gallery. One would suppose that everything was for sale, had just been moved in and would soon be moved out. Two maids and two bartenders had been hired for the night. All were white. About two dozen of the two hundred guests were black. There had been an opening that night of a black militant play which ripped the hell out of white Liberals and had been financed, attended, and applauded by white Liberals.

And the upshot of my informant's information—for after browbeating me, he had grown kindly again—was that if we had drawn up a legitimate project for studying the feasibility of such a school as we had actually run, the funds would have been forthcoming. For "there is a great need in this city for schools like yours."

I told all this to Mabel, and said glumly, "We should have financed a project and run the school in secret."

"People who think that way," she said, "don't start schools in the first place."

(I think that if we were applying for our grant today, we would receive it, and perhaps not from one but from several sources. The climate has changed that much. The despair of the poor is now anger. Their demands are too strong—and too justified—to be ignored. It is becoming clear, too, that many teachers and supervisors, trapped in an outmoded bureaucracy, would welcome the very changes I have been describing.)

Yet it was not merely the lack of money that closed the school. We ourselves were not strongly enough motivated to make the sacrifices that would have been necessary to sustain it. I had gone back to full-time writing, and during the second year my place was taken by Michael Eigen, who was working toward his doctorate in psychology. Mabel was nursing our baby (and lugging her to school almost every day, where she became an important piece of educational equipment). Gloria had gotten married. Susan, by the end of the second year, was exhausted, and was hungry for an adult milieu. This is par for the course, and perhaps in itself is not an evil. Nevertheless, we did withdraw from our community of concern, and these were the forms our withdrawal took. We had hoped to raise money and turn our school over intact to younger workers. That was a pipe dream. Yet the dream, and our return, as it were, to private life, revealed an important truth: enterprises of this kind—community functions—*cannot be performed as services.* They are the life concerns of those who live in the community, and they must arise in the community. It is absolutely essential that members of the community be empowered for this work, financially and by training, for the closer we come to the homes and neighborhoods of the children, the truer, the more correct, becomes the motivation of those who work with the young. I would like to return to this thought in a moment.

We closed house at the end of the second year. We loaned our microbus to LEAP, just a few streets away, and gave them some books and equipment, for at that time they were running a school of their own under the direction of Martin Greenhut, who is one of the ablest people I have seen anywhere in community work. (We had hoped briefly that he would take over First Street.) We also gave some equipment to a group of parents who, against enormous odds, were trying to start a school of their own.

And what of the children? Long before the second year was out, several of the families had moved away. Eléna and José (who visited me several times) now lived in Brooklyn and could no longer attend First Street. Michael Hasty moved to the Bronx. Vicente, Julio, and Willard also moved, and then moved again, and we don't know where. New children took their places. The school was slightly larger the second year.

We still have contacts with certain of the children. Mabel and Gloria—now with infants of their own—have taken a crowd to the country again during summer vacation. We know that Maxine and Eléna, after progressing so much at First Street, managed to keep their gains. José is treading water, and very likely will go under again. Michael Hasty is in trouble. Dodie and Rudella, who had been such lively children, are now somewhat angry and embittered young black girls, fully aware of the cruelty massed against them and the privilege that surrounds their island of want. Michael, Dodie, and Rudella were in the crowd that came to the country. All miss the school. Some miss it grievously. Many resent us for having failed them, as fail them we did.

Stanley came to the apartment one day. I was writing in the back, and I heard the buzzing of the bell and a lot of shouting in the street. I looked out the window, and there he was, with four Negro youths all much larger than he. I told them to come up.

Stanley spun me a yarn: one of the Negro youths had been absent from school and would get in trouble unless he had a note from home—which he couldn't get. Would

I write him a note? ("Why don't *you* write it?" "Naw, my handwriting doesn't look grown-up.") I poured sodas for them. While we talked, his pals eyed the apartment. Two of them went over to the door and looked very closely at the Fox Police Lock, standard equipment in these parts. Since I believe that hooky is one of the few constructive conventions in the public schools (how well Stanley knew me!), I wrote them their note, though I didn't much believe the yarn. As I escorted them to the door, the chief Lock Studier leaped away. I asked him what it was he found so interesting, and he grinned and said, "Nuthin'."

And so we can boast of very little in the way of long-range effects. Our short-range effects were often impressive. How easy it would be to extend them! How easy indeed—if it were not almost impossible.

I would like to close this book with a word to parents and teachers, for we are not faced today by simple choices among methods of mass instruction—as if any of them were working—but by the Biblical question in all its severity: *If the salt hath lost its savour, wherewith shall it be salted?* This is as much as to say that any hope for a new spirit in education lies quite outside the present establishment. It lies among parents themselves, and in revitalized communities, and among younger teachers. I would like to say why this is so, why our school professionals, taken as a class, an institutionalized center of power, are fundamentally incompetent and must be displaced. My purpose is not to castigate the bureaucrats, but to recall parents and teachers to an awareness of one crucial truth, a truth that should be, but is not, the gut-wisdom of everyone: that in humane affairs—and education is *par excellence* a humane pursuit—there is no such thing as competence without love. This is the sort of statement that strikes many people, and especially our technocrats, as being sentimental, and so I would like to speak of it in some detail and make clear its truth. And I want to stress that I am not speaking here of excellence of performance, but of mere competence. Let me stress, too—because the question of competence comes down in the end to the characteristics of individuals—that I am not saying that among our fifty thousand bureaucrats there are no persons of real worth. The issue is precisely that of the effect of the institution upon the individual. The institution, the educational system in all its branches, is corrupting to the individual, and though the corruption may in many cases take the form of considerable expertise, the fact remains that competence is destroyed.

In naming love as the necessary base of competence in humane affairs, I am referring not only to the emotion of love, nor just to the moral actions and feelings that belong to caring, but to loving and caring in the very generalized, primitive sense in which they constitute a background condition of life, as we say of young children that they live "as if in love," and as adults, when they are simplified by disasters and extreme demands, reveal a constructive energy and compassion which are obviously generalized and basic.

There is nothing in this background of generalized love that is inimical to speculative thought or formalized research. On the contrary, where the issues are humane, where the field of attention is living persons, as in philosophy, psychology, and education in all its branches, we are more than ever aware of this background of love, and especially when we encounter excellence. The reason is obvious: the events of the field—which are often of the most subtle and elusive kind—cannot even be discerned unless there is a responding sensitivity in the observer. This sensitivity, if we are to speak of competence, must span a considerable range; and a range of any magnitude cannot be sustained except on some active principle of concern, attraction, care. What we call curiosity is no mere matter of the intellect, but is itself a generalized form of love. Einstein called it "holy." Often, in reading humane studies, we infer the background of love from the number of things observed, from the finesse of observation, and the unwavering insistence upon values. Quite simply, these are the qualities of one who cares. Sometimes, as in the pages of Darwin, Kant, Whitehead, or Freud, one feels a positive glow of benignity, or the flush of enchantment with the host of real events which form our lives. Dewey, in his knotty way, writes with love; and what else but this deep, ineradicable caring can give such sharpness to the eye, such patience, integrity, and persistence to the whole labor of a life? It does not matter, then, whether love is *expressed*, or whether it be a love of causes and meanings and not of individual persons. We are aware of it as a background, a source, the condition of the writer vis-à-vis his world. We are aware of more than this, however, for we also see that this generalized caring is the meaning of the speaker's very presence before us. It is the motive of his address. It is the justification of his words. Communication, in its true sense of communion and change, is inconceivable apart from this background of love. One might also speak of the sensual elements that belong to caring. The world is attractive. It is attractive in its sensual forms. Our knowledge of its forms begins in response (which soon becomes creative), and we cannot respond except with our senses. We cannot know feelings by analysis, but only by feelings. The generalized love that I have been describing is a criterion of wholeness. When it is diminished, we progressively lose our world, and as our world is fragmented, so are we. One might put it this way: that there is no other path except this original ground of attracted care by which the events and forms of the world can reach fruition as mind. When this background is corrupted, or held inoperative, true mind, true thought, is not to be attained. What we see instead is mere intellection. In Goethe's words: "All the thinking in the world will not bring us to thought. We must be right by nature, then thoughts present themselves to us like the children of God, they jump up and cry, 'Here we are!'" Thomas Mann calls this harmony the joy of the artist: "thought that can become feeling, feeling that can become thought."

It is in this sense, then, that failure of mind is, at bottom, a failure of love. The conditions which nullify caring as the vital breath of being in the world are ruinous to thought, and render competence in humane affairs quite unattainable. There is no need to point out that the deathly rigidity of bureaucratic institutions nullifies the organic demands of attracted care. It is enough to say that scientists, artists, professionals of all kinds (provided they have integrity), men of independent spirit, and all children are profoundly unwilling to surrender sensibility and will to the demands of the bureaucrat.

I have given three examples of the speech of our educationists. Let me refer to them now in order to contrast briefly the characteristics of the philosopher and the Expert, the scientist and the technocrat.

What is the social action of jargon? I have said that true communication is communion and change. Jargon is not innocent. The man who speaks it, who prates in front of us of roles and reciprocally operative groups, and evaluative maps, and the aims of the curriculum, and better fits, and superordinate and subordinate persons means to hold us at a distance; he means to preserve his specialty —his little piece of an essentially indivisible whole—precisely as a specialty. He does not mean to draw near to us, or to empower us, but to stand over us and manipulate us. He wishes, in short, to remain an Expert. The philosopher, by contrast, wishes all men to be philosophers. His speech creates equality. He means to draw near to us and empower us to think and do for ourselves. He does not isolate little specialties and cling to them, but reconstitutes large forms, forms toward which he is modest and toward which he teaches modesty. He is *of* the community, and neither he nor we can escape it.

And how does the technocrat differ from the scientist? We need mention but one fundamental way, for it is decisive. Where the scientist recognizes no authority but nature, or truth, and will not accept premises at the hands of government, class, or superiors, the technocrat reverses this essential attitude of free thought and accepts precisely his premises at the hands of others. It matters very little if he calls himself a scientist, and makes a lesser divinity of Research, and a greater one of Basic Research. His methods, in the last analysis, are not serious. His objectivity is not objective. It is without gravity or risk. Is it objective, for instance, to say that we must change our schools, *but only within the framework of existing authority?* Scientists in our time have discovered that the very act of observation influences the phenomena. They include themselves in their equations. Our technocrats have not yet, and never will, take that decisive step.

Now what is the point of all this? For one might say simply, "Our educators have failed. They have done nothing but fail. They are incompetent."

I have put it in this form in order to say that any solution which perpetuates the existing authoritarian bureaucracy is doomed to failure. And I have wanted very much to say that competence is impossible without love, for in this centralized, technological, Expert-ridden age of ours it needs desperately to be said. To say it indicates, too, the direction of the essential change. We must transfer authority to where concern already exists. We must place it where there is nothing in the environment which will *inevitably* destroy the vital breath of concern. Authority must reside in the community. It must be local, homely, modest, sensitive. And it must be tied, once and for all, to the persons who not only *do* care, but will go on caring. In my opinion, there is no other hope but this.

Community, of course, is a much-abused word, and often a vague one. It does not mean neighborhood, though neighborhood is indispensable to community. I have tried to make clear why I believe that parents and teachers, "laymen," "ordinary persons," possess the potential—and many the actuality—of true competence in the education of young children; and why the technocrat, isolated in his cubicle, does not and cannot possess it. But in fact no community need want for wisdom. The greatest of minds are, in effect, its permanent residents. Just as some men are of the bureaucracy, of the state, others are of the community. All philosophers are of the community. All scientists are. All artists are. It does not matter how difficult or elevated their work may be; its action is to create peers. And so the authority that needs to guide the educational function, in being local and close to home, need not forfeit one jot of its resources. Or put it this way: a community is not a true community unless, in principle, it is universal.

Let me close with the words of two men who are of the community. Between them they provide both largeness of conception and the vital breath that animates.

I see at bottom but two alternatives between which education must choose if it is not to drift aimlessly. One of
them is expressed by the attempt to induce educators to
return to the intellectual methods and ideals that arose
centuries before scientific method was developed. The appeal
may be temporarily successful in a period when general
insecurity, emotional and intellectual as well as economic,
is rife. For under these conditions the desire to lean on fixed
authority is active. Nevertheless, it is so out of touch with
all the conditions of modern life that I believe it is folly to
seek salvation in this direction. The other alternative is systematic utilization of scientific method as the pattern and
ideal of intelligent exploration and exploitation of the po-
tentialities inherent in experience.

The words are Dewey's, in *Experience and Education.*
Tolstoy is the other man, though these are not his words,
but the words of a former pupil, recalling in his old age
the school at Yásnaya Polyána.

We would surround Leo Nikoláievich, catch hold of him
before and behind, try to trip him up, snowball him, and
rush in and climb on his back, eager to overthrow him. But
he was even more determined than we, and like a strong ox
would carry us on his back. After a while from weariness,
or more often for fun, he would fall into the snow. Then our
ecstasy was indescribable! We at once began to cover him
with snow and threw ourselves on him in a heap, crying,
"The heap's too small! The heap's too small!"
We enjoyed school and worked eagerly. But Leo Nikoláievich worked yet more eagerly than we. He worked with
us so eagerly that he often missed his lunch. In school his
appearance was serious. He demanded of us cleanliness, care
with the school things, and truthfulness. . . . He never
punished anyone for pranks, disobedience, or idleness; and
if we became too noisy he only said, "Quieter, please!" . . .
In such pleasures and merriment, and with rapid progress
in learning, we grew as close to Leo Nikoláievich as a
cobbler's thread is to wax. . . . We spent the day in school

and passed the evening at games, sitting on his balcony till late at night. He would tell us tales about the war, or of how a man-cook cut his aunt's throat in Moscow, and how he went hunting and a bear bit him, and he showed us the scar near his eye. There was no end to our talking. We told him terrible things—about wizards and wood demons. . . . He told us tales, terrible or funny, sang songs, suiting the words to us. . . . He was in general a great jester and never missed a chance to have a laugh. . . .

Fifty years have passed since then. I am already an old man. But my recollections of Leo Nikoláievich's school and of himself are still clear. They always cheer me, especially when I am in trouble. . . . The love of Leo Nikoláievich then kindled burns brightly in my soul and lights my whole life; and the recollection of those bright and happy days I have never lost, and never shall lose.

—AYLMER MAUDE's *The Life of Tolstoy*

Perhaps the emblem for our American primary schools should be a medallion without words, showing Tolstoy with the children on his back.

*

My wife's influence runs through these
pages in a number of ways, and I would
like to thank her for it. In fact, I would
like to thank her for the book.

Thank you, Mabel.

*

* Appendix *

One of the few encouraging things in our country to-day is the self-aware yearning for community among certain of the radical young. The days of petitioning aloof and ignorant politicians are over. One must do it oneself, and (hopefully) carry the "leaders" along. The same might be said of the many parents who are desperate for a humane school environment for their children. One hears more frequently now of parents banding together, finding teachers, and starting little schools of their own. There are no signs that a movement exists, but there are many signs that one might. One of the important considerations in this regard is that the needs of such parents strike a deep response in the very best of the radical young, who see in small, libertarian, community-oriented schools a meaningful increment of a better world. And so I would like to describe briefly how the First Street School was set up, so that others might have an idea how to go about it; and then I would like to say a few words (rather, quote the words of other, more experienced teachers) about materials, i.e., how to spend the too-few dollars usually available.

In order to exist at all, an independent school must satisfy certain demands of the federal, state, and city governments. Some of these demands are disastrous to private initiative, especially among the poor. But let me describe them, at least in their essentials, as they now obtain (they are subject to change). If community action should ever succeed in reducing them, the next writer on the subject will have a simpler tale to tell.

You can start a private elementary school without a charter, and you'll have no contact with city or state officials—until your pupils arrive. One of the responsibilities of the Board of Education is to prosecute parents for the truancy of their children. As soon as a child is transferred from a public school to your private one, you must be able to prove that you actually have a school. The Board will want to know, too—another of its duties—that the education you provide is at least the equivalent of that provided in the public schools. And so you will be called upon to assure them and reassure them, and a charter—not essential in itself—exerts a calming influence on everyone. You can get it from the Board of Regents of the University of the State of New York. Write to them for an instruction booklet: "Incorporation of Educational Institutions by the Regents." You must already know a certain number of things about your school. The provisional charter is granted after the school is in operation and has been visited by an inspector. Write also to the state Education Department for information on the state education laws. Employees' withholding tax must be paid to the state Department of Taxation and Finance at the same time that you send in your federal taxes (described below).

First Street received no document of approval from the New York City Board of Education. They wrote us saying that they had "no jurisdiction over private schools"; and we still don't know what they meant, for they could have closed us down very easily. We *did* receive the Board's approval, but it was by word of mouth after an inspection visit by the District Superintendent, accompanied by someone from the central office. In approving us, the Superintendent followed this procedure:

1) He checked that we had favorable reports from the relevant city agencies: the Fire Department, the Bureau of Sanitary Inspections (a branch of the Health Department), and the Department of Buildings (which issues a certificate of occupancy).

2) He asked the District Supervisor from the Bureau of Attendance to help us set up attendance procedures.

3) He satisfied himself that we were providing the equivalent of a public-school education. There were six criteria for this:

    a) provisions for health and safety
    b) teacher qualifications
    c) officially prescribed course of study
    d) appropriate textbooks
    e) instructional facilities and materials
    f) organization for instruction and grouping

Few public schools meet all these requirements adequately. The unorthodoxies of First Street mattered very little compared to the advantages we were creating for the children, and these were so obvious that no issues arose. For instance—because our school was small—the number and variety of books on hand per child was much greater than in the public schools. The same was true of other materials: Cuisenaire Rods, workbooks, art supplies, tools, etc. Our organization for instruction was ideal, and this mattered much more to the Superintendent than the fact that the children themselves had had such an important say in determining it. Our lunches— often cooked by the children's mothers—must have seemed like banquets compared to cafeteria fare. In a private school, not all of the teachers need be certified, though some must be. The officially prescribed course of study means the kinds of knowledge you touch on. If it seems that you are equipped to cover it, you need not account for your way of doing it. I doubt if the Superintendent would have believed (though he might have) that we were accomplishing in fifteen minutes what the public schools could not accomplish in weeks. The Publications Sales Office of the Board of Education can supply you with curriculum outlines. The Supply Division of the Bureau of Attendance will send you forms to fill out daily, monthly, and annually. We wanted our older pupils to be free to leave the school, or not come to it, and so we were prepared to fake the attendance records. As things turned out, the kids came to school devotedly and on time, and our records—considering the previous histories of most of the kids—must have seemed like outrageous lies. We were never questioned. The meaning of such records lies almost entirely in their existence. Their function is to be handed up the chain of command, and to be filed. Therefore they must exist. The Bureau of Attendance not only sends out attendance forms, but sends out truant officers disguised as citizens, who look for unattended school-age children. They usually look near the schools and near the homes of known truants. They do not look on Sixth Avenue south of Central Park, or on the grounds of the Cloisters.

Under the Department of Health are 1) the Bureau of Sanitary Inspections, 2) the District Health Office, and 3) the Division of Day Care. You must request that the first of these inspect you. Their report will come from the Health Department and will take several weeks. They have a reference manual you can use as a guide. The District Health Office can help you with medical reports on the children, and can advise you on emergency procedures. X-ray reports on the teachers and a copy of the health code must be kept at school. If you are handling children between the ages of two and six, in groups of six or more, you must apply to the Division of Day Care for a temporary permit. The Division maintains a consultation service for initial planning of facilities, programs, and teacher certification.

You must write to the local Fire Department and request an inspection. They issue a report quickly. When you are considering different buildings for a school, it's wise to ask them for a preliminary inspection. A negative report at such a time will save you many wasted days. Your school must conduct fire drills and keep records of them as outlined by the Fire Department. We took this very seriously.

You must obtain a certificate of occupancy for public use from the New York City Department of Buildings. This can be a long and intricate process, especially if alterations are required, for then you must submit architect's plans, have them approved, make the alterations, and have them inspected. When you are considering a location for your school, you can go to the Buildings Department and look up the block and lot number of the building and find out its existing classification. This Department, more than any other, is an obstacle to the spread of independent schools, and should be made the target of community action. Small groups of children, for instance, do not need the space required by hundreds, but the logic of the Department is to place the same restrictions on all schools.

Your relations with the federal government will be simpler than with the city. You must write the Internal Revenue Service of the U.S. Treasury Department and apply for the status of a tax-exempt institution. Ask for Form 1023. It cannot be filled out until after the school has been in operation for several months. It is a complicated form. The tax-exempt status allows you to make purchases without paying sales tax, and allows you to receive tax-exempt gifts. You file an annual report instead of an income-tax return. Employees' withholding taxes are due monthly, and additional forms have to be filed quarterly and annually. A bookkeeping system for the school should be set up by an accountant, or someone familiar with fund-raising, tax forms, and the annual state and federal reports of a tax-exempt institution.

The first thing to do, because it takes the most time, is to get the certificate of occupancy from the Department of Buildings. Next, consult the Health Department. If you are running a nursery, consult the Health Department right away.

Some of the things mentioned here can be done by friends of the school or by someone hired especially to push them through. Fund-raising may require outside help. First Street is obviously not the one to consult on this. There is federal money from the U.S. Office of Education and Welfare, state money for education, and federal money administered by the Board of Education of New York City. There is a book in the public library listing all the foundations of the United States. Some of our parents tried to get money from the Department of Welfare of New York City to be used as tuition, since the

Department does provide money for certain kinds of special schooling. The parents were unsuccessful, but it is probably a good strategy to push. The state will provide milk and the city will provide lunches, but there are so many strings and regulations attached to these services that we preferred to do without them. Workmen's Compensation should be looked into, and insurance to cover accidents to children in and out of school. Once your school is running, a daily coordinator, or teacher-in-charge, must handle transit passes, attendance records, fire drills, and health records. Our teachers and parents were in unusually close contact and cooperated on a great many things, including fund-raising and assaults on the Welfare Department. We found it very useful to keep a good supply of petty cash on hand, to which all teachers had access, so that books and supplies could be purchased when needed (and not six weeks later), and so that transportation and entrance fees would be available for events of special interest. The cash on hand also made it possible to pay children for special jobs, to provide allowances once in a while, and to buy presents for birthday parties.

The mass of regulations, standards, and customs governing the existence of a school should become the target of community groups backed up by legal advice. Some of the regulations—fire and health—are sensible and are attached to services of the kind any community would wish to provide for itself. Others are class-oriented, are expensive to comply with, and are undemocratic. Still others—the buildings codes especially—are narrowly conceived and play havoc with pressing needs of the community. A good strategy, provided you are actually (and safely) meeting community needs, is to ignore the specific restriction that threatens you—and then raise hell when the officials move against you. Often they will not move at all, and this hastens the demise of crude and out-dated codes.

I would like to mention here, in connection with the problems of organization, a strategy employed by the newly formed Children's Community Workshop School, at present the most exciting development in New York City. The school is located in exactly the kind of borderline area recommended for mini-schools by Elliott Shapiro. Its seventy-five pupils include middle-class whites, blacks, and Puerto Ricans, and impoverished whites, blacks, and Puerto Ricans. The races are evenly represented. The school was organized by a group of parents whose first concern, certainly, was the education of their children, but who saw clearly that the current trend toward decentralization would in no wise lead to community schools but would simply subdivide the bureaucracy. And so the Children's Community Workshop School was set up *as if its own immediate neighborhood constituted a school district.* Their elected governing board was drawn from among parents of the children. The strategy in short was to organize, by private means, a public school, that is, a school of open enrollment and charging no tuition, and then to petition the state to accept the neighborhood as an independent school district and provide funds. It will be an uphill fight, obviously. Nevertheless, this point of attack is an excellent one, and at present there is no other model of true community control. In the meantime the school must raise funds. They have been struggling along on grants of various sizes and from many sources. They are in an urban renewal area, and the city has made available three storefronts and the ground floor of a brownstone for classrooms, offices, and playrooms. I recently visited and talked with Anita Moses, the director. Taken all together, it is the most heartening project I have ever seen. Internally, the school is modeled on the British Infant Schools (described in Joseph Featherstone's *Report*). In all essentials it resembles First Street, and so I won't describe it in detail, but will say only that the children, teachers, and parents all seemed elated, even a little wonderstruck at how well they were doing.

As regards teaching materials, First Street was not experimental. Our toys, tools, teaching aids, etc., were the more or less standard items of small or progressive schools. We shopped a lot at Bank Street, had some items from Creative Playthings, used the Cuisenaire Rods, and made a great many things for ourselves. Gloria found that some of the young kids from the poorer families were not on a par with middle-class kids in their perception of figure/ground relations and of visual boundaries. She invented games with crayons and paper and cutout cardboard that would involve coloring within boundaries, sorting out figures from grounds, and noticing differences and similarities of easy symbols. Workbooks of this kind can be purchased, but it's much better to make them up for and with the individual child. This sort of highly structured play—together with a great deal of physical experience of coordinates: up/down, hard/soft, quiet/loud, slow/fast, careful/sloppy (Montessori is very good for this)—is very valuable in its own right, and makes learning to read a great deal easier. She used Ashton-Warner's word-card techniques. When I asked her to think of materials she had used, she frowned and said, "I can hardly remember. It was mostly spontaneous—whatever I thought might work with a particular child at a given moment." Gloria has taught young children for about six years, in public and private schools and in settlement houses. Her answer, as I have discovered, is the standard first answer of all good teachers. Later she wrote me a list, as did Susan, but it's clear, looking at our total First Street list, that we have nothing new to offer in the way of materials. I have written other teachers and directors of schools, and I would like to quote them here to show both the variety and consensus in the field concerning materials. Our own experience is worth stressing in this regard, however: that whatever materials are used, the close contact of teacher and child converts them into highly specialized items. The materials become the occasion for individualized improvisation. Susan, for instance, was not satisfied with our workbooks in math (a well-known modern math series). We had standard public-school books on hand as well, and she picked and chose and made up special sheets according to the needs of each child. The same for reading. The close contact allows the teacher to make up for the deficiencies of particular books. The Dick and Jane books are dreadful little puffballs, but they are well laid-out, use a repetitive vocabulary, and illustrate the text very closely. They should not be used with beginning readers, but they are useful to throw in now and then for what they do with vocabulary. The Bank Street graded readers are much better, but do not repeat their words often enough. And so one goes from book to book, writes stories oneself, and gets the kids to write them. Some of Tolstoy's tales and fables are excellent for reading aloud to older children, especially boys. Leskov is good, too—both simple and dazzling. I had thought that Twain's *Huckleberry Finn* would be good, but for our particular boys it was not. The child's own response is the most important guide. A Golden Book of fairy stories—$1.25 at the A & P—just happened to fascinate Dolores, and she learned to read from it. After our school collapsed, Susan taught for a while at LEAP with teen-age "delinquents." One of the boys was fascinated by a fifty-cent booklet put out by the *Reader's Digest,* and so that was his book, and he learned to read from it. (Teachers who are radicals should refrain from foisting their attitudes on children, especially their highly rationalized sense of alienation, however justified it may be.) When I asked Susan about her curriculum at First Street, she said, "Talk, talk, talk, talk—that was the curriculum at First Street."

I have already mentioned certain other items that we used and were popular—the typewriter and microscope, the book closet open at all times, the closet full of costumes and fabrics, a tape recorder and movie projector. We had a fish tank and raised plants in window boxes. Much of this comes naturally and need hardly be described. Let me go on now and give the words of people more experienced in these matters than we, from schools more durable than ours.

I wrote first to John Holt, whose books, *How Children Fail* and *How Children Learn,* are on their way to becoming classics in the field. He answered as follows:

I still like the Cuisenaire Rods, though I think the best things about how to use them have been written by Madeleine Goutard (her stuff is available from the Cuisenaire Corp. in Mt. Vernon, N. Y.). I have lost my enthusiasm about the Dienes materials. I like very much a set of materials called Attribute Blocks, or A-Blocks, developed by my friend Bill Hull and sold by the Webster Division of McGraw-Hill, in St. Louis, Mo. The best Math series for elementary-school kids is the one developed in England by the Nuffield Foundation. It can be bought from any British bookstore and is gradually being brought out (at a higher price, naturally) by John Wiley and Sons here. ESS (Elementary Science Study), at EDC, 55 Chapel St., Newton, Mass., has de-

veloped some very good materials. They have quite a bit
of stuff, some of it quite highly structured and leading the
children toward predetermined "discoveries," but some of
it imaginative, open, and flexible, like their units on shad-
ows, or musical instruments. Though I am not enthusiastic
about the idea of "teaching" reading at all, the best materials I have seen are in a kit called Modern Reading, ob-
tainable from HUMANITAS, Orange City, Fla. ITA isn't
bad, except that most teachers stick with it too long, perhaps overencouraged by the publishers. Another useful reference book is *Let's Read*, by Bloomfield and Barnhart, published by Wayne State Univ. Press.

I think the cassette tape recorder is an excellent piece of
classroom equipment. So is a typewriter. So are old adding
machines. There are good things in the catalog of Creative
Playthings—one, particularly, a $5 stopwatch.

I also wrote to Wilbur Rippy, who since 1949 (when
I first met him) has been teaching and directing in primary schools, and experimenting with school materials.
For several years he was teacher and director at Orson
Bean's Fifteenth Street School. Rippy is an acute and
deeply thoughtful observer, and his answer to my simple
question about materials raised an issue that is central to
educational reform today. Since we did not have to face
it at First Street, it is especially worthwhile to describe
it here. This is the question of what to do about the
susceptibility of children to the expectations which per-
meate (especially) the middle class, and reach into all
corners of a child's life. The demands are often not expressed overtly by parents, relatives, and friends, yet they
are among the most compelling features of the child's
environment. They appear in school, Rippy tells us, in
the form of peer-group assumptions, and also in the behavior of adults, who though they may cling to an ide-
ology of freedom, act in accordance with the top-down,

class-oriented structure of our society as a whole. How can we free the true motivations of individuals from this web of unspoken demands, which has the effect, always, of leveling differences and directing everyone toward illusory norms?

I would prefer a school [Rippy writes] in which the child could learn basic skills at the age most agreeable to him, and in ways agreeable to the teachers. The child must set the priorities, and we must be guided by individual differences. In a society that makes such a big deal out of learning, and out of, say, learning to read in the first few grades, a child will be made to feel like a dummy unless he complies. The freedom of choice—which ideally would protect his own needs—becomes illusory because he is swayed by pressures that are almost ubiquitous. The school must give him every conceivable support in this; and I would favor teaching methods which increase the child's own effectiveness and independence as fast as possible. In the teaching of reading, the best method is one that aids the child in "breaking the code." The method should be clear, decisive, and quick. The child's increase in competence will bring pleasure. At the beginning stages of reading, subject matter is not too important, though it needn't contain the absurdities of a Dick and Jane reader. It is crucial that the child be given many experiences with relevant literature. These will come primarily through his own experiences, drawing cartoons, telling and illustrating stories. A "codebreaking" reading program must be suffused with the child's own language, whether spoken or written. I am talking about the early primary grades, for as soon as the child has broken the code he can exercise his ability and choose as widely or as narrowly from the available literature as he wishes.

For the above reasons, I've used the Sullivan Programmed Reader, the Merril Series, and the Stern materials. The Sullivan Programmed Reader is quite a shock to an adult who is concerned with good literature, whatever that is. Yet it quickly teaches the child to read. Too, it relieves him of

gratuitous adult aid and of much well-meant but superfluous (and often confusing) adult attention. I've found
that children who have started with the programmed material have quickly branched out to other reading. They
also become more able to "do their own thing," for they
gain the skills quickly and then are able to write their own
stories, cartoons, and books without relying all the time on
adults.

Some kids dislike the Programmed readers, or might start
on them and soon tire. In such cases I've made other material available—the Merril, or Stern material. The teacher's
manual recommends using the Programmed reader day
after day, as an unbroken series, but this is unwise and I
have never done it. Some teachers feel that programmed
materials will create a programmed child, but I have never
seen any evidence of this. The Programmed reader seems
more likely to rescue the child from the diffuse and inef-
fective teaching so often seen in schools.

I am still surprised that I can recommend these materials.
You know my interest in literature, but perhaps you don't
know that for many years I supported and taught an individualized reading program somewhat akin to Sylvia
Ashton-Warner's. In using the programmed materials I was
forced to the conclusion that the child was soon liberated
from his dependency, and was able to communicate the
images, ideas, and feelings which lie at the heart of the
"basic skills."

I've found no Math workbooks that I can heartily recommend. The Cuisenaire Rods are extremely helpful. Unfortunately, the instructions which accompany them are not
as clear as they might be. The Dienes *logic* blocks are also
a marvelous material. Children are intrigued by the problems they present, and they seem to hook into the child's
pleasure in solving puzzles.

I can make no recommendations about science and social
studies workbooks, and it is not for lack of searching. Some
of the ESS programs are certainly elegant. If used in a very
open-ended way, as suggested in the manuals, they can be
helpful. It's best to make a social studies program for yourself, building it around the children in the school, how they

relate to each other, how they solve or fail to solve problems arising in their own social group. Films can often be helpful here, as can live—not educational—TV, especially at times when the children's interest is high, as at the launching of spacecraft and the death of Martin Luther King. Excellent science materials can be found in junkyards and surplus stores—old gas-pump meters, random electronic parts, discarded TV sets, gyroscopes from planes, etc. Cameras, projectors, duplicators, and tape recorders are all very helpful. I have seen them used to produce and duplicate stories and cartoons and newspapers, to record conversations, and to make fanciful explorations of unusual sound and color phenomena. It is important that they be introduced to the children in such a way that they can be used as soon as possible without adult supervision.

I have mentioned the Collaberg School several times throughout this book. Mabel taught there before starting First Street. The school was organized about twelve years ago by Robert Barker, who had prepared himself by going to England and working two years with A. S. Neill at Summerhill. The original Barker School—the name was changed later to Collaberg—represented, as far as I know, the first full-fledged use of Neill's methods in this country. Vera Williams has taught there from the beginning, and Jack Carson for the last few years. Together they have kept the school going, often at great personal sacrifice. The Collaberg setting is beautiful. They're in Stony Point, New York, at the foot of steep-wooded slopes on the edge of Harriman State Park. What I have seen of their program and teaching has been impressive. Jack Carson once told me he was using Paul Goodman's *Empire City* as a text. Since I knew that he was working with twelve- and fourteen-year-old boys, I was surprised, for the novel is extremely intellectual. Then I remembered that I had pointed out myself, reviewing the book years before, that much of it was hard to grasp at first because it was so disarmingly simple and direct. Carson had seen what few of its critics had noticed, that the book is a grand-scale educational romance; and he was using it in exactly that way: to make manifest the romance of learning to his pupils. One of the novel's heroes is an eleven-year-old boy—Horatio—who learns sociology and economics (and a great deal more) on the streets of New York. Carson and his pupils hiked and biked over many of the sites that figure in the book, repeating the observations of its young hero and verifying those of its author. Readers of Goodman will know what a range these covered. The First Street visits to Collaberg were among the high points of the year. I wrote Vera and asked her to say something about their equipment and materials.

We do not have much money to spend on equipment, so we mostly use things that you find around or that you can make yourself. Of our own making, and the most popular equipment here, are 2 rope swings with tires on the end. One is 35 feet long, and one is 70 feet long. On these you can get a variety of thrilling rides and learn a range of things I shudder at. Almost everyone at our school uses these untiringly. For the little kids we have a kind of very secretive place, 5 feet off the ground, built against the wall, entered by ladders (something like a projectionist's booth). This gets constant use. Also a large sandbox. (Wherever you are, you should try to have a very big sandbox.) The little kids use the swamp and marsh a lot too, for frogs, and getting wet, and being hidden.

We have a large set of homemade blocks, plywood, notched on both ends, from which can be made a 4 foot sq. house, or bigger, that you can get in. We've papered a whole wall of one of the rooms with a very detailed map of our area (Coast and Geodetic series). We put pins on it to mark our trips.

We make lots of trips, try to use all the things that are

available—museums, parks, old mines, reconstructions of historic sites, markets, docks, demonstrations, factories, architecture. We have taken long trips of a week with everybody over 8 years old. Our VW buses, though needing frequent repair, are among our most valued equipment. We have made many trips to the local dump and have supplied ourselves with a great deal of cloth, cardboard, spools, cylinders, boxes, books, a complete set of *Life* magazine from its beginning, and lots of odds and ends. We've used lots of electronic parts, because we had an associate who was doing electronics and we got him to put his shop in our basement and help the kids make things. In the same way we have had the use of a jewelry-making shop and of weaving equipment. One of our parents made a potter's wheel, and that gets a lot of use too.

Purchased equipment includes very little—besides art supplies, and endless glue, scissors, etc. Cuisenaire Rods are something we bought and use a lot and recommend highly. A small number of Math textbooks. A subscription to the *Scientific American.* Two microscopes acquired in exchange for part tuition. We have dug our own clay, ground grain, gone to the mill and seen it ground, made our own bread, milked our own goat, fixed our own car motors, cleaned our own well, surveyed our own property, designed, repaired, painted, and built our own buildings— all with the help of those children who were interested. We use our kitchen a lot to cook with the kids, make candles, and dye things.

We have lots of books. People give them to us. You don't need to buy many, between the library and gifts. We get films from the library, too.

For social studies classes we use the newspapers, magazines, WBAI, televised events, people in the streets, demonstrations, interviews with active people. We use our local community college for all kinds of performances and movies, which they give free.

We have homemade shop tables that we use, simple woodworking tools. Teachers have more advanced tools when needed. The kids like to have a typewriter and an adding machine that they can use—good for learning reading, writing, and numbers. Also a large rubber alphabet stamping set.

The last teacher I would like to quote is Bill Ayers, the young director of The Children's Community, in Ann Arbor, Michigan. This school is one of the most exciting and admirable ventures I have heard of anywhere. It is beautifully oriented toward community life, and provides an excellent demonstration of the fact that there is no cutoff point in politics, properly understood, for its political activism has grown directly out of its concern for individuals and families. Ayers, together with Joan Adams, a thirty-five-year-old Negro mother with four children, campaigned for election to the Ann Arbor School Board. Their platform reads like a summarization (which it is) of the best that has been written on libertarian, community-oriented education. The school was started by parents and teachers. Its financial difficulties have been considerable, and one of the things I most admire is the fact that the teachers themselves have kept the school alive by all kinds of expedients, devotion, and plain guts.

The school was started [Ayers writes] in 1965 as a pre-school and kindergarten. We've been building each year, and this year we're accredited by the state for the equivalent of K-4 (we're ungraded, however). The school was started by a handful of parents who were dissatisfied with the existing schools, but had no definite ideas of where to go educationally. One had read Summerhill, a few had seen Goodman, but no one was particularly sophisticated nor committed to a specific direction. Whatever hard ideas we have now (few indeed) are much more the result of three years' work than anything we've read or heard.

Our money has come largely from small donations and small fund-raising efforts. We've put an incredible number of hours into movies, bucket-drives, sales, etc., with a very small return. We've found that big money doesn't like us; and that if we're going to exist, we have to depend on a strong (if impoverished) base of our own committed people.

We've learned how to hustle in three years. And we've learned how to hustle for things as well as for money. We know how to get lumber, paper, paint, clay, toys, etc., for nothing; we know how to use laboratories, displays, projects, etc., for nothing; we know how to get junk and make it useful. And most important, we know how to live inexpensively. The school ran for two years on approximately $5,000 a year. Last year we spent around $8,000. This was with 24 kids and 6 staff people. There are lots of people who helped and received no pay. This included parents, university and high school students, a musician, a retired engineer, and many others. The staff existed by living collectively. We made group decisions about what to spend and where to spend it, about how much money was needed, who should get a job which month, who should travel to see prospective donors, who should ask his father or brother for a loan, etc. Living collectively isn't the easiest thing to do, but we felt that it was the only way the school could survive.

I'll tell you briefly some of what we've used.

Books: We own a lot, although there are few that aren't either racist, judgmental, stupid, or irrelevant. The kids particularly like Dr. Seuss and Ezra Jack Keats (*Snowy Day, John Henry,* etc.).

Word-related stuff: Lots of old typewriters, and a new primary typewriter (big print); magnetic and linking letters; picture/word matching games with a homemade machine; recipes; discarded street signs; kids' letters, diaries, stories; songbooks made from tape-recorded versions of soul music, including words and pictures of the group.

Math and science: Cuisenaire Rods; Attribute games; Spinning tables; tri-wall; science units (ESS). Our kids made scales to weigh things, drew a map of how to get to Chicago, mapped the area around Ann Arbor, made Num-

ber Lines on adding-machine tapes, kept notebooks record-
ing the growth of every growing thing in sight, including
themselves; tended an incubator with eggs; tended plants
and live animals.

I would like to add to Ayers' list the publications of
The Children's Community itself. Ayers' own *Thoughts
on Our Schools* (his campaign document) is a lucid and
persuasive analysis of the interdependence of community,
political, and educational issues. His suggestions for
changes can serve as a guide for other community groups.
Ayers' *Education, an American Problem* is a brief critical
bibliography of recent literature on education and community problems. Teachers especially will find it useful.
One of the insights that runs through Ayers' work, and
which arose in practice at The Children's Community, is
that integration is a two-way street; it does not mean
bringing the blacks into the culture of the whites, but—
to the extent that the cultures are distinct—intermixing
them and fertilizing each from each. Prominent in Ayers'
and Joan Adams' campaign platform was: *Include an
adequate treatment of black history as a part of the regular history curriculum at all levels.*

Let me end by going back to the kids and teachers of
First Street. Susan said that the curriculum was "talk,
talk, talk, talk." What this means, of course, is really intimate relations between teachers and pupils. I have already mentioned how such intimacy transforms the materials on hand. I would like to quote Susan again to show
some other effects of it . . . and from an angle I would
like to have included more of in this book. Her observations here are from a letter written in response to my
request for some notes about her kids.

Eléna.

A wild girl at first, desperately jealous for love and affection. The day Dolores first came to school, Eléna said to me, "Keep me away from her, Susan, or I'll kill her." They later became best friends and often rolled body-to-body together on the floor.

Eléna was a thief when she came, but eventually would return exact change after making purchases for the school. I was never able with her, or other of the Welfare kids, to get them to pay tokens in the subway. They instinctively went under the turnstile, leaving me to deal with the irate stationman. The best I ever achieved was a halfway compliance, intended to save my face. The kids wanted to keep the tokens for themselves. I insisted it was the school's money.

One day, during the first year, Mabel's Aunt Frances gave a birthday party for Mabel at the school. She brought cake, daffodils, small cookies for the kids, tablecloths, fancy napkins, paper hats, etc. The girls helped her set it up. The party went O.K. during the preliminary eating, then a fight broke out, food was hurled, and most of the kids were taken down to the gym. I stopped off at the third floor in my room. One by one the girls in my class entered, carrying bunches of daffodils. Each one asked me to hide them while she was at the gym. I said I wouldn't be responsible for guarding daffodils. So each girl hid her own—and in the process discovered those that had been hidden already. Each one stole the ones she found and added them to her own pile. Each one too insisted that I help her hide the stolen booty. When they all came up from gym there was a grand confrontation scene, Dodie, Rudella, Eléna, and Dolores, all shouting about daffodils—in the midst of which walked Mabel. She sized up the situation immediately, and cried, "It's MY birthday!" and took all the daffodils back. She then gave each girl three and walked off downstairs with the remainder.

I left with Rudella and Dolores to wait outside for the parents to come. Dodie came down with a strange look on her face and said, "Eléna just tore up all the bulbs and seeds in the window box." Eléna then came down yelling that she wanted to take daffodils home to her mother, Mabel was unfair, the school was no good, Dodie was a liar, I was a stinker, etc.

I'd had it, and said disgustedly, "Oh, Eléna, go home. We'll see you tomorrow." The next day Dodie brought seeds for the window box completely on her own, and she and Eléna planted the box again.

I remember another ghastly day with Eléna. I'd taken her, Dodie, Rudella, Dolores, Kenzo, and some of the little ones to the Old Merchant's House on East 4th Street. An old white-haired lady took us around and repeatedly asked the kids not to put their hands on the antiques. Eléna persistently disobeyed, and sassed the lady, with "fuck you" and the like. After some expostulation I said, "O.K. That's enough. We're going since you don't know how to behave." Out we marched, and once outside I burst into tears and told Eléna I'd never felt so embarrassed, she should have respect for older women, and other true enough middle-class pieties. (I'd had about three hours' sleep the night before, and so basic themes were coming out!) Eléna ran off down the street. The next day Dodie and Rudella begged me, "Susie, don't cry again. We'll be good so you won't have to." Eléna usually kept a civil tongue in her head after that. I felt silly for having cried.

Eléna came in reading at about the end of first-grade level, doing beginning second in Math. She "wouldn't" do school-work. My battle with her on the subject turned on the themes that a) she *was* intelligent, and b) she could learn for herself, not for the teacher. This established, she did brilliantly. When she left, a year and a half later, she was reading the middle of fourth grade and doing beginning fourth Math. She would occasionally go on learning jags and chase me around the school, workbook in hand, demanding that I check her answers or give her a "test."

When Eléna paid attention to something she wanted to learn, she grasped it almost always on the first explanation.

Part of her difficulty with reading was a vocabulary one. She had school English when she came, but didn't know the names for simple household things. I recall schlepping over the Lower East Side with her, looking for a store that sold a special Spanish ingredient necessary for making "Puerto Rican" chicken that afternoon at my house. The ingredient turned out to be regular black pepper. I told Eléna she could buy it at the A & P next time.

About 80 percent of my reading work with her was vocabulary definition. Unfortunately, she got turned on to Mary Poppins after having seen the movie—and I went nearly out of my skull trying to explain Victorian middle-class notions to this East Side barrio hellion-in-transition.

Eléna's energy was phenomenal. One day, at the end of the first year, we had to pack up all the books to store them for the summer. Eléna heard me mention the problem to Gloria, and said, "Oh, wait a minute, I'll get some boxes." She vanished for an hour, and reappeared with enough boxes to pack up the entire school—which she promptly did. It was a most relaxing day for me.

Hannah.

Hannah came to First Street from a Catholic school, to which her bohemian mother had sent her for a year. Her face was closed and tight when she came. She was intelligent and sweet, with an underlay of malice. Her family ran an avant-garde theater, and (like some of our Puerto Rican kids) she was held responsible for the upbringing of her younger siblings, carrying the wash to the laundry, and shopping.

Hannah had a dreadful conscience. Once Gloria lectured the whole school at lunchtime about not making noise and running in the hall (which was getting the Y's secretary down, for her office was right off the stairs). Gloria spoke in the tone of the firm public-school teacher. Hannah afterwards stopped me and said, in a worried voice, "Gloria wasn't talking to me, was she, Susie? I don't run up the stairs." I laughed and told her the lecture was meant for others and she shouldn't take such across-the-board statements personally. But it was characteristic of her to feel guilty for what she hadn't done.

Most of my "educational" work with Hannah consisted of taking the pressure off her and trying to get her to stop being such a good, good girl. Her reading level went up and up practically on its own, anyway.

I have a vivid memory of her face toward the end of her stay at First Street. It was on a trip to the Metropolitan with my class. They were playing hide-and-seek outside before going in. Hannah was running after Kenzo, her face brilliant with happiness, looking like the perfect joyous little girl. Left unread on my lap was *Little Women*, which a year ago she would have been reading, sitting quietly at my side while the others played. Hannah and I got on extremely well—probably because she reminded me so of myself. She too brought presents of strange books to the teacher.

After Hannah had moved to the country, the school went on a trip to visit her there. Before we left, Eléna said to Dolores, "Hannah's family's rich, isn't it?" Dolores shook her head. "No, Eléna. They're very poor. They probably have less money than your family. They just use it in a different way." Dolores, whose Puerto Rican mother was uneducated, and whose stepfather was a student of Zen and a restaurateur, knew the economies of both worlds.

ABOUT THE AUTHOR

George Dennison (1925–1987) was best known for his account of the First Street School, but he also wrote fiction, plays, and critical essays, most notably his novel *Luisa Domic* and a collection of shorter works, *Pierrot and Other Stories*. Having grown up in a suburb of Pittsburgh, he joined the Navy during World War II, attended the New School for Social Research on the GI Bill, and took graduate courses at New York University. Although he devoted himself primarily to his art, he also taught school for a number of years, at all levels from preschool to high school. He trained at the New York Institute for Gestalt Therapy with Paul Goodman and later worked with severely disturbed children as a lay therapist and teacher. His plays were produced at the Judson Church in New York and elsewhere, and his essays and fiction appeared in many periodicals. In the late Sixties George Dennison and his wife Mabel Chrystie, the founder of the First Street School, moved to rural Maine, where they raised three children.